TEACHING THE 'SLOW' LEARNER IN THE PRIMARY SCHOOL

Edited by
M. F. CLEUGH

LONDON AND NEW YORK

First published in 1961 by Methuen & Co. Ltd.
Reprinted 1965

This edition first published in 2021
by Routledge
2 Park Square, Milton Park, Abingdon, Oxon OX14 4RN

and by Routledge
605 Third Avenue, New York, NY 10158

Routledge is an imprint of the Taylor & Francis Group, an informa business

© 1961 Methuen & Co. Ltd.

This book is a re-issue originally published in 1961. The language used is a reflection of its era and no offence is meant by the Publishers to any reader by this re-publication.

All rights reserved. No part of this book may be reprinted or reproduced or utilised in any form or by any electronic, mechanical, or other means, now known or hereafter invented, including photocopying and recording, or in any information storage or retrieval system, without permission in writing from the publishers.

Trademark notice: Product or corporate names may be trademarks or registered trademarks, and are used only for identification and explanation without intent to infringe.

British Library Cataloguing in Publication Data
A catalogue record for this book is available from the British Library

ISBN: 978-1-03-200270-5 (Set)
ISBN: 978-1-00-317552-0 (Set) (ebk)
ISBN: 978-1-03-200458-7 (Volume 2) (hbk)
ISBN: 978-1-03-200468-6 (Volume 2) (pbk)
ISBN: 978-1-00-317426-4 (Volume 2) (ebk)

Publisher's Note
The publisher has gone to great lengths to ensure the quality of this reprint but points out that some imperfections in the original copies may be apparent.

Disclaimer
The publisher has made every effort to trace copyright holders and would welcome correspondence from those they have been unable to trace.

Teaching the Slow Learner
in the Primary School

EDITED BY

M. F. CLEUGH

*Senior Lecturer, University of London
Institute of Education*

LONDON
METHUEN & CO LTD
11 NEW FETTER LANE . EC4

First published 1961
Reprinted 1965
© *1961 Methuen & Co Ltd*
Printed in Great Britain
by Billing & Sons Limited
Guildford and London
Cat. No. 02/6379/46
1·2

CONTENTS

I SOCIAL, MORAL AND RELIGIOUS TRAINING.
R. W. Bannister — *page* 1

II PHYSICAL EDUCATION AND HEALTH. R. C. Ablewhite — 21

III BASIC SKILLS: SPEECH AND ORAL WORK. H. Purt — 39

IV BASIC SKILLS: READING. M. F. Boote — 63

V BASIC SKILLS: ARITHMETIC. D. A. Ray — 92

VI EXPRESSIVE WORK: ART. Geo. A. Edmonds — 115

VII EXPRESSIVE WORK: MUSIC. D. H. Cleife — 135

VIII EXPRESSIVE WORK: DRAMA. A. F. Harris — 152

IX HANDICRAFT. J. B. Hawkins — 164

X ENVIRONMENTAL STUDIES. W. A. Hollingbery — 179

XI THE KEEPING OF RECORDS. Cyril E. Saunders — 195

XII EQUIPMENT AND APPARATUS. I. R. Miller — 212

XIII THE SLOW LEARNER IN THE INFANT SCHOOL.
Mary E. Middleton — 241

XIV BACKWARD CHILDREN IN VILLAGE SCHOOLS.
K. I. Marshall — 251

XV REMEDIAL TEACHING. Joan M. Gordon — 264

PREFACE

The hard core of the problem of backwardness is in the ordinary junior schools. The writers of these chapters (all experienced primary teachers, and all holding the E.S.N. Diploma of London University) have tried to give suggestions which will be useful and practicable in ordinary classrooms, bearing in mind the usual difficulties of widely varying abilities, limited equipment, and above all large numbers. They have not written of ideal situations which are unlikely to be realised in more than a few 'very special' classes, believing that it is more helpful to more teachers to write in terms of conditions that are generally applicable. For the most part they have in mind children of 7-11 in urban areas, so the needs of slow infants, and of slow children in small village schools are considered separately. Finally, the concluding chapter assesses the more elaborate work of the specialist remedial teacher.

The opinions expressed in the chapters are those of the writers and are not to be taken as the official policy of any Authority which employs them.

Acknowledgments were made in the first volume of this work and will not be repeated here, but mention must be made of Mr. D. C. W. Pettegree, who undertook the arduous task of providing an index.

M. F. C.

Chapter I

SOCIAL, MORAL AND RELIGIOUS TRAINING

He would have been referred for special educational treatment – like John Ridd, he is somewhat 'heavy in the head' – but in his day special educational treatment belonged to the future. Yet for many years he has worked regularly, paid his own way and lived a quiet, law-abiding life. Pleasant and unassuming, he has won for himself a wide circle of friends and is a man of some authority in the life of the church which has done so much to make him what he is.

His church served him best as it gave him a way of life to follow in the company of others. Sunday and weekday meetings settled him in a comfortingly secure routine; he had somewhere to go and something to do. Church membership put him under discipline and gave him a basic code of conduct. There were people to talk to, inside the church and outside in the street; others to visit in their homes, where he learnt many of the simple social graces. By degrees, acquaintance gave place to friendship. Bound by the ties of mutual interest, respect and affection, he came to live as his friends lived.

The man of whom I am thinking, although 'dull', is gently and attractively good and well able to manage his own modest affairs. However, what one church has done for him, many schools are doing now for others like him. He is what he is because he was taken into a close-knit community actively practising the good life and held there by friendship.

The slow-learning child has acquired something of a reputation as a ne'er-do-well, but it is wholly wrong to conclude, as some do, that by his very nature he is doomed to delinquency or worse. The danger is there, for he is impulsive, often unable to foresee the consequences of his actions, and at times shows a bland disregard for right or wrong which amounts to amorality. Nevertheless, he is not without hope. Perhaps he senses his own insufficiency, for more than anything else he wants to 'belong.' Not that he shows any moral discrimination in his choice of company. He goes where he is made to feel most at home and as if to tie the bonds more closely, he will readily adopt the ways – and way of life – of his companions. His hope lies in the fact that he may be most powerfully affected, for good or evil, as he is a member of a community. For many years, those the earliest and most formative, he must attend school. His teacher may not be the only influence in his life, but he is both a constant and a sympathetic one. Out of his own experience of the good life and his knowledge of the child, he is better able than most to create for him that stable, wholesome community life in which his social, moral and religious training can best take place.

Like the teaching of English, social, moral and religious training cannot be confined to set periods of the time-table; it is continuous and never-ending. Put another way, the teacher's opportunities are many and varied. But a start must be made. Then where? Perhaps with the classroom itself, for after all, the slow-learning child must do much of his living and learning in there.

'Atmosphere' is one of the teacher's powerful aids. In no small measure he will create it simply by being what he is, hence the need for honest (though not morbid), self-examination when things go wrong. Nevertheless, skilful use of the physical environment can do much to quicken the mental and spiritual environment. Desks in groups, rather than long, regimented rows, can suggest intimacy and a personal approach; neatly stored, easily accessible apparatus, polished wood and clean floors can impart an air of brisk, orderly purpose. Even in repose, a classroom should not want for character. Carefully arranged illustrations, living things, collections of tree-bark and sea-shells, all these bespeak lively curiosity and exciting discovery. The teacher's contribution does not always go unnoticed. One boy said, after looking at a drawing of a stage-coach, 'You don't 'alf work 'ard for us, sir.' Then, with evident satisfaction, 'We've got a smashing room.' In many simple but effective ways the scene may be set. Better still, the child himself can help to set the scene and in some way make the room his own. His paintings, his models, his illustrations, his captions, gracefully accepted and faithfully used can give him a place, literally, in his community – and nothing can compensate for knowing that his work is acceptable. So with classroom chores. Sweeping, dusting, tidying, checking apparatus, even cleaning the blackboard, he may experience, if only at a simple level, a sense of orderly living, a feeling of being capable and responsible, a willingness to serve others. Helping in his classroom, he might well come closer to the spirit of his community and the more readily take his place within it.

Like teacher, like class. As he lives the good life, so will his pupils. Practice is more persuasive than precept, and perhaps in no way can the teacher put precept into practice more effectively than he can in planning the day-to-day work of the class. Nothing can be more confusing to the slow-learning child than the complete change of method which too often occurs between class and class and perhaps more often between school and school; nothing more frustrating than the still too common practice of beginning all over again. Confusion and frustration so often bring in their wake despair, indifference, even resentment. Continuity of method; graded work; individual treatment – these are more than teaching techniques, they are indispensable means of promoting his personal growth. For him, nothing succeeds like success. Progress, however slight, can make for poise, for confidence, for a feeling that all is well with him and the world. Indeed, it may work a near-miracle in his attitude towards life in general.

Moral training has its roots in a balanced, harmonious personal relationship between teacher and child which may be built up in a variety of incidental ways – casual conversation, a joke, a game of ludo in 'choosing time' – but most surely through individual treatment. Working together in a common cause, the good of the child, each will come to know the other better. The teacher may bring to his work a sharpened awareness of the child's academic needs (and so keep him adequately supplied with purposeful, interesting work) together with a deeper understanding of him as a person. Most of all, he is better able to bring 'the personal touch' to his teaching . . . a sympathetic, not sentimental understanding of difficulties; handmade material, perhaps done on the spot; advice rather than instruction on how to set out his work so that 'I may read it easily and quickly'. It is with his teacher and because of his teacher that he will learn to work independently and with some degree of self-sufficiency; to put his basic skills to practical, social use – writing a 'get well' note to a friend or measuring lengths of skipping-rope for the class. But so often the teacher will succeed as much for what he is as for what he does. The child will catch something of his calm purpose, something of his belief in success. He will warm to the feeling that here is someone who understands him, who accepts him as a person, not a 'C-streamer'. Of course, it is not always easy to accept him – he may be surly, indifferent, uncouth even – but the teacher will be better able to do so as he can see his needs clearly and seek to meet them adequately.

Community is 'a living together' and if the teacher is to foster a lively sense of community, then he must bring his class together regularly and as a group in pursuit of some common interest. Music, poetry, art, nature study, literature – all these may draw him and the children closer together as they share a communal experience ... perhaps the quiet pleasure and ease in one another's company which may come of painting together; the laughter which may follow upon the saying of a tongue-twister: the delight in listening to a worm's 'bristles' scraping across paper. But there are other, deeper experiences. In a story well told, with no concessions to maudlin sentimentality, children may thrill to high endeavour; fight in a just cause; feel for the helpless; respond in a very real way to human goodness in action. Not all lessons can, or should be, inspirational in this sense, they would place too great a strain upon the teacher and the children; but used discreetly they can build up a feeling for what is fine and noble. However, no lesson need be without its inspiration. As the teacher appeals directly to interest, draws freely upon information offered (interest is a great loosener of tongues) and in his turn offers some new knowledge or experience, he will evoke a sense of common, unifying purpose; a feeling of doing something worthwhile together.

'No impression without expression' is an axiom of sound teaching. Play groups and model groups can make their contribution to the common cause and as they do so their members may learn some of the basic disciplines of community life – amicable discussion, the acceptance of leadership, the sharing of responsibility, working

SOCIAL, MORAL AND RELIGIOUS TRAINING

faithfully and well as a member of a team. Too, they may acquire a new respect for one another. Billy passed largely unnoticed by the rest of the class, and the teacher, until it was discovered that 'he can't 'alf draw smashing 'orses'. From then on he was a very different person, and very much in demand. Wherever possible, the children ought to play a part, however simple, in planning the work of the class. One sympathises with the child who said, with some bitterness, 'Our teacher does everything himself.' Of course, the teacher must guide; sometimes suggest a more practicable alternative; bring in the shy and retiring; deflect the over-bearing; but as he can step aside, the class may come closer together, learning community from the bottom up. Experience can be a great teacher.

'Wholesome community life' is compounded of many things, but it finds expression in an ordered, purposeful routine; in lively, confident children; in warmth of manner and ease of conversation; in work done wholeheartedly; in many spontaneous and kindly acts of service; perhaps most of all in the 'togetherness' which characterizes the ebb and flow of classroom life. Inevitably, some kind of community life will grow up around teacher and class, if only because they are thrown so much into one another's company. How far it can be made to serve the needs of each child will depend upon how deeply the teacher believes it is his duty to bring him up 'to be as good a member of the community as possible',[1] and to what extent he can accept him as a 'unique personality, having physiological drives, instincts and emotions which crave satisfaction, intellectual abilities, social potentialities, and the capacity to acquire modes of behaviour, interests, attitudes and skills'.[2]

Social training might very well begin with the child's appearance and manners. He is more likely to want to fit in as he is accepted by others, but many people are put off by a dirty appearance and graceless ways. Given tact, the teacher can do much to help him, by setting a personal example of course, and more effectively perhaps by dropping broad hints here and there in the classroom itself. Mirrors and clothes-brushes with the question, 'Are you tidy?'; soap and towels with the invitation, 'You may use these.' Combs can be something of a problem at first, but a little persuasion goes a long way,

---

[1] *Special Educational Treatment* (Min. of Ed. Pamphlet No. 5), p. 38.
[1] *Educating the Sub-normal Child* (Frances Lloyd), p. 8.

5

particularly if the persuasion takes the form of a few minutes 'tidying time' at the beginning of each session. Hints on how to look after clothes may bear surprising results. In one class a group of girls volunteered to sew on buttons and do simple running repairs. So with manners. The teacher who slammed the staffroom door in the face of a child with a curt 'Go away!' need not have wondered why 'children are so rude'.

Despite large numbers and perhaps two sittings, sometimes in the school hall, sometimes in the classroom, school dinners may still offer valuable practical experience of the simple social graces – laying tables, serving, waiting, eating in a quiet and pleasant fashion. School functions – Open Days, Sports Days, football fixtures, cricket matches, concerts – are no less useful means of providing sound social training. There are programmes to be sold, people to be taken to their seats, or around the school, refreshments to be served, so many little things which the slow-learning child may do graciously and with quiet, good manners. In one junior school, 4C was frequently visited and each visit was turned into something of a social occasion by the class. A programme would be drawn up . . . 'They'll want to see us work, won't they?'; 'Let's do a play'; 'Would they like to play stoolball?' A welcoming party was chosen to wait at the school gates, and a good deal of 'spit and polish' went on. Once someone, remembering Open Day, suggested name-cards on the desks 'so they'll know who we are'. Invariably, the teacher was reminded to buy some biscuits and at play-time two girls would clear his desk, arrange flowers and set chairs in place – then tea and biscuits would be served. As one of them said, 'Well, you've got to make things nice.' However, concerts and visits do not happen every day, school does. It is through the daily round, the common task that the teacher may do most to help the slow-learning child to acquire the rudiments of sociable behaviour.

Reference was made earlier to the sense of well-being which follows upon continuing and recognizable success. Each achievement, however slight, should bring the slow-learning child nearer to realizing that goal of reasonable self-sufficiency which the teacher must set for him. Mrs P, middle aged and 'rather simple', was quite unable to manage herself or her money. Frequently in debt, she just as frequently found herself short of food. At first she was considered

SOCIAL, MORAL AND RELIGIOUS TRAINING

rather a joke, but her repeated importunities – a shovel of coal, a rasher of bacon, half-a-crown for the milkman – wore the joke thin. She became the most thoroughly disliked person in her neighbourhood. People kept their doors closed against her and crossed the road to avoid speaking. Her pathetic but irritating lack of self-sufficiency alienated her from all hope of the help and understanding she so badly needed, as it had already alienated her from her family. If the slow-learning child is to achieve a thorough-going mastery of the basic skills, then it must be in the basic skills of 'everyday' . . . making pleasant conversation; dropping a line to a friend; or writing a more formal letter of application; reading for meaning (instructions, directions, even making sense of the popular press) as well as reading for pleasure in leisure; finding out how much? working out can I afford it?; learning by practical experience to plan his day for himself. The better he is able to manage his own affairs, the more likely is society to accept him, and the more certain he is to hold down a job. Once free of the relatively calm and stable school environment, he may begin to drift away from society. The regular routine of a work-a-day life can be a steadying influence. Clocking-in, clocking-out, drawing a wage-packet can give him some sort of equality with his fellows, a certain status which may help to anchor him more firmly within society. No doubt he will marry. Money does not make a marriage, but a steady income helps and so does the ability to use it wisely.

Of course, he is unlikely to be working more than forty-eight hours each week – with perhaps a few hours extra 'overtime'. The school would be failing in its duty to the child if it did not encourage him in the right use of leisure time, for the devil still finds mischief for idle hands. It might persuade him to join some outside organization, always provided that the leaders are told beforehand of his special needs and disabilities and invited to consult the school whenever they feel in need of advice. It ought also to teach him some of the traditional crafts. One man, who spent all his school life in a C stream, makes small historical models from a variety of odds and ends. Another grows prize dahlias. Neither have time to get into trouble and both enjoy the respect of their neighbours.

Moral training has been defined as training in Man's duty to Man, yet it is in the faithful performance of his duty towards others that

TEACHING THE SLOW LEARNER IN THE PRIMARY SCHOOL

the slow-learning child can make perhaps his most valuable contribution to society. Indeed, it is difficult to say where moral training begins and social training ends. There are many ways in which he may learn to serve his fellows, possibly most effectively as he shares with his teacher some responsibility for the efficient administration of day-to-day routine . . . keeping the class calendar up to date; checking and re-ordering supplies of powder paint; issuing and accounting for exercise books. It may begin as a co-operative venture, with him working under the direction of his teacher, but service is self-giving and as soon as possible he must be left to carry out the task by himself and in his own way. The teacher will not always find it easy to step aside, yet it is only as the child can assume complete responsibility that he can give fully of his own talents and his own judgement; that he can learn to keep faith with others. From time to time, and within the teacher's discretion he should undertake a new and different responsibility. The wider his field of service, the deeper his sense of service.

Almost every day, opportunities for 'casual service' will arise – repairing damaged apparatus, cutting and mounting illustrations that have come to hand unexpectedly. Odd jobs may be used in a variety of ways . . . to divert the troublesome child; to provide practical application of some new skill; and so often they enable the teacher to draw even the least favoured child into the service of his fellows, if only for a few moments at a time. Frank was a boy of extremely limited ability. The simplest of tasks seemed to be quite beyond him. One day, almost as a last resort, he was asked to take a written message round the school. From then on he became a most efficient school messenger. He would leave a classroom as unobtrusively as he entered it, and acquired a reputation for 'never interrupting'. Indeed, he brought to his task a tact and a quiet politeness which won him many sympathisers. At one time never particularly forthcoming, he took to volunteering for odd jobs in the classroom and around the school. Perhaps his greatest academic achievements flowed from his new-found sense of service. He became label monitor, copying his teacher's rough draft in a laborious hand. In the process he built up an illustrated work book which helped to set him on the road to reading and writing. Not that he became literate there and then, but he came by a

SOCIAL, MORAL AND RELIGIOUS TRAINING

feeling of worth which made a more promising person of him.

The child himself is surrounded by many services of which he is only vaguely aware, if at all. Surely some study of 'the people who help us' will form a useful part of his social training. Listening to the school nurse talk about her work, or visiting a milk-bottling factory may help him to mark the difference between earning a living and serving the community.

'The ultimate test (of the school) must be whether it assists in the development . . . of men and women . . . who care for all that is lovely and of good report.'[1] Moral behaviour may begin quite simply with a desire to please, to emulate a respected, well-loved person. The teacher must not under-estimate his own powers for good in the life of the slow-learning child. Indeed, the stronger the bonds of affection and respect which exist between them, the more wholeheartedly will the child adopt for himself that code of conduct which the teacher lays down by his own consistent example and the more readily will he reject behaviour which the teacher, out of his concern for him, condemns as wrong. It is easier to be good amongst good people, and moral behaviour is very much a matter of atmosphere, a pervasive feeling of 'this is what we do here'. There must be rules – they may be likened to guide ropes, marking the way and inspiring a feeling of security – but let them be as few in number as possible; fitted to the child, asking no more of him than he can offer; easily understood and having the common good as their aim, not the teacher's convenience. Above all else, let the rules be positive – 'Do' not 'Don't' – inviting his active co-operation in the maintenance of law and order. However much, if not everything, will depend upon how the teacher conducts the day-to-day affairs of his class. From time to time he must dispense justice; he must be careful to do so calmly, without bias, not forgetting that justice may often be tempered with mercy. Mercy may succeed where punishment will fail, though should the teacher feel that punishment is necessary (and generally speaking, the punishment should fit the crime) then he must make it a principle that the punishment wipes out the crime. There must always be a way back. Certainly no good will come of flinging past offences in the child's face. The persistent offender needs help, not abuse. Sauce for the goose is sauce for the gander, and the

[1] *Handbook of Suggestions for Teachers* (H.M.S.O.), p. 15.

teacher must never resort to force or fear to get his way; indulge himself in sarcasm; fail to keep a promise once made. In short, he must not make the mistake of assuming that there is one moral law for him and another for the children. Often he may work by inference. A 'Lost Property Box' suggests plainly his assumption that missing property is lost, not stolen, and will be returned through the box to its owner. Free access to answer cards implies his belief that they will be used honestly. As he shares responsibility, he expresses his confidence in the trustworthiness of his monitors. At times moral training will be something of a trial of faith for the teacher, though he may temper faith with practical caution by removing possible causes of temptation. His faith will not always be rewarded, yet the child will find it all the harder to be good when the teacher suspects nothing but the worst of him.

The best kind of moral and social training goes on in the classroom community where the child is made to feel at home; is treated with respect, affection even; is always busily occupied in a variety of interesting pursuits; can find someone to share his satisfaction in success and guide him through his failures; is made to feel capable, responsible and trustworthy; is prompted into many little acts of kindness; is given a basic code of conduct. Where in fact, he can find fellowship – a common way of life to follow in the company of others.

Religious training has as its goal 'a life of worship and service within the Christian community'.[1] What practical steps consistent with good taste, can the teacher take towards realizing this purpose? He will find the Agreed Syllabus a most valuable guide, but it is only a guide. Having selected from it what is strictly relevant to his theme, he should bring to his preparation something of 'his own study, thought and faith',[2] looking especially for points of contact within the child's experience. Many though not all, R.I. lessons will take the form of story and expression. If the story is to achieve its purpose, it must be concise; the characters and situations must live. Enthusiasts are notoriously indifferent to the other equally pressing demands on the teacher's time but one feels bound to recommend a careful study of the Bible as an essential part of his preparation. There are so

---

[1] *Syllabus of Religious Instruction* (Sunderland), p. 13.
[2] *Syllabus of Religious Instruction* (Durnam), Preface, p. viii.

SOCIAL, MORAL AND RELIGIOUS TRAINING

many excellent Commentaries; popular studies of 'Life and Times', 'Social and Economic Conditions', 'Religious Beliefs and Practices' readily available that he will not find it too difficult to build up a wide background knowledge. Much of what he knows will not come out directly in the story, but the wider his background knowledge, the clearer will be his appraisal of the issues involved; the sharper his delineation of the characters; the more illuminating his touches of local colour; indeed the better he will be able to bring the child into 'such vital contact with the religious experience of Mankind as recorded in the Bible'[1] that he will 'want to worship the God about whose dealings with Mankind he has been learning.'[2] How far he can prepare the child for the central experience of the Christian Faith – communion with Christ – will depend upon how sensitively he can portray Him as a living person. At no time will the teacher need to draw more deeply upon faith informed by study.

It is sometimes said that religious training is wasted upon the slow-learning child because there is much of the Bible which he can neither read nor understand. This is a counsel of despair. There were few in the early church who were able to read, yet none can doubt the reality of their religious experience. They heard the Bible read by those who could read; listened to others who had built up a repertoire of Bible stories; memorized key passages; watched and took part in religious plays. The teacher may use the same means of making the slow-learning child familiar with the appeal and language of the Bible. Certainly it need not be a dead book, for there are so many ways in which the child may make active use of it . . . finding the gospel from which the next story will be taken, or a text to be memorized and illustrated; practising a choral reading or the reciting of some familiar passage for the school assembly. A Bible Library may help – small detergent packets backed in brown paper, each representing a book of the Bible, arranged in two main sections, the Old Testament and the New Testament, and perhaps sub-titled Law or Poetry or History. The stories told may be re-written, illustrated and mounted sometimes by the teacher, sometimes by a child, then slipped inside the 'books', so providing him with a useful, if simple means of both finding his way about the Bible and reading it for himself. There are stories about it too – how the books came to

[1] *Syllabus of Religious Instruction* (Sunderland), p. 13.   [2] ibid.

be written; what it cost in terms of human endeavour to bring it to him here in England; stories of the men and women who spent, and are spending their lives translating it into other languages and carrying it to remote corners of the world. So it may come to stand for much of what is best and most inspiring.

But of course, religious training is not only an 'ordered presentation of Biblical knowledge'.[1] The child may see, and in some measure experience, Christianity in action as he sees Christians at work in other countries; through the ages; here and now. Thus he may sense if only dimly, the universality and continuity of the Christian Faith.

The teacher must not depend solely upon words. Flannel-graphs, film strips, movies, puppets, plays should be pressed into service. The R.I. lesson, and the school assembly, which never changes, will quickly become flat and lifeless. Nor is religious training all one-sided. The child must be encouraged to play his part. During the expression work which follows upon the R.I. lesson, he may restate the experience he has shared in his own terms and in a variety of familiar ways, modelling, painting, acting 'live' or with puppets, building up a display. At such times, helping here and answering a question there, the teacher may do much incidentally but effectively to deepen the child's religious experience. One model of the village of Nazareth took some time and several art and craft periods to complete. Gradually, other work grew up around the model – a 'Jesus Book', to which many children contributed short illustrated accounts; a 'Jesus Museum', containing models of scrolls, phylacteries, things that Christ would have seen and handled. The barriers between the sacred and the secular were broken down. Jesus became more of a person and less of a character; R.I. made use of, and stimulated a fresh interest in the traditional subjects.

'Be still and know that I am God.' Without worship, a sense of the worthiness of God, there can be no real religious experience. The teacher cannot leave it all to the school assembly, he must help the child to 'practise the presence of God' in the classroom. Much will depend on how clearly he is able to show God active in the lives of men and women whose religious faith inspired their work; and no less upon the reality of his own faith, for it may be that the child will first see God through his eyes. As always, 'atmosphere' is an

[1] *Syllabus of Religious Instruction* (Sunderland), p. 13.

SOCIAL, MORAL AND RELIGIOUS TRAINING

invaluable aid; certainly it is easier to worship in a bright classroom where the children are on good terms with one another and the teacher. Again, a display or model developed around the current theme and placed where it can be seen easily may arouse interest and become, in an informal but appealing way, the focal point of classroom worship. The children may take an active part in evening prayers as they help to compile a class prayer book in which they are free to write and illustrate prayers remembered, copied or made up. It might be compiled in three sections, Thank-You prayers, Remembering prayers, Promising prayers. Deciding into which section a prayer should be put could be a useful means of teaching 'the elements of worship' . . . Thanksgiving, Intercession, Consecration. In many such simple ways the teacher may evoke a sense of God, a readiness to worship as sincere as it is spontaneous.

Sometimes one is asked the question, 'What can the C-streamer, with all his disabilities, hope to get out of the junior school assembly?' A more constructive question might be, 'What can he bring to it?' Surely, it is the main purpose of the assembly to fuse several differing capacities for worship into a corporate experience of God. The slow-learning child may make his contribution, a sense of God and a readiness to worship acquired in part in the classroom. Nor is it beyond him to help in the ordered preparation which must precede the assembly – opening windows, arranging flowers, putting up hymn numbers. He may even read the Call to Worship or take part in a short, carefully rehearsed play in celebration of one of the Christian festivals.

The same question, 'What can he offer?' may guide the leader in his conduct of the assembly. Clearly, he cannot hope to cater exclusively for the slow-learning child (nor is it desirable that he should) but he can meet many of his needs as he meets the needs of all children at worship. What then can children in general offer? A natural piety, provided they are helped not hindered in their devotion, and a relatively short span of attention. Music as they enter the hall – preferably one feels, orchestral music on records – may encourage quiet, orderly behaviour; a gradual fading out into silence can evoke that stillness of body and mind which should precede corporate worship. 'Then it is well to set some vision of God'[1] by a hymn of

[1] *Syllabus of Religious Instruction* (Sunderland), p. 98, paragraph (ii).

praise, following upon a very brief and pertinent introduction by the leader. From then on the order of worship should proceed unhurriedly but it must never lag and so 'beget inattention'.[1] Modern school hymnals have reached a high standard and the leader will not find it difficult to choose the right kind of hymn, that is one which the child can both understand and sing. The tune must be simple and in good musical taste, and it is very important that the words are written in language which appeals to his own limited experience of life. Understanding as well as joy should characterize the assembly. The leader need not always use the Bible, there is a rich field of sacred literature from which he may choose, and sometimes a modern translation of the Bible may prove more helpful, but the reading should be brief and in keeping with some theme clearly stated, perhaps at the beginning of the week – the child will worship all the better for knowing why he is worshipping. For the same reason, prayers should be few and very much to the point – this does not preclude the use of many lovely traditional prayers – and except where the children can say them together or join in the responses, they should be short. The dedication of the school's life and work to God must never become the occasion for veiled references to slacking, late-coming or rudeness. Long homilies have no place in the assembly, neither have impromptu hymn practices nor speech-training exercises. They belong to another time and another place. All might best end as it began, punctually and on a note of praise 'restoring the vision of God',[2] followed by a moment of silence. Then and only then, should notices be given out. Nothing can be so anti-worship as the hurried beginning, the confused ending. But what can the C-streamer get out of all this? A growing feeling of school-community, a deepened sense of worship; the dawning realization that he belongs to the school and to God. Moreover, he will begin the day happily and in the most hopeful way.

'Each kindly deed a prayer'. . . . J. G. Whittier makes the point that serving others can be worship. Nothing could excuse the highly dangerous and thoroughly distasteful practice of constantly urgign 'holy works' on children, but there are times when opportunities for 'worship in service' arise quite naturally and healthily. Remembering

[1] *Syllabus of Religious Instruction* (Sunderland), p. 98, paragraph (vii).
[2] ibid., paragraph (iv).

the sick should not stop short with prayers, it can find practical expression in get-well letters, perhaps small gifts of flowers and fruit. Some act of service undertaken in the wider out-of-school community will help to give point and purpose to the celebration of the Christian festivals . . . gifts of toys to the local Children's Home at Christmas; food distributed amongst old-age pensioners after the Harvest Festival Service. These are exercises in Christian living without which the child's religious experience would be incomplete.

It must be the school's purpose that each child will want to be 'actively associated with the Christian Community',[1] and the Christian community is the Church. How far a school would be justified in persuading parents whose children do not already do so to send them to Sunday school and enroll them in some church organization, many would hesitate to say. Yet has the Church no part to play in the after-care of the slow-learning child? True, not all churches are worthy of the name, but there are many able to offer him that stable, wholesome community life which he will need perhaps most of all during the early and difficult post-school years. Would it be wrong if, from time to time, the school did no more than circularize parents with information about local church organizations, stating times and places of meetings and the names of the leaders? It might even arrange letters of introduction.

Even assuming that the Special Schools have taken the very slow children, it is obvious that there is a large number of slow-learning children for whom the ordinary school must accept responsibility, and there can be little doubt that the responsibility will lie most heavily upon the junior school. It is there where he will reach the 'readiness stage', that degree of maturation, physical and mental, at which he can best begin his more formal education. It is in the junior school where the early and most hopeful opportunities will arise for helping him on his way towards reasonable self-sufficiency through a thorough-going mastery of the basic skills of everyday; it is there where he may come by a healthy self-respect and a feeling of worth; where he may at least begin to learn to live a stable, law-abiding and co-operative community life. Four years of failing to live well and learn well will almost certainly send him on to the

[1] *Syllabus of Religious Instruction* (Sunderland), p. 13.

secondary modern school where he will enter upon the last and decisive phase of his education, at odds with the world in general and with school in particular.

What provision can the junior school as a school with equally pressing responsibilities towards other children, make for his effective education? One still meets with the feeling implied, if not openly expressed, that the 'educationally sub-normal' are also sub-human, creatures apart, who have no proper place in society, and certainly not in the ordinary school; for whom nothing can be done, save to keep them in order; of whom nothing can be expected, save failure. The school must begin by accepting him as a person. True, he is a tail-ender, but he comes at the tail end of the scale which includes ordinary folk. Good will may be expressed in many simple, but to the child encouraging ways. It is no small thing for him that he should be appointed school monitor for a week, taking his turn with the other children; that he can compete for a place in the school teams. He may fail to qualify, so will many others, but at least he will be made to feel eligible. There are schools where, as one boy put it, 'They won't even let you try.' He is quick to sense the unspoken belief that he is incapable and for him feeling eligible is almost as important as success. And there is the practical consequence that the more he is made to feel eligible, the deeper will be his regard for the school and all for which it stands.

Parents are not the only ones given to judging a school by its results. The more the slow-learning child learns, the more he is likely to believe his is a good school, working in his best interests. A 10-year-old moved from one school to another, then visited his old school some weeks later. When asked how he was getting on in his new school he said, 'It's a rotten school, they don't teach you nothing.' In many junior schools of course, teachers change classes with each academic year, excepting perhaps those who take the so-called scholarship and pre-scholarship classes. All too often at least one C class is thrust upon a junior member of staff, not infrequently newly arrived from training college. Others may be taken by teachers who feel that in doing so they are releasing a colleague to work in the more congenial atmosphere of an A or B stream. Worse still, the C-stream teacher must so often work alone, with the barest knowledge of what has gone before, and no better guide to the

SOCIAL, MORAL AND RELIGIOUS TRAINING

year's work than a truncated B-stream syllabus. Little good can come of what is in fact a caretaker system, for only an experienced and sympathetic teacher can meet the needs of the slow-learning child adequately. Indeed, the most hopeful means of providing special educational treatment exists in those junior schools where the four C classes are organized as a co-ordinated unit by a team of mutually interested teachers. Together they may plan a four-year progressive syllabus designed to meet the child's growing needs and abilities; equally important, they may devise a common system of cumulative individual records. A factual account of the child's growth both as a person and a scholar, is an invaluable aid to the teacher. It helps him to make personal contact earlier and more surely; moreover, he need not adopt the chancy expedient of beginning all over again and in the dark. There are still too many slow-learning children failing because they are expected to be their chronological, not mental, age; because they are being taught by what are, for them, the wrong methods. Who are in fact, being confirmed in failure for want of a record card or for want of its proper use. A big, pretty, well-dressed child was referred to a remedial group because she was 'lazy, unco-operative, almost $9\frac{1}{2}$, but extremely childish'. On investigation, her mental age proved to be a little more than $6\frac{1}{4}$. Small wonder that her behaviour was extremely childish, or that she was still struggling with her Reading-book Two! Her record card was later discovered in a locked cupboard. No action had been taken either to refer her for ascertainment or to provide her with special educational treatment. Her teacher was genuinely surprised to learn that she was so 'mentally backward'. It cannot be said too often that successful learning makes for successful living. A team of mutually interested teachers can build up an adequate supply of the supporting apparatus and carefully graded work material so necessary to the C-stream. Moreover, they may help each other in many practical ways – exchanging opinion, sharing experience, pooling knowledge. Too, their unfailing interest will do much to win the support of parents and colleagues. So, as he passes from class to class, the child will be spared the strain of making new adjustments to methods of work and attitudes of teachers. Always he will begin where he left off, moving steadily onwards; always he may expect the same calm and helpful treatment.

TEACHING THE SLOW LEARNER IN THE PRIMARY SCHOOL

Obviously, the smaller the class, the more effective the teaching, but it is not unusual for a C class to be made larger than it need be by the deliberate inclusion of some brighter, difficult children – the highly strung, the downright awkward and sometimes the bright foreign child who cannot speak English. It needlessly complicates the teacher's task to ask him to cater for children who could be dealt with adequately elsewhere in the school, and who might prove to be a disruptive influence in the life of his class. In any case, he will no doubt already have his fair share of difficult children. If the school is to serve the best interests of all its children, then it must guard against interpreting special educational treatment too widely.

However, the most hopeful means do not always obtain and many argue that where the child requiring it attends a two – or perhaps a one-stream school, then special educational treatment presents insuperable difficulties. It would be foolish to minimize the difficulties, nevertheless it is possible to go at least part of the way towards meeting his needs in meeting the needs of his class-mates. One may expect a wide spread of ability within an unstreamed class. No doubt there will be a few bright ones and certainly there will be a small group of slow learners. The thoughtful teacher will readily see that he can teach most effectively as he employs some form of group and individual work in the basic subjects. In one single stream class a set of class readers was replaced by a series of graded readers. Over a year the results were encouraging. Capable readers were happily employed at their own steadily rising level of competence, so freeing the teacher to give individual instruction to the slow learners. Very good readers were able to read children's classics they might never have read otherwise and so acquire the rudiments of a literary taste. The best interests of the A-child and the C-child are not altogether incompatible.

Techniques make for better teaching and there ought to be at least one specially qualified member of staff in every junior school able to advise his colleagues, but so often it is the manner rather than the method which makes for success. Her colleagues said that if Miss F. could not teach a child, then no one could, yet her methods could hardly be described as modern. Nevertheless, she managed to inspire the children she taught with her own quiet determination; and they warmed to her obvious interest in all they did. The school which,

SOCIAL, MORAL AND RELIGIOUS TRAINING

like Miss E., can make the slow-learning child feel wanted, cared for and in some way responsible, will have done him a great, if not the greatest of services.

Suggestions for Reading
Educational
BURT, C., *The Backward Child*, U.L.P.
— *The Juvenile Delinquent*, U.L.P.
— *The Sub-normal Mind*, U.L.P.
FLEMING, C. M., *Individual Work in Primary Schools*, Harrap.
ISAACS, S., *Social Development in Young Children*, Routledge.
— *The Children We Teach*, U.L.P.
ISAACS, S., OLIVER R.A.C. and FIELD, H.E. *The Educational Guidance of the School Child*, Evans.
KENNEDY-FRASER, D., *The Education of the Backward Child*, U.L.P.
LLOYD, F., *Educating the Sub-normal Child*, Methuen.
VALENTINE, C., *The Difficult Child and the Problem of Discipline*, U.L.P.
VERNON, P. E., *The Measurement of Abilities*, U.L.P.

Religious
ALINGTON, C. A., *A new approach to the New Testament*, Bell.
BARCLAY, O., *The Making and Meaning of the Bible*, S.C.M.
BRALEY, E. F., *Blackboard Drawing for the Sunday School Teacher*, S.P.C.K. Now out of print.
COOK, S., *An Introduction to the Bible*, Pelican Books.
COOK, H., *Heroes of the Faith*, S.C.M.
DEANE, A., *The World Christ Knew*, Guild Books.
— *How to enjoy the Bible*, Hodder and Stoughton.
— *Rabboni*, Hodder and Stoughton.
— *How to understand the Gospels*, Hodder and Stoughton.
ENTWISTLE, M., *The Bible Guide Book*, S.C.M.
HALL, H. F., *The presentation of the Bible to children*, O.U.P.
MANSON, T. W., *A companion to the Bible*, T. T. Clarke.
MACKIE, G. M., *Bible Manners and Customs*, Blackie.
PATERSON SMYTHE, J., *How we got our Bible*, Low.
READ-MUMFORD, E., *How we can help children to pray*, Longmans.

SMITH, J.W.D., *Bible Background*, Methuen.
SOMERVELL, D. G., *A short history of our religion*, Bell.
WALKER A. H. and EVANS M., *Biblical models and how to make them*, National Society.
WILSON, D., *Child Psychology and Religious Education*, S.C.M.
YOUNGMAN, B. R., *Background to the Bible* (Books 1-4), Hulton Ed. Publications.
— *Teaching Religious Instruction*, Hulton Ed. Publications.
YEAXLEE, B., *The Approach to Religious Education*, S.C.M.

R. W. BANNISTER

Chapter II

PHYSICAL EDUCATION AND HEALTH

'I'm fed up with Fred's colds. Why don't his teacher make him put his coat on when he does games?'

'I'm not letting Charlie go bathing any more till he can swim as he gets his hair all wet.'

'Please excuse John being away yesterday as my Mum can't write proper and he has a touch of consumsion.'

'Billy isn't too well but he'll be alright if you let him sit nere the pipes and don't let him out.'

Yes! They are all genuine and I know my colleagues who deal with backward children in the ordinary junior school could give many more examples. So often the backward child is just another member of a backward family and these notes are the products of ignorance – ignorance not only of the English language but also of the basic rules of health. It is quite evident, if only from these notes alone, that the backward child is in great need of physical education in its widest possible sense and yet I cannot help but note with dismay that in many junior schools he gets little or nothing beyond what is known as the P.E. lesson on the time-table. Indeed, where administration is weak, he often misses that, for P.E. is a favourite lesson for some teachers to skip. It is skipped for a variety of reasons: 'Too cold'; 'Too hot'; 'No time to change'; 'They would be better off doing arithmetic'; 'It's the County Test next week'; 'I feel whacked'; or 'They have their corrections to finish'.

Most teachers today would agree with Professor L. Arnaud Reid in his definition of education. He said, 'Sound education is the art of helping human beings of all ages to grow and develop to a fuller stature of mind, body and spirit and to live well in their world. It should be remembered that education is for every type and variety of life.' It seems to follow that as all forms of communication with our fellow human beings are limited to the five physical channels of touch, sight, sound, taste and smell, any influence we may have in the mental, emotional and spiritual spheres will be achieved only through the physical. Would it not be wise, therefore, to rid ourselves of the notion that physical education exists only in the P.E. lesson, for surely this is as foolish as the idea that children learn to read only in the lesson labelled 'Reading' on the time-table.

Perhaps it would not be too much to claim that, at least in the early stages, all education is physical education. The baby learns about his environment by physical contact. Finding the difference between rough and smooth, hard and soft, hot and cold, etc., is all physical education. At a later stage, learning to read involves very complex physical skills. Later still come the physical skills required by writing, painting and drawing and many of the basic requirements in arithmetic are physical, such as the concepts of more and less, heavier and lighter, longer and shorter. In fact it is not until the child has progressed to the stage of abstract thought that we can begin to distinguish with any clarity at all between what is physical and what is mental and even in the most isolated academic atmosphere there is still much physical education apart from P.E. and games. When one considers that many a backward child will never reach the stage of abstract thought it begins to appear that most of our work is physical education.

The idea of a sound mind in a sound body is not new, but too often physical education has been thought of in terms of body building of the 'You too can have a body like mine' type. Our aim should surely be to see that each child each year is in a little better physical trim – a little fitter, a little more alert, a little quicker to move, a little brighter in the eye, a little more upright than he was last year. Would not many of our problems be solved if our charges were fitter, more alert, quicker off the mark, brighter in the eye and more upstanding?

It is most important that every child showing signs of backwardness is sent to the school medical officer to make quite certain there is no actual physical defect. It is not good enough to send the child to the minor ailments clinic unheralded. Medical officers and school nurses are busy people and they cannot be expected to read the teacher's mind. It should be remembered that the teacher is the person immediately responsible (where there is parental inadequacy) for the overall welfare of the child. It is the teacher who stands *in loco parentis* – not the doctor or the nurse. The school medical service is an ancillary service which will provide you with specialist assistance if it knows what you are looking for. It is essential, therefore, that the M.O. should know why the child is being referred to him and that the teacher should ask for his specific assurances along relevant lines. The correct way of doing this may vary from district to district, but each Head teacher would find it of value to know the medical officer and school nurse personally. It is so much easier to ring up a personal friend and ask for help than to suffer the delays associated with 'normal channels'. In the same way the Head teacher might find it well worth while to know influential people in the other ancillary services. 'Could you pop down to 47 Dismal Street on some pretext and let me know what sort of a place it is?' Some class teachers like to visit homes themselves. The sight of Mum and Teacher being friends over a cup of tea might well give little Tommy a new slant on life. In any case it is worth while to make a list of the many people who could help if their co-operation were secured. They are often as shy of consulting you as you are of consulting them.

From the knowledge gained the teacher can plan ahead. It may well be that spectacles will help to clear up one problem or that the knowledge of a slight hearing loss may help the teacher to cope with another. Other services may be brought in to assist, the dentist, the child guidance service or the speech therapist. These people, like the teacher, are professional people doing a professional job. It is for them to give the advice but it is up to the teacher with his broad picture of the whole child to decide how that advice may best be followed. The child is the teacher's problem and the obtaining of the very best advice does not solve the problem – it merely points the way. I stress this because I know of many cases where the teacher has said in some form of words, 'Oh him! We don't bother about him, because he's under the psychologist.' The teacher may be able to arrange for the better nourishment of the child by telling parents how to go about applying for free meals or by arranging for him to take cod-liver oil at school. It may be possible to arrange for him to be included on a school journey or to arrange through the appropriate channels for a stay at some camp school or convalescent home. Often, of course, there will be no obvious physical defect . . . the child is physically normal.

We all know that the bounds of normality are very wide and it is within these bounds that the teacher often has to work. These children are well known to teachers everywhere. There is little wrong with them, but they are frequently away. He has a cold, she has a tummy upset; this one has a sore throat, that one a temperature. He isn't up to the mark, he doesn't feel himself or he's had a touch of that horrible thing they cannot spell. Many of them suffer from that distressing complaint known to teachers as 'Fridayitis'. In our depressed moments we feel the only thing they are sick of is school, but in our saner moments we know perfectly well that it is quite true that they are invariably below par physically. They are never quite fit. Their parents often become as weary as we do of this chronic condition because they do not understand the reason for it. Where both parents are working one has to stay at home to look after the child and lose money thereby. The parents are annoyed and vent their emotions on the school. They blame us for every sneeze as indicated in the first two notes at the beginning of this chapter. Often the first job is to try to educate the parent and anyone who has tried this approach knows the difficulties and pitfalls in store for the unwary. It is certain, however, that once the teacher has convinced the parent that he has only the child's welfare at heart, the battle is largely won. It is equally certain that the exchange of rude notes will only serve to aggravate the problem.

So far I have tried to indicate that, where for any reason the home has failed, it is the teacher's primary duty to take every step open to him to ensure that every child in his care is as physically fit as the resources of the Welfare State can make him. But this is not enough. Education is much more. If the child is to keep fit he must be taught how to look after himself, how to keep himself in good health and how to make himself fitter than ever. He must be shown that fitness brings its own rewards. I am certainly not suggesting that there should be on the time-table of the junior school a lesson called

PHYSICAL EDUCATION AND HEALTH

'Hygiene', but there must be some definite and deliberate teaching of the simple rules of health. The teaching must be both positive (Do this) and negative (Thou shalt not). Under no circumstances should the teaching develop into a course of anatomy or human physiology, but should arise in the course of informal chats and simple stories like 'The Microbe Man' or be centred round a simple theme such as 'Where there's dirt, there's danger'. At present there is a move towards more science teaching in the junior school and the imaginative teacher could include a great deal of useful teaching under this heading. In simple, but dramatic ways at least the following matter should be covered:

1. Cleanliness and tidiness of clothes and body.
2. How and why we sweat.
3. Why we should change for P.E. and games.
4. The most suitable wear for different times.
5. How colds and other illnesses are carried.
6. Footwear.
7. Care of eyes, teeth, nails and hair.
8. Moderation in all things.
9. Cuts and bruises.
10. Dangers of sticking pens into others, pulling chairs from under others, etc.
11. Burns.
12. Handkerchiefs.

A word of caution is necessary especially for the benefit of the less experienced teacher. Many teachers have been brought up in a socially favoured environment and tend to expect too much. It is the height of folly to expect a child to take a daily bath when he lives in a house without a bathroom and when his parents have only a nodding acquaintance with water themselves. Progress is slow – very slow. Remember that the child who pulls out a dirty rag is perhaps doing his best to comply with your requirement that every child shall have a handkerchief. Avoid the public rebuke and remember that the fault often lies with the parent and not with the child. In the hands of the skilful teacher the few health talks that appear to arise by chance will have a great impact on the child. The boy who looks after his bicycle and the one who does not can be used to explain the importance of looking after the most complicated machine of all. Make him understand that he cannot buy another. The fascinating topic will lead to pertinent questions, the teacher will side-track the morbid stories about Uncle Tom's contribution to medical case history, a good deal of ignorance and a good many old wives' tales will be swept aside and a little breath of the fresh air of understanding will be administered, all helping to make the new generation a little better informed than its predecessor. If things go well, the cleaner, more careful and more thoughtful child will be a little easier to teach, a little keener to learn about other things and a little more willing to co-operate. In the lower reaches of intelligence, training may have to be substituted for education – e.g. toothbrush drill daily until it becomes a habit – but this is (under a progressive authority) rather in the sphere of the Special School than in that of the ordinary junior school.

In the realms of what is usually understood by the term Physical Education, the teacher has far more allies at his elbow than he has when struggling with the Three R's. Dad and Mum got on quite well without the latter. In any case, where he lives, it is 'cissy' to speak properly. But to be a footballer or a high-jumper – well, perhaps that's not too bad. It's worth a try, anyway.

The P.E. lesson or games will, then, start off on the right foot. The trouble is that backward children want to be able to do it all at once and are discouraged when they find they fail in this activity as they have failed in others. This sense of failure is the biggest bogy of all in the treatment of the backward child. The teacher must so set the stage as to ensure a fair expectation of success. All success is as bad as all failure. They need sufficient successes to give them confidence and sufficient failures to allow them to learn to accept their limitations. The activities of the good infant school, the free play, the directed play, the music and movement and all similar things have usually set the child off to a good start. In the junior school he finds considerably more formal work in which he is already beginning to understand that he doesn't shine and only too rarely a P.E. lesson where he can really express himself. And express himself he does, with a vengeance, which is yet another reason why Teacher may often decide that life is brighter when Tommy is chained to his desk and why Teacher dreads – and if possible skips – the P.E. lesson.

It seems that there are three ways in which the junior school can direct the child's undoubted pride in his physical strength and agility into healthy educational channels:

(1) The systematic teaching of the basic skills required in games.
(2) The development of music and movement.
(3) The development of physical skills required in other subjects.

1. The Systematic Teaching of the Basic skills required in Games

As I have indicated earlier, it is not the slightest use to take a backward boy on the football field and set him various practices in ball control. He doesn't want to do that at all. He wants to play football – all at once – just like that. We all know many places where that happens. A class of boys is let loose between two goalposts and for the next forty minutes a bundle, made up of about sixteen boys and a ball, galumphs about the pitch, its teacher-satellite orbiting erratically, while six other boys freeze solid in outer space. Now I am not denying the advantages of this system. If it is the only time in the week when a class of city children get on to a grassy space, the rough and tumble alone, together with the mile walk to get there, is definitely physical education. It is true also that some of the brighter children will learn something about football and that the backward ones will be so busy getting either cool or warm afterwards that they will be quiet for the rest of the afternoon.

The problem is this. Youngsters expect to play football when they go on a pitch, yet they have to be taught the basic skills and unless there is some system clearly understood by all concerned it is fatally easy that only the most promising children will be picked out by the teacher responsible for the school football team and taught the skills, while the huge majority go on chasing a ball and missing the wonderful educational opportunities that the teaching of the skills affords.

There are, no doubt, many ways of ensuring that the skills are taught to all. To my mind there is no doubt that the proper place for the teaching of the skills is in the P.E. lesson. Perhaps this sounds obvious, but it is my experience that so often the P.E. lesson is divorced from everything else on the time-table. Progressive teachers in the junior school have for many decades longed for freedom from the set syllabus and now that freedom is gained many do not know what to do with it. Working to the spirit of the recent publications calls for personal initiative and a large number of fainthearts seek the comfort of their shackles again. Classes still go in orderly (or disorderly) fashion through a series of carefully (or carelessly) devised exercises and activities watched by teachers who do not engage in one single point of teaching or coaching throughout the whole of the 'lesson'.

Perhaps the best way to proceed is to devise a system that will make the child proud and keen to improve his skill. Some schools run a House system, while others will not hear of it. It all depends on your system. It is certainly true that a child of this age can become fanatically loyal to a group, especially when it is a real live group to which he belongs and which has caught his imagination. A House system which is dusted and brought out once a year at the annual Sports Day cannot possibly catch the imagination. It is also well known that a junior loves a badge. Why, then, give your House or group badges away or sell them? Why not take the line that only a useful member of the group is fit to wear its insignia? It is simple enough to devise a series of tests of basic skills to meet your requirements. Here is an example:

Tests for Award of House Badges and Stars

To be taken as opportunity permits in P.E. and games lessons. Any *five* completed tests entitle a child to be recommended for the award of a House Badge. For each extra three tests completed a star will be issued to be worn on the gym vest or blouse. Maximum award: One House Badge and five stars.

Test 1. Reasonable ability to dodge a football when thrown below knee level by ring of children surrounding candidate and at a reasonable distance from him.

Test 2. Ability to catch a small rubber ball with both hands when thrown to him under-arm by another child at a distance of at least 5 yards.

Test 3. As Test 2, catching with right hand only.

Test 4. As Test 2, catching with left hand only.

Test 5. Ability to throw small rubber ball through smallest hoop from a distance of at least 5 yards. (2 out of 3.)

Test 6. Ability to hit a target drawn on playground wall in the form of a circle of 1 foot diameter using an overarm throw from at least 5 yards. (2 out of 3.)

Test 7. Ability to hit a rounders ball with a rounders stick. (3 out of 5 fair rounders serves.)

Test 8. Ability to keep a small rubber ball bouncing on a padder bat for at least half a minute.

Test 9. Ability to skip, turning the rope himself, to a count of at least 20.

Test 10. Ability to skip, others turning rope toward the competitor. Run in, skip 5 and run out.

Test 11. As Test 10, but rope turning away from competitor.

Test 12. Ability to hit wicket twice in 6 balls bowling overarm at a distance of 18 yards.

Test 13. Ability to dribble a football with inside of foot and outside of foot around obstacles 2 yards apart. Ball to be kept under perfect control.

Test 14. Ability to walk balance bench correctly.

Test 15. Ability to crouch jump in good style over bench.

Test 16. Ability to perform a correct forward roll.

Test 17. Ability to perform hop, step and jump in good style.

Test 18. Ability to knock over a basket with a football, taking a place kick from 8 yards. (2 out of 3.)

Test 19. Ability to perform a correct forward roll through a medium sized hoop held with its centre approximately 2 feet above the mat.

Test 20. Ability to juggle with two small rubber balls.

Recommendations for these awards should be sent in to the Head teacher on a convenient day each week and the awards should be made publicly, perhaps after Morning Service. A clear record should be kept in alphabetical order showing the name, the tests completed and the awards made. Each of the badges and stars should also carry the automatic award of a House Point. If the tests are carefully devised, the majority of children (including the backward ones) in the first year will manage to obtain the House Badge and will experience the thrill of belonging to their House as they make their way to the platform to receive the badge and to hear their

House announced. It will be found that those few who fail to obtain the badge in the first year do so for physical reasons and are from all ranges of intelligence. It is rare indeed to find any child who has not obtained the badge by the end of the second year. I have also found it very useful to arrange to have the House Captains sitting on or near the platform and to encourage them to give a smile and a pat on the back to the little ones as they come forward. I regard this sense of belonging as a useful member to a group as a fundamental attitude to be encouraged throughout the junior school. At the end of the Primary Course I have also found it useful to issue school colours for P.E. These take the form of a properly printed certificate and are awarded to five (and sometimes four) star holders. They are restricted to a maximum of six each year and the secondary schools to which these children go have been persuaded to take considerable notice of these awards. It is true that the backward children rarely qualify for these high awards, but the fact that they are available to them does serve to stimulate the maximum effort. Over the past four years two of these children have received colours for football, two boys and one girl have received colours for rounders and two boys and two girls have received them for swimming. Only one boy succeeded in obtaining his P.E. colours. The important point is that it is evident to the backward child that these awards are within his reach. At the time of writing four boys from the third and fourth year backward classes have been selected, on merit, for the school rounders team.

All the skills involved are taught and tested during the course of the normal P.E. periods. In addition to teaching these skills, which are basic to both boys' and girls' major team games, the teacher is expected to devise activities and minor team games in which the skills taught may be practised and further developed.

Running and jumping may also be dealt with in the normal P.E. and games periods, but under a slightly different scheme. It is necessary to remember that it is the teacher's duty to encourage every child in the school to improve his or her individual standard of attainment in running and jumping rather than to train junior children in the specific techniques involved. It is certainly not our aim to pick out an *élite* and coach them for the town sports. Nevertheless, if a sound scheme is followed, there will be no lack of more able children well fitted to represent the school at any sports meeting.

PHYSICAL EDUCATION AND HEALTH

Perhaps the best time to begin is in the second half of the Spring Term each year. Occasional P.E. lessons should be devoted to running. After a preliminary warming up activity a very slow trot around the yard or field should be interspersed with short bursts of sprinting called for on a whistle, changing back to trotting on a second whistle. Children should be reminded that you cannot run efficiently until you are warmed up and that it is not good to stop suddenly after a sprint or to throw oneself on the ground. A short rest should be given while the teacher talks of these points and also points out the value of taking long strides and the importance of remembering that the shortest distance between two points is a straight line. This can be followed by running with giant strides and then the class may be allowed to watch one individual running to a set point so that they may see for themselves how much further he runs than is necessary.

The teacher should then set his class into groups, skipping, playing minor team games, etc., while he marks out a distance appropriate to the age of the class. (I suggest 50 yards for first year juniors and 80 yards for fourth year juniors.) One of the groups may then be sent over the course timed against a stop-watch. Then the other groups should be dealt with in turn sending each group back to team games when finished to avoid standing about. The lesson should be finished with a posture exercise and the class brought back into school in good order. Back in the classroom the times should be posted for all to see.

In following weeks the pattern should be repeated and House Points awarded for those children who make the best improvement on their previous timings. Avoid praise for the 'best in the class' and aim to show that the only kudos involved is the best improvement in individual timing.

During the final week of the Spring Term teachers concerned with the same age group should confer and, after considering the recorded times, fix two standards for the age group. A High Standard should be fixed at such a point that only some 25 per cent. of the age group are likely to reach it and a Main Standard at such a point that only 25 per cent. of the age group are unlikely to reach it. These standards should then be published in order that the children may, should they wish, practise during the holiday.

TEACHING THE SLOW LEARNER IN THE PRIMARY SCHOOL

In the first few weeks of the Summer Term the Standard Tests should be held and a list sent in showing the name of each child in alphabetical order, his House, a tick under High or Main Standard if obtained, his best recorded time and the House Points gained (say 2 for High Standard and 1 for Main Standard).

Over the same period the various jumps should be practised – perhaps as one of the group activities – and standards reached in the same sort of way.

When all the class records of standards are in, the Head teacher, sports secretary or school secretary should break down the class records into House records and supply the details for each House to the teacher in charge. House meetings may then be arranged to pick competitors for the inter-House school sports. At the beginning of this sports meeting the points already obtained by standard-holders will be on the recording table and points gained at the meeting itself will be added, so that a child who is not actually competing can say to his mother or father, 'I have gained three points for my House.' The results of the sports meeting will easily pick out the obvious people to represent the school at the town sports. In a way such as this it is, therefore, possible for every child to make a personal contribution to his community, irrespective of his age, mentality or physical condition.

It may also be possible to bring outside schemes into line. For example the swimming instructors at the local baths have a scheme of awards. A green badge is awarded for the ability to struggle from one side of the bath to the other, then comes the elementary certificate and later a yellow badge, which confers the right to use the baths for a year without paying entrance fees and so on, right up to the County Badge. By arrangement I have found it possible to have these awards collected from the baths and duly presented after Morning Service with an appropriate award of House Points. Cycling proficiency awards could also be included. Inter-House contests in all kinds of minor and major team games all play their part.

If the House system, or any other system, is to be successful its operation must be continually in front of the children's eyes. A cloth for the table in the Hall could be embroidered with the House symbols in each corner, so that the winning House may have its symbol draped to the front. The actual point score should be clearly

PHYSICAL EDUCATION AND HEALTH

displayed on the wall above the platform. All the boards, embroidery, etc., should be made by the children in the various craft lessons and each House should have its own notice board and hold its own meetings regularly. It will be found that the children will naturally pick captains from those who have obtained several stars in P.E. and who have good running and jumping standards. These are usually the children who have striven the hardest over the years and are thus fitting persons to lead the House. In fact I overheard one of our captains telling a first year boy, 'I couldn't jump when I was your age. You just have to try and if you try you'll be good.' Needless to say, the House system should cover all aspects of the school life and not only the Physical Education side.

I have talked a great deal about the House system in order to illustrate the principles involved. There is no particular merit in the House system itself. I have spoken of the whole school because every teacher has to consider the school as a whole and the teacher responsible for backward children is constantly striving to find ways and means whereby his children can play their part in the larger community of the school and is continually striving to avoid the disadvantages of segregation. There is no reason at all why the principles set out above cannot be applied to any system, to any type of child, to school organization or to class organization. These principles may be summarized as follows:

(1) A clear cut, easily understood, series of aims.
(2) P.E. lessons devised to teach, to give practice in and to strengthen the necessary muscles for sensory-muscular co-ordination.
(3) A testing programme to encourage effort in the individual child.
(4) Games lessons to give opportunity to use, progressively and intelligently, the newly acquired skills.
(5) At least an annual check to see that all the necessary apparatus, playground marking and material are available to all and are in good order, for it is quite impossible to learn first class skills with second rate apparatus and facilities.
(6) A staff of teachers who all clearly understand and work together to achieve these aims, even if some of them are not too skilful in this sphere themselves.

There are many books which may be consulted as source books from which the teacher can select exercises, activities and games to bear upon the skill he has in mind to develop. A selection is given at the end of the chapter.

2. The Development of Music and Movement

It is to be hoped that the teacher or the school which has developed the P.E. and games lessons along sound lines will not consider the task of physical education completed. The poise, the gesture and the flash of the eyes can be more eloquent than the tongue. The grace of Alicia Markova and the grace of Stanley Matthews are at once so very different and so very much alike. There are other things in life beside football that are equally dependent upon physical skills. I will briefly comment on three – drama, music, and dancing – confining my remarks to their relevance to Physical Education. A fuller treatment will of course be found in Chapters 7 and 8.

(a) Dramatic Work

Much useful Physical Education is found under this unlikely heading on the time-table. From the foundation of the music and movement taught in the infant school it is both easy and useful for the backward child to progress along the lines of imitative mime. Miming the man with the pickaxe, the pneumatic drill, the try-your-strength hammer at the fair, the man playing tennis, the window cleaner and a thousand and one other familiar situations demands the development of easy and graceful massive movements of the body. Similarly imitation of things like threading a needle, watching a fly, using a typewriter, folding a letter and putting it in an envelope give a great deal of useful practice in the finer, more delicate movements which are so necessary to develop in the backward child. Remember that it is on memory, observation and co-ordinated fine movements of hand and eye that most of our more academic achievements depend, even down to the mechanics of turning over to the next page of this chapter. Remember, too, that for the backward child action may well be the only easy form of expression. It is especially useful because a child can quickly find success where before he found only failure. This work, to my mind, is a part of physical education we neglect at our peril.

PHYSICAL EDUCATION AND HEALTH

(b) *Music and Choral Speaking*

These are two other obvious developments from music and movement, but perhaps they are not often considered as a part of physical education. We talk of the poetry of motion: there is motion in poetry. Singing together is well known to the teachers of backward children in the Special Schools for its therapeutic value. We could do well to use it more with our backward children. When all attention has flagged, when all concentration has vanished, the wise teacher gathers them around the piano, or around himself if he cannot play, and a few minutes are spent in singing for the sheer joy of it. On another occasion he sends them for a quick romp in the yard. Music or physical romp, the effect is just the same. They return refreshed, cheerful and ready to carry on. And how they love and respond to the rhythm of a poem like 'From a Railway Carriage', 'Tarantella' or 'Night Mail', and what physical activity the fertile mind can think up to accompany the rhythm of the poem to build it up into a fine piece of choral speaking. Rhythm is the very stuff of physical education.

(c) *Dancing*

No chapter, however brief, on physical education could possibly omit to mention the importance of dancing. Here, again, it grows naturally out of the music and movement. The backward child should take part and progress as far as possible. It is absolutely essential in a mixed school that both boys and girls should take part in this activity every week right from the first year. If this is not done naturally and without fuss the boys are apt to scoff, but if it becomes accepted as the natural thing to do they will enjoy it immensely. Quite apart from the obvious advantages of dancing as a form of physical education leading to perfect control, poise and carriage, it is a most desirable social accomplishment, helping to promote tone, courtesy and the easy, unembarrassed mingling of the sexes on terms of mutual respect. In fact, in many of these skills the boys find, to their obvious surprise, that the girls are not so 'cissy' as they had imagined. I have seen quite a number of boys skipping since this skill was required in Tests 9, 10 and 11, at first rather shamefacedly in a remote corner of the playground and then, later, joining in with some of the more complicated efforts of the girls. I was surprised recently to see a mixed group of girls and the most unlikely collection of boys playing skipping, running in, skipping three and running out. All were quite natural, all were enjoying the game and the boys were quite cheerfully taking their turn at turning the rope after an unsuccessful run in. Patting a ball against the wall they have not found too easy either.

3. The Development of Physical Skills required in Other Subjects
Great attention should be paid to the physical manipulations that are needed every day and in every subject and which are too often forgotten. A child needs to be taught how to hold a pen and a pencil, or how to sit in the most efficient position for the job in hand. Time and motion studies and organization and method teams have shown us how much adults have to learn in these matters. The sloppy way in which some of our children sit has to be seen to be believed. The pity of it is that many teachers seem to think that it is old-fashioned to do anything about it. The child also needs to be taught how to hold a ruler so that it does not slip and why ink will smudge the paper if he does not make use of the bevelled edge of the ruler. He needs to be shown how to use an eraser so that the paper is not rucked up. He needs to be led to take a pride in overcoming these small physical disabilities in the same way that he takes a pride in beating his last year's standard in the high jump.

The great majority of skills required in puppetry, scrap work, painting, drawing, clay work, needlework, bookcraft, weaving, toy-making, potato and lino cutting, and all those other things I hope your children have an opportunity to try out, are physical skills and their acquisition a matter of physical education. The thoughtful teacher will also realize that these are also the very skills that are required for efficient reading, writing and arithmetic. It seems very clear that academic skills are based upon physical skills and that the products of these skills will be a help or a hindrance according to our success or failure to influence the child's moral and spiritual development. Thus is shown the importance of the fourfold approach envisaged in the 1944 Act. The skilful and successful teacher of the backward child is the one who uses all the forces at his disposal to influence for good all the various parts, be they mental, moral, spiritual or physical, that go to make up the individual.

PHYSICAL EDUCATION AND HEALTH

Success, then, can never come while reading is in one compartment and P.E. in another. Success or failure will be noted in some twenty years' time when Johnnie, now himself a parent, writes in on decent paper, correct in spelling, punctuation and address:

'Dear Mr ——,
I regret to hear you have been unable to find a place for my son in the winter swimming class. I had hoped . . .'

Or will it be on the back of the familiar sugar bag in the well-known illiterate scrawl:

'Why did you tell my boy to wash his feet before he went . . . ?'

Teachers can do much to break the vicious circle of illiteracy, and problem families. If in your lifetime you manage to do something towards breaking even one of these circles you will deserve a medal. You will not get one. You, who deal with the whole child, will get just a few more in your class and be regarded as worth just a little less than those clever people who teach one subject to older children who are keen to learn. But you will be a first class teacher – the salt of the earth.

Recommended Books
BUCHER, *Foundations of Physical Education*, Kimpton.
EDMUNDSON, *Technique in Physical Education*, Harrap.
London County Council, *Syllabus of Physical Education for Junior Schools*, Staples Press.
Ministry of Education, *Physical Education in the Primary School:* Part 1 (Pamphlet 24), 'Moving and Growing'; Part 2 (Pamphlet 25), 'Planning the Programme', H.M.S.O.
RANDALL, *Modern Ideas in Physical Education*, Bell.
(Many ideas may also be gleaned from the pages of the old 1933 *Syllabus of Physical Training for Schools*, H.M.S.O.)

COOKE, *Simple Climbing Apparatus for Nursery and Primary Schools*, Bristol Education Committee.
HEAD, *Agility Apparatus for Primary Schools*, Evans.
MUNDEN, *Suggestions for use of small apparatus in Physical Education*, Ling Physical Education Association.

TEACHING THE SLOW LEARNER IN THE PRIMARY SCHOOL

DUNN, *Games Activities for Girls*, Blackie.
EDMUNDSON, *Games and Activities*, Pitman.
KINGSTON, *Activity Games for Playground and Classroom*, U.L.P.
KOHL and YOUNG, *Games for Children*, Faber and Faber.
LAING, *Games and Games Training for Junior Children*, Arnold.
MACCUAIG and CLARK, *Games worth playing for school, playground and playing field*, Longmans.
PATERSON, *Handbook of Physical Activities and Games*, U.L.P.
Various books of the *Know the Game* Series, Educational Productions.

BRUFORD, R., *Teaching Mime*, Methuen.
LANDER, B., *Music for Mime*, Methuen.
These two books go together.

ALFORD, V. (ed.), *Handbooks of European National Dances*, Max Parrish. (A very wide selection of books each containing instructions, music, colour plates of costume, etc.)
JARVIS, *Dances and Musical Activities for Juniors*, Faber and Faber.
SHARP, C., *The Country Dance Books*, Novello.
Folk Dances from Many Lands, Ling Physical Education Association. (Several Series – music and instructions are published separately.)

ASH and RAPAPORT, *Creative Work in the Junior School*, Methuen.
Various Dryad Leaflets dealing with wide variety of crafts.

Chapters bearing on the health of the child in the following two series:
BARNARD et al., *Science-Life*, Macmillan (New York) (6 volumes).
SCHNEIDER, *Elementary Science*, D. C. Heath and Co. (U.S.A) (4 volumes).
Junior Posture Charts, Ling Association Educational Productions. (Three charts – Feet, Sitting, Standing.)

R. C. ABLEWHITE

Chapter III

SPEECH AND ORAL WORK

> *The job of the school is to help its children to grow in their power of using their mother tongue, just as it helps them to grow in their power of using their bodies.*
> Ministry of Education pamphlet *Seven to Eleven*

Speech and the Child

The skill of talking is a natural one to a child and, as is pointed out in the Ministry's publication *Seven to Eleven*, 'children are always talkative'.

The normal child learns to talk before coming to school; but even by the time he is seven he still has much to learn about the art of talking. His speech has been based initially on the satisfaction of his personal needs and the quality of his experiences, in the home and in the small personal world that surrounds him. The extent of his vocabulary has therefore been governed by a number of factors:

(1) His home background.
(2) The vocabulary he has heard from those around him.
(3) The amount of opportunity and encouragement he has received to expand the use of speech.
(4) His own ability to put into words the thoughts and feelings which he has experienced.
(5) The quality and depth of these experiences and his ability to give expression to them adequately within the framework of the vocabulary he has mastered.

For the dull and backward child there are a number of retarding influences which slow up the natural development towards mastery of the art of oral communication. His home background is likely to be much poorer in the provision of:

(a) Opportunities for experiences which provide much of the material of background knowledge. Such things as trips to the seaside or country, shopping excursions, holidays away from home and the provision of well illustrated books and interesting pictures are all likely to be much fewer in the poorer homes from which the majority of our children are drawn.

(b) Similarly the vocabulary surrounding the child from an early age is probably going to be far smaller, inaccurately used and altogether less varied than that from the more favourable home.

He is going to have less perception of the situations and experiences through which he has lived; his experiences are dulled and he will receive from them a much simpler 'picture' than the brighter child. I recall a discussion in a class of 10-year-old boys following a visit to a well-known circus which was in the town. They had all received a great deal of enjoyment from it, but the brighter ones had noticed many tricks and antics of the clowns which had been missed by the C group at the bottom of the class. In many cases they could see how the trick 'water spouts' and magical bouquets of flowers had been made to appear from about the clowns' persons. Their enjoyment was heightened and the experience enriched by this ability to appreciate the artistry which lies beyond the surface gaiety – an appreciation beyond the ken of those duller ones in the lower reaches of the class.

Furthermore the child who has had from an early age an ever increasing succession of failures in his endeavours to cope with school and all that it stands for, is less likely to want to express an opinion, even when he has something that he really wants to say. He knows from past experience that most people seem to know more than he does and that very few have the time or patience to listen to him to try to understand what he wants to say. The result is that the backward child is likely to withdraw even more into himself and reserve his use of speech merely for the absolutely essential. Anything beyond this in the way of classroom discussions, oral lessons, general small talk with his neighbours, etc., is likely to be completely non-productive unless we prepare the way with the utmost care.

This brings us to the point where we should stop to consider the

BASIC SKILLS: SPEECH AND ORAL WORK

essentials that should be looked for in a scheme of work designed to improve the oral vocabulary and speech of the backward junior.

Firstly we must bear in mind the advantages that we hope to gain from the whole scheme. The acquisition of good speech is a basic educational requirement. Practice in the spoken word provides a corner-stone in the foundation of a sound education. For consider:

(1) The basic element of communication from man to man is speech. The larger and more accurate the vocabulary in use the easier and more exact that communication is going to be.

(2) Spoken communication is the prerequisite of all communication and good reading and writing habits depend in the first instance on a sound basis of speech.

(3) Words form the basis of the advance of thought and the pathway towards abstract reasoning. It has been said that thought is conducted along verbal channels so it must follow that the better and more accurate the vocabulary the higher the chance there is of an improvement in the standard of thought.

(4) The ability to converse freely and express oneself with clarity and ease is of paramount importance in the creation of a feeling of confidence and a sense of 'belonging' to the group. How many of us have felt at times 'cut-off' and unwanted because we happen to have become involved in a discussion or conversation outside our sphere of interest or knowledge? This feeling constantly perpetuated must surely be the worst type of atmosphere in which to attempt to educate our pupils. We recognize the importance of producing a sense of well-being, elimination of a constant sense of failure and the possibility of early success in all our work with the backward child.

Originally I suggested that the child's vocabulary grew through a variety of factors, but summarized we could say that these would reduce to three in number; his experiences, the type of language he hears and his own opportunity to voice expression and opinion. Surely then it must be around these elemental factors that we must fashion the work which we intend to do. Those things which have been lacking in the child's experience to date are to be put there by us. We know how the normal child grows towards a fluency of speech and we are convinced of the vast importance of the task before us. How shall we begin to rectify the earlier faults and failures and commence in the building-up of a satisfactory and satisfying vocabulary?

Underlying all our work I think that there are three major factors which must be kept in the forefront of our minds. We must provide (*a*) activities and experiences; (*b*) opportunities of appreciation and finally (*c*) opportunities for expression. The activities and experiences must be in concrete form, capable of interpretation by the type of child we are dealing with and within his sphere of interests at his own particular stage of development. Linked with them at all times we must provide opportunities of hearing and using words which centre around those experiences but reach out into wider spheres. We must give the child a reason for talking; provide him with something to talk about; help him with the words that are necessary in talking about it.

Amongst the millions of words which flow past the child's ears there must be many thousands which leave no mark or trace of any description for the simple reason that they go by unexplained, without illustration or definition. We must aim therefore at a deliberate enlargement of a 'hearing' vocabulary recognition. The teacher must provide opportunities for appreciation of the words which he uses within the classroom. This means that at all times we should ensure that the meanings of new words being introduced are fully understood. We can do this by the provision of some form of concrete connection by illustration (picture), demonstration (by teacher) or participation of individual pupil or the whole class. Apart from the obvious immediate results of clarification at the time this will also increase the child's interest in the idea that all words are capable of being understood and possibly increase his desire to achieve that understanding.

It has been said that the mind is like the stomach; it is not how much you put into it that counts, but how much it digests. And we all know the truth of the fact that no body of knowledge or particle of skill really becomes part of our own make-up until we have had an opportunity to practise it. When an art has received expression our impressions and experiences become clearer, more lasting and part of a genuine body of knowledge. The child must be given ample opportunity, and every encouragement, to translate his every experience into language and further be given the opportunity to relate these experiences. There are still many classes where teaching is a one-way process, rather like a broadcasting system with the teacher at the microphone and the children acting as immobile receivers. If we are to achieve our objective we must ensure that our classes are not like that all the time. There will be times when the class sits and the teacher talks, but there must be many more occasions when the class talks; as individuals in controlled discussion; as members of a social group sharing interests and experiences; as individuals seeking advice from one another or from the teacher; or as individuals talking to the rest of the class as a body. This needn't result in the chaos and lack of discipline which those who haven't attempted it may fear. If the teacher plans the course and remains at the helm throughout the journey then it will be a peaceful, enjoyable and most fruitful experience for all taking part, even if it's not a quiet one. Apart from all else this opportunity for expression and practice in the use of the spoken word is an absolutely essential feature of our programme. The art is dead without expression.

Story-telling and Reading
The first factor in achieving greater vocabulary control is the gathering-in of new words, the 'intake' side as it were. This requires real listening with interest and powerful motivation. What better for this purpose than stories? These have been an accepted part of the education of children since time immemorial and we use them in the primary school in our history, geography and R.I. lessons to put the background facts before the pupils, be they bright or dull, because we acknowledge them to be an extremely good way of holding interest.

If approached too easily and without proper preparation and thought there can be a great danger though of our using a perfectly valid and well-tried medium inadequately, missing altogether the particular objective that we are aiming at in this context. We, as adults, readily accept the meaning and form of the words as they unwind themselves during the story. The flow carries us along, and it will carry our class along as well. At the end the main facts, the outline of the plot, will have been understood. But I say that this is not all that you and I are after.

I have said that one of our aims must be to enlarge the scope of interests and appreciation held by the child. This can be done in a vague sort of way by presenting the story as I have just suggested. But there is a value beyond this where stories can play a vital part in actually increasing the usable vocabulary possessed by your child. Do you want the child to understand by merely skimming through the words presented to him, comprehending perhaps one in three, or do you want him to gain a much deeper experience through which he can build up his own stock of words, and eventually use them with a true knowledge of their meaning? These are definite alternatives.

One of the main difficulties in the proper use of stories is, paradoxically enough, its very easiness. Children will sit and be read to. They will listen to your story, as long as your voice isn't too hard on the ears, almost irrespective of the subject or its treatment – within reason of course. Perhaps it is because of this that listening to a story is often a very passive type of occupation. It so often calls for no active response from the listener – at this level I would say that it is becoming merely a 'time-filler' and hardly a part of education at all.

From the teacher's point of view also it can become a dangerous thing, for how easy it is to pick up a book of stories and say, 'Now we'll have a story.' For the busy teacher, and aren't we all, this is a big temptation. A lesson with the minimum of preparation, possibly none at all.

But of course to really use a story, to get as much as we can out of it, we must be prepared to spend as much time and thought on it as we do on our other subjects. We must examine our aims, know our story, and then stage its presentation with care and thought. This applies as much to the story we are reading for enjoyment, as the one we are using in our history or geography topics. The real enjoyment of the story will depend to a great extent on how much of it can be comprehended whether it is the story of *The Babes in the Wood* or *How Alfred Burnt the Cakes*. The amount of comprehension will be governed by the method of presentation, always remembering that the mental images invoked by the words we use are dependent on the

BASIC SKILLS: SPEECH AND ORAL WORK

ability of the child firstly to understand them, and then to link them with something within the confines of his own previous experiences.

Perhaps before going further it would be a good thing to define some of our aims in the use of stories within the context of this particular chapter. I would suggest these five. You can probably think of some more:

(1) To enrich the child's experiences and widen his bounds of knowledge. To introduce to him new facts about the world around him; knowledge of other people both here and abroad; how people once lived and how his present world is related with the past.

(2) To give him an appreciation of the enjoyment to be found from the tales of the experiences of others by following the characters in the stories and living with them through their experiences.

(3) To introduce to him new words and phrases, as well as facts, and to show him how these words are related to meaning in as concrete a fashion as possible. To enlarge his 'hearing' vocabulary.

(4) To present a situation which will provide him with a common experience which he can use in communication with the rest of the class, in class discussion and conversation. To enlarge his 'spoken' vocabulary.

(5) To provide an opportunity for the appreciation of the lyrical quality of words. Providing a pattern for him to imitate in his own writing efforts.

Many of these points are common to all children, some apply specifically to the slow learner. The first two aims in particular are those which have guided our choice of stories for some time now, and those of you who have had some experience in this field will find that the next paragraph or two are purely revisionary in nature.

Choosing a story which is suitable to the particular age and interests of the child is a matter which has been the subject of some research and there are a number of books which can be referred to for information.

Susan Isaacs in her study of the primary school child of 7 to 11,

TEACHING THE SLOW LEARNER IN THE PRIMARY SCHOOL

The Children We Teach has given us a broad outline which will guide us in our choice of suitable books and stories.

She points out that at the beginning of the period simple nature stories (those in which animals, the wind and weather and other natural phenomena are given personalities and speak like human beings) are enjoyed by both girls and boys. More realistic stories of animal life, if told vividly and dramatically, are also enjoyed, but this more detached type of presentation belongs more properly to the 8 and 9 year level where the cruder 'talking-beast' tale is hardly tolerated.

Fairy tales like *Jack and the Beanstalk, Tom Thumb,* and *Red Riding Hood,* delight the 7-year-old, but the more classic type of fairy tale as told by Grimm, Andersen and Andrew Lang are appreciated more by the 8-year-old, and even into the 9-year range.

Stories of real events enthral children and they appreciate tales of children of other lands. The boys enjoy hearing and reading about animals in the wild and heroic exploits in tracking, hunting, and taming them. But the girls enjoy more the stories about domestic animals and those of the farms.

The interest in fairy tales is still shown by the girls even up to the age of 9, but by this time most of the boys have become realists and prefer stories of boy-life and real heroes.

At the age of 10 the interest in fairy tales falls off sharply, even among girls, but myth and legend still hold some appeal. Such stories as *Pandora's Box* and *The Miraculous Pitcher* are well loved. So are the well-known legends *Robin Hood, William Tell* and *Morte d'Arthur*. There is also a growing interest in the more realistic stories of travel and exploration, and in biography, which creates a new link with the geography and history studies of the school.

This interest in the world around them extends, at the age of 11, to include tales of inventors and their inventions, machinery, aircraft, engineering, and the tales of mystery and adventure. Henty, Jules Verne, Fennimore Cooper and Edgar Wallace are favourite authors of the 11-year-old boys.

The girls' interest at this age follow their brothers in the realms of adventure, but they prefer hearing and reading tales told of girls' schools and domestic life rather than those of the more mechanical realms of engineering and science.

BASIC SKILLS: SPEECH AND ORAL WORK

A useful list of books and story references can be found in the first volume of *Primary (Junior) Teaching To-day*. The chapter on literature, contributed by R. K. and M. I. R. Polkinghorne, is full of interest and information for the teacher studying the use of stories. For further study there is also an interesting and informative analysis of the reading habits of children in a junior mixed school in the book *Juniors* by G. H. Pumphrey.

I have found that the interests of the slow learner, in this particular connexion, are very close to those of the normal child. There may be a degree of immaturity in comparison with a child of similar chronological age, but in the main the research and information provided in the books referred to will give a very useful guide to the type of material we should be using. Allowances are always made by the good teacher so that she can choose those stories which she knows will be suitable for her class, for she is in a position to know better than anyone else their tastes and fancies. But I think it can be a very dangerous thing to imagine that mental age, rather than chronological age, will determine the interests of the child, as has been suggested in some quarters. It would be wrong to imagine that a 10-year-old boy with a mental age of $7\frac{1}{2}$ is going to be interested in the type of story that has been found to appeal to the 7-year-old child. His interests are much more likely to be nearer his own chronological age.

The greater difficulty is going to be found when we consider the third of our aims; the use of the story in introducing new words in a meaningful context.

Writers and publishers have produced their books with the normal child in mind and they go to great trouble today to ensure that they are written in the style and form which is suitable for the age intended. Consequently the sort of vocabulary used is going to be in advance of that which we know is suitable for our children. Overcoming this difficulty is one of our main concerns. The Ministry in their *Handbook of Suggestions* suggest several times in the chapter on 'English Language and Literature' that there is a danger in watering-down the language used in a story, particularly when the effect of the narrative depends on the nature of the words used. The teacher must employ system and foresight in her aim to increase the children's understanding of and command over language by deliberately introducing and explaining new words within the text. This is our aim, and to steer a steady course between the dangers of ruining a story by expunging the difficult words, or presenting it in its original, and probably incomprehensible, form requires a great deal of planning and study on the part of the teacher.

I think we are faced with three alternatives when we want to present a story to our class.

(1) We can read the story from a book written in a language suitable for the normal chronological age of the child concerned, and adjust the vocabulary accordingly.
(2) We can use a book which has been written as a 'reader' for backward children, which will then have a more or less suitable vocabulary structure.
(3) The story can be 'told' to the children without the aid of a book during the performance.

Of the three I would say that the last method is perhaps the best, and the first is a reasonable substitute. As for the second method, this suffers the disadvantage of being a distortion of the original intention of the publisher and author. The words will be repetitive, sentences short and stilted, and the whole presentation rather dull and uninteresting when read aloud. In short, this type of book would be normally quite unsuitable and only to be used as a last resort.

Story 'telling' is undoubtedly the best method of putting the story across. It has the advantage of creating an immediate link between the story-teller and the listener without the intermediary of a book. It is an art which requires practice and a lot of patient preparation, but the amount of enjoyment which it gives to all participants makes all the work more than worthwhile.

Perhaps the main cause of concern to those who would like to use this method, but fear the results, lies in their reluctance to rely on the memory, which may fail at the crucial moment; and what could be worse than this in front of a class all agog for the climax of an interesting story? To those I would recommend Elizabeth Clark's book, *Stories to tell and How to tell them*.

In this, Miss Clark advises that the first essential in story-telling is the creation of a bond of friendship betwixt the story-teller and the story. One has a certain freedom and delight in relating one's own

BASIC SKILLS: SPEECH AND ORAL WORK

experiences because whilst doing so one relives the events, and the scene passes before the eyes as an unrolling picture. We remember so clearly because we have all the details at our finger-tips. Our interest is a living one and we have a complete command of the essential details. This is what we must also acquire in the case of the stories we want to tell.

Systematic, intelligent preparation is essential. Having read, and re-read the story until we have gained a full and sympathetic realization of its mood and character we have to reduce it to its basic fundamentals, the essentials in outline. Jot down the order of events, the introduction of characters in their order of appearance, and formulate a 'ground plan' which can serve as a basic guide.

Once having mastered this plan, the time is ripe for experiment in telling the story to one's self, scribbling it on odd pieces of paper whenever the opportunity occurs, and generally practising the art of re-telling it, without an audience, until it becomes a familiar thing. Then the story is yours, like some past personal experience ready for recall on demand.

When giving the story to the class the main essential is to remember that story-telling is a 'homely', restful thing. Any hint of hurrying, strain or worry will come between you and the listener. The thing to do is to live in the story and forget yourself. As the story unfolds it will bring a shared sense of wonder, beauty, surprise and delight. You will find opportunity to add words of explanation if some of the children look puzzled at some particular point, or elaboration of detail if dealing with something which is outside the range of experience of some of them. The rigid formality of a 'book' story is dispensed with and it becomes truly a shared adventure into realms of phantasy and imagination.

It won't be possible to do this with all the stories that one wishes to deal with and there must be times when the teacher will read the story from the book. Nevertheless plenty of preparation must still be done. It is still necessary to know the story before you start. You must read it beforehand, not just once, but twice or more. This is to give you not only a feeling of confidence and knowledge of the character and order of events, but also an idea of what type of alterations are necessary to make the vocabulary more suitable for your purpose. I find that it is usually possible to amend the text by using pencilled notes on the book itself, substituting simpler words where needed, omitting or re-phrasing unsuitable passages, even whole sentences, which are not simple or clear enough in the original.

Most of these alterations can be made before presenting the story to the class, but there will still be a need to keep a watchful eye open for any sign of bewilderment or obvious lack of appreciation when particular points are being made in the story. This is the time when the observant teacher adds to the script his own words of explanation or illustration.

The standard of vocabulary used must depend entirely on the level of the class, according to the teacher's own judgement, remembering that there is a great difference in the comprehension level as between the written and the spoken word. Even your non-readers are going to be able to understand a fair percentage of the story read to them.

Even so I think it would be wise to remember that whichever method of story presentation is used, successful interpretation is going to depend on the ability of the child to create abstract mental images from possibly unfamiliar words, which may have no link with anything which has yet come within his range of experiences. It is in providing for this difficulty that I think the major part of our story preparation lies. What can we do to link the abstractions of speech with an available concrete experience?

First and foremost we must provide a definite visual link with the atmosphere and background in which the story is set. If it is in the country with the characters enjoying life on the farm then we must have available in the classroom some large, coloured, and not too complicated, pictures of the farm. What will the words, 'The ducks waddling across the farmyard,' mean to a child who has never seen a duck or a farmyard in his life? The excitement of a story about a storm at sea is going to be brought home more clearly and with greater intensity if they can see the Atlantic breakers tossing a steamship about in a picture on the wall. For the child in the small country town who has never experienced the hectic hustle and bustle of busy city streets, a well-chosen picture can give an immediate impression where no amount of descriptive phrases would have any effect.

Now having set the scene and given the story a firm background

BASIC SKILLS: SPEECH AND ORAL WORK

it is usually necessary to develop it visually as the story moves along. This you can do by introducing small cut-outs which can be added to the main picture or put up separately. The characters can be introduced. The old farmer, his jolly wife, the farmyard dog, will all be far more real and impressive if they can be seen. Descriptive words and phrases will mean far more when they have some visual image that they can be linked up with.

One word of warning. It is most necessary to be on guard against the possibility of interrupting the flow of the story by too much movement. If you are continually bobbing up and down to attend to the pictures, the interest is likely to become gradually focused on whether they are going to stay on the board or not, rather than the story itself. A flannelgraph can prove very useful in providing an easily manipulated form of picture background, and sometimes it is even possible to get one of the children to put the pictures up as they are needed. In those classes where the reading ability is sufficiently high, the pictures should be accompanied by their word labels for quick identification and to assist in both comprehension and reading.

If you are running a 'serial' story or a series of stories on the same topic, or about the same characters, it is possible to extend the use of your pictures. They can be left on the wall of the classroom and used for conversational periods; as a link between the successive stories; subjects for art, and so on. A further extension of this is to utilize small models on a baseboard instead of, or in addition to, the pictures. The impression they create will be far more real and lasting, for they can be touched and handled.

I have seen a number of film-strips which have been prepared for the teacher to use in the illustration of stories and poems, but although this method of presentation would undoubtedly be very suitable for our purpose, there seem to be none as yet that really meet our requirements. We need a simple, clearly defined illustration without too much superfluous detail. The strips produced to date are those to accompany poetry, which have an artistic interpretation rather too sophisticated for our children, and some very detailed ones produced to assist in story-telling.

So far we have dealt with the 'intake' of vocabulary and its interpretation as provided by the teacher. Important as this obviously is, perhaps even more important is the work which will follow – the practice which the pupil will have so that he can master the words and make them part of his own 'spoken' vocabulary.

Our object is to encourage the child to talk, not only in the stilted language which so often passes for conversation as between teacher and child, but more freely and in other relationships besides the 'teacher-child' one. The story can be used as a basic starting-off point for all forms of work in the classroom, most of which will provide us with opportunities for the consolidation and practice we are seeking.

(a) Dramatic Work, Self-expression, Puppetry
This is an ideal and probably the main form of work which can be used as a natural follow-up. It is in these periods when the children will feel most free to let themselves go, and with this freedom will come the most fertile practice of the vocabulary you have been supplying. In a permissive atmosphere the natural mimicry of the child will reproduce and re-create much of what you have given it.

(b) Painting and Handwork
Used to illustrate characters and scenes from the story, these periods are bound to give opportunities for informal discussion and conversation in which the new words will arise as a natural thing.

(c) Written Work and Reading
Although properly outside the bounds of this chapter, we can say that both of these subjects can be stimulated and given both direction and purpose through the medium of the story.

(d) Conversation, Discussion and Criticism
Perhaps one of the most difficult things to get is an atmosphere of conversational discussion, in abstraction as it were. When the conversation is centred around some concrete activity, as suggested under (*a*) and (*b*) above, there is less self-consciousness and consequently a greater freedom. Nevertheless it may be found possible in the later years in the primary stage to stimulate discussion by using topics related to the story and arousing the critical faculties of the children by reference to the authenticity and background of both story and author. I have found that 9 to 10-year-olds, even slower

BASIC SKILLS: SPEECH AND ORAL WORK

ones, are interested in knowing whether the story is true or not. They like to know about the author, country of origin, etc., and anything which will stimulate interest will further their willingness to talk – if you are prepared to let them.

It is often possible to find one or two who are willing to re-tell the story in their own words, either in its entirety or by taking parts and sharing the job between them. The pictures you have been using are a great help here in the matter of prompting.

I have dealt with the subject of story-telling and reading at some length because it is through this medium that one can provide all that is necessary; an interesting experience, examples of new vocabulary in a natural context and opportunities of practice in an interesting situation. Anything which can promote one or more of these aims is of value, and reference to other chapters will give an indication of what can be done in order to achieve this, but I think there is still a place here for me to mention more particularly some of the activities which will be found useful.

Classroom Games

The use of games has the obvious advantage that whilst the child is concentrating on his own particular part of the game, his mind is released from the anxiety which has been built up through continued failure in a 'lesson' situation. Furthermore it provides opportunities for necessary repetition and checking which in other contexts might prove boring and abortive.

Games can be arranged as individual affairs, where the child is competing against himself, in pairs, small groups or as class items. In the lower forms of the school it will probably be found advantageous to keep the groups as large as possible, very rarely having anything much smaller than the complete class as a group. This is necessary so that the teacher can always be readily available, and virtually in control the whole time, in order to keep the spirit of the game alive and help to overcome those awkward moments which arise when Jill isn't bold enough to take her turn, or John is too bold and wants to 'run the show'. The more experienced and abler classes will be able to dispense more and more with the services of the teacher as leader and she will be wise to fade quietly into the background, leaving the children with a greater sense of freedom and new-found sense of responsibility.

Remembering that our aim is to achieve a freedom and fluency of speech we should choose games which will promote these ends. We want to get the child thinking, keep him interested and then give him an incentive which will produce a desire to express those thoughts as clearly and lucidly as possible.

A number of games based on pictures of 'familiar objects' can be devised. For these you will need a collection of small pictures of everyday objects which are familiar to all the children. (I use coloured advertisements from magazines, catalogues, etc.) Each picture is mounted and clearly numbered. The mounting is a refinement which can be dispensed with, but I would recommend it if you want to use them more than once or twice. Basically the idea is for each child to have a picture and tell the class all he can about it. I have found that the best way to start it off is for one of the children to stand up and call out the name of one of the others in the class, and a number – say: 'Joan, twenty-three.' Joan collects picture twenty-three and says all she can about it; before sitting down she calls out another name followed by a number, and so the game continues.

The idea can be varied in a number of ways:

(1) By using different collections of pictures: e.g. toys, animals, pets, games and amusements, tools and simple implements, means of transport, occupations, etc.
(2) By specifying what the children should do: e.g. describe the object, say how it is used or how it works, what the person does, how to look after the pets, or just give a general talk about it.
(3) By varying the method of distributing the pictures. You can have them given out around the class so that each child has one in front of him for a short while before being called on. Alternatively each child can be given a number so that when his turn comes he takes the picture with that number on it.
(4) The game can be used as a guessing competition. The rest of the children are asked to guess which picture the individual has been talking about. You can embody this into a team game. Each team takes it in turns to provide a speaker whilst the

BASIC SKILLS: SPEECH AND ORAL WORK

other team has the job of guessing what has been described.
(5) The older children who have had some experience with the simpler games, and who have some reading skill, should reach a stage where they can dispense with the pictures. Then words written on slips of paper can be substituted for them. e.g., tiger, football, express-train, etc.

Any variations of the popular 'parlour' games can be introduced. For example 'I Spy' can be played with enjoyment as it has been for years. 'Hunt The Thimble' can be varied by having the child who is 'hiding the thimble' tell the teacher which particular hiding place he has chosen. The rest of the class try to guess the hiding place by questioning the 'hider' who has to answer their questions. Reference to any good book on popular party games for children will suggest any number of others which can be modified in this way so that thoughtful speech is brought into play.

There are a number of very useful suggestions for class games in the chapter on 'Oral Work' in *Primary (Junior) Teaching To-day*, Volume I. Also a number of valuable ideas and a good source of pictures can be found in Longman's *Fluent Writing and Speaking* course by J. Hemming. There are several variations of the above games included in the 'A' and 'B' books of that series.

Speech and the Curriculum
In considering the use of speech in connexion with other lessons on the time-table it is necessary to return to some of the first principles outlined earlier.

It has been said that an essential background for the development of verbal ability is a 'richness of living'. If we provide the child with interests which are vital enough we can foster and stimulate the desire to communicate which is after all the main element in our programme. This can be done by providing the child with experiences which are immediate, vital and personal ones.

This sort of stimulation will come through experience of concrete situations, by meeting people, and through practical work, far better than through abstractions or contact with second-hand ideas. The child needs to have provided for him opportunities for human contacts within the neighbourhood of the school and locality. By going out to meet the world around him and by having contacts from the outside brought in to him, the world will grow more alive and interesting.

For this our lessons must be centred more around 'interests, activities, projects' – the word you use for it matters little. It means the type of study which substitutes for the artificial sub-division of the time-table into history, geography, nature study, etc., a more realistic approach through personal experience and seeking after first hand knowledge. The curriculum needs to be based on an idea imbued with the spirit of exploration. The children become seekers and finders, with the school acting as the link between the child and the community. In this way we can provide a wealth of background and incentive.

(For those who haven't seriously considered this type of work before, and for those of you who would like to gain fresh inspiration, I would recommend a thorough study of *Exploration in the Junior School, Junior School Community* and *Actuality in School*, as well as Chapter X of this book.)

As far as 'Speech' is concerned, I don't believe that any purpose can be served by trying to impose it as a special feature or aim which must be brought within the periphery of the 'project' or 'activity'. It is almost bound to arise naturally. What we must do is to provide the atmosphere in which conversation and discussion can flourish. As I said earlier, the children must have opportunity to hold conversations. The atmosphere must be a permissive one. It may be possible in some classes in the last year of the school to introduce the simple formalities of classroom discussion, with the teacher acting as a chairman in the opening stages, but gradually coaching some of the children to take over this office so that he may step more into the background. But one must watch closely to see that this type of discussion doesn't become a feature superimposed to the detriment of the development of truly free discussion and conversation.

To sum up I would say:

(1) We should aim at providing as many first-hand experiences and personal contacts as possible.
(2) The atmosphere of the classroom should be such as to encourage 'live' conversation and discussion.

BASIC SKILLS: SPEECH AND ORAL WORK

(3) The teacher must learn to adopt that difficult role of leading without monopolizing or obtrusively guiding the discussion or conversation.

(4) Progression can be made in two directions.
- (*a*) Towards an ability in the child to profit from vicarious experiences which are based on first-hand knowledge.
- (*b*) Towards more formal discussion, with the teacher retreating more and more into the background as leader of the group.

Mechanical Aids

In this scientific age quite a few of our primary schools are now being equipped with those extremely useful items such as the film and film-strip projectors, radio, and even, if they are lucky enough, the tape-recorder. All of these can play their part in our plan, to provide background knowledge, examples of good speech, and practice in the use of it.

(1) *Film and Film-strip Projectors*

Generally speaking I think there is a certain danger in using films too indiscriminately. Only too often the sound commentary employs a vocabulary which is rather beyond our slow learners. Similarly the action of the film is too fast, so that it becomes merely a kaleidoscope of incidents, and impressions only a few of which may be retained. Nevertheless, I find that used with care, both the film and film-strip can be employed most valuably to provide a richness of background knowledge. The pictures can give to the child a vivid presentation of the subject, provide accurate illustrations, and certainly, if well chosen and presented, will leave a lasting impression.

My personal feeling is that the film-strip and the silent film, both of which allow the teacher complete control of the vocabulary content which is so important, are of more use to us than the sound film in this particular connexion.

(2) *Radio Programmes*

(*a*) The use of broadcast programmes again has the obvious advantage of the vast resources behind them, and of a presentation which is vivid, varied and compelling. They can bring a spice of variety into the school, bringing in that outside contact. Unfortunately they have a big disadvantage in that the vocabulary employed is outside the control of the individual class teacher. For this reason alone they are a source which I feel must be used with great forethought and caution.

(*b*) In the later years in the junior school it is possible to employ the technique of the broadcast programme by getting the children to make their own broadcasts. Schools wired for sound programmes usually have facilities so that a microphone can be plugged into the circuit. Others can make or buy suitable equipment for this purpose without too great an expenditure.

I have found that a personal school broadcast programme provides two important factors:

(1) A big incentive to speak.
(2) A good corrective influence to improve poor speech and increase fluency.

Complete organization of such a scheme is outside the scope of this chapter, but it may be useful if I mention that a normal programme would include such items as: Simple news items, schools events and local news; Short readings of simple stories; Poems, recited and read; Variety through songs, solo items, etc.

After some experience and practice it is possible to present simple plays over the circuit. These are always enthusiastically enjoyed by both listeners and broadcasters.

(3) *The Tape-recorder*

This machine is still at the stage where its very novelty is of immense use to us in catching and holding the interest of the children. But beyond this it has some much deeper and lasting advantages.

In the first instance the children will be happy to speak into it merely to have the pleasure of hearing their own voices played back to them. At this stage, which may last for only a short while, it has its value in encouraging even the slowest child to make an effort in speech. It also has a great self-critical and self-corrective influence for they like to hear their voices 'sound right' and will strive to achieve a reasonable standard. The amount of development beyond this point lies in the hands of the discerning teacher and there is scope for great experimenting.

In use I have found the following schemes to work quite well and produce a lot of interesting results:

(*a*) Poems, recitations, short stories, etc., are recorded by individual children. This is usually done during lunch-time and playtimes when the rest of the class are not around. These are then played back to the class as a miscellany for amusement, and interest and often constructive criticism.

(*b*) Programmes similar to those outlined in the section on broadcasting are recorded. These have certain advantages over the 'live' broadcasts as they can be edited and corrected during the recording so that the 'play-back' is a more polished performance.

Although an expensive item, the tape-recorder is an aid which deserves its place alongside those others which are coming to be accepted as part of school equipment. If you haven't one yet, press for one. It is a very worthwhile cause.

(4) *The Telephone*

Imaginary telephone conversations have long been a feature of 'English' and 'Speech' lessons in the classroom. Having the instrument in the classroom is a logical step beyond this. Simple battery telephones are readily available now from army surplus stores and are not expensive. They give good reproductions and are simple to use, involving only the two instruments and a length of wire across the classroom.

They are rather limited in scope because the conversation tends to be a far more personal thing involving only the two who are using the instruments, but their use cultivates a lively interest and can be included in many periods of play, private activities, dramatic periods and so on.

Summary

The development of oral vocabulary and speech is a matter which must be regarded as of as great importance as are the traditional subjects of reading and number. I would say that of the three it is probably the most vital, for not only does it provide the essential link between the child and the world around him, but also on this development of verbal ability depends the quality of thought which is the foundation for all other education.

This is not to say that 'Speech' is to be regarded as another SUBJECT which must be fitted neatly into its own pigeon-hole in the time-table. Rather we must be continually aware of how we can find an opportunity to develop it adequately within the curriculum as an integral part of the whole.

Our aim throughout must be to provide:

(a) Background

A good background of experience, knowledge and interest forms the essential framework. It can be developed through:

(1) First-hand experience and contact in activities, local study, etc.
(2) Using visual and auditory aids – pictures, tape-recorders, etc.
(3) Reading aloud to the children, or telling them, stories which they will enjoy and understand and those which will enrich their cultural heritage.
(4) Reading and talking about any material to make unfamiliar and vague ideas clear ones through association with the child's own experiences.

(b) Experience of New Vocabulary

We must remember that children think in terms of concrete things and visual images and not as we do in terms of words themselves, so with all the above we must be prepared to provide a background of both familiar and unfamiliar words which are actively linked with the concrete and visual images invoked. This will provide a new background of words available for use by the child himself.

There should also be provided opportunities when the child can be given an enjoyment of the rich cultural beauty of language even when every word isn't understood.

(c) Opportunity for Practice

Children talk more freely in the informal situation than they do in the formal atmosphere of the traditional classroom pattern. They

BASIC SKILLS: SPEECH AND ORAL WORK

need to be given the encouragement of a 'permissive' atmosphere and a classroom arrangement of furniture and furnishings which permits of a more informal grouping for 'conversational' opportunities. Formal rows of desks are not conducive to the development of good language skills.

Practice must be varied, involving informal conversation and discussion in varying sized groups progressing towards the more set type of discussion group when the situation and maturity of the children warrant it.

Whatever the situation the children need the feeling of security and confidence which can only come when they know that their freedom is under the control of a sympathetic but resolute teacher.

Finally, a word to those who expect to see some reference to the formal teaching of speech as a speech training lesson. I must say that I regard the freeing of the child to speak as of prime importance and something which must be done before any formal speech training can be attempted, but there is a need to work on the speech of a child:

(*a*) If there is any conspicuous deviation from the speech that is accepted as good in that geographical area.
(*b*) If it is sufficiently different from standard usage to cause difficulty in reading and spelling.

Probably the word formal is the wrong one to use, for too much 'formality' in the way it is normally interpreted is likely to make matters worse in this particular type of lesson. Briefly I would say that effectiveness in speech training depends, firstly, on the teacher's own daily example and, secondly, on the way in which she approaches the subject. It is necessary if you intend to introduce speech training to do it in an interesting and amusing way, with more emphasis on good usage rather than on the defects which are found.

There are many good books which approach the subject in this way and I would recommend the section in Book 1, *Primary Teaching To-day* where the topic is fully dealt with.

When definite speech defects are found it is of course a question for reference to a speech therapist who is in a much better position to deal with them, and who will undoubtedly work closely in conjunction with the class teacher.

TEACHING THE SLOW LEARNER IN THE PRIMARY SCHOOL

We must always remember that development of speech is an integral part of the development of the child's social awareness. The skill he develops influences his future ability to fit into the social framework which man has built up mainly through his ability to communicate and by using the art of communication to enrich and develop the human inheritance. The speech pattern the child adopts influences his ability to earn, the pattern of living he builds up for himself and the friends he draws around him.

Book List

ATKINSON, M., *Junior School Community*, Longmans.
CLARK, E., *More Stories to Tell*, U.L.P.
— *Stories to Tell and How to Tell Them*, U.L.P.
CONS, G. J. and FLETCHER, C., *Actuality in School*, Methuen.
GANS, R., *Guiding Children's Reading through Experience*, Teachers' College, New York, U.S.A.
ISAACS, S., *The Children We Teach*, U.L.P.
MELLOR, E., *Education Through Experience in the Infant School Years*, Blackwell.
Handbook of Suggestions for Teachers, H.M.S.O.
Ministry of Education, *Seven to Eleven*, H.M.S.O.
PHILLIPS, H. and MCINNES, F. J. C., *Exploration in the Junior School*, U.L.P.
POLKINGHORNE, R. K., and POLKINGHORNE, M. I. R., *Primary (Junior) Teaching To-day*, Volume I, Newnes Ltd.
PUMPHREY, G. H., *Juniors*, Livingstone.
SHERIDAN, M. D., *The Child's Hearing for Speech*, Methuen.
STRICKLAND, R. G., *The Language Arts in the Elementary School*, Heath, Boston, U.S.A.
WATTS, A. F., *Language and Mental Development of Children*, Harrap.

H. PURT

Chapter IV

READING*

The teacher desiring advice on the teaching of reading may well be deterred by the number, scope, and technicalities of the books dealing with the subject. Comfort, however, may be derived from the knowledge that upon certain major points their authors agree.

They stipulate, for instance, that before formal instruction is given the child should be 'ready to read' (i.e. from an intellectual standpoint), otherwise ultimate success is jeopardized. In this connexion a junior school teacher may safely assume that in the majority of cases this stage was reached at the top of the infant school, or will be reached at some time during the first year in the junior school. She must, nevertheless, remember that intellectually some of her pupils are bound to mature more slowly than the majority, and for this minority she must be prepared to adapt her teaching methods accordingly, seeking chiefly to stimulate and keep alive a desire to read, while she waits for maturation to take place.

This brings me to the second point which research has made clear, namely, the importance of early training in forming those habits of observation and discernment which are helpful towards acquiring reading skill. First and foremost comes the establishment of correct directional attack upon words to be read. A left to right eye movement is demanded when we ask a child to read a word or a group of words; furthermore this movement does not come naturally to him at the initial stages of learning to read, for previously he has identified objects by allowing his eyes to rove at will over them, in search

---

* Publisher's Note to 1965 reprint: Sir James Pitman's Initial Teaching Alphabet (i.t.a.) has brought a new factor into the reading situation. Its efficacy as a medium for slow-learning children (and others) has to be weighed against the necessity for subsequent transfer to orthography. Information on it may be obtained from Pitman's Initial Teaching Alphabet Foundation, 9 Southampton Place, London, W.C.1.

of distinguishing features. Hence, in reading, he must acquire a new habit and needs help in doing so. His attention must be deliberately drawn to the necessity for making this controlled eye-movement, and he should be allowed to indicate the left to right direction by pointing, if this appears to help him at the outset. The teacher herself should remember to emphasize direction by making some indicative gesture when reading to beginners. Various other more detailed devices are suggested in certain pre-reading schemes, e.g. in the *McKee Readers*. Other useful habits to be cultivated concern an active response to differing sights and sounds, sometimes classified more grandly as 'visual and aural stimuli'. Suggestions for quickening these responses are usually available in the teachers' manuals issued to accompany modern infant reading series.

Lastly, we are enjoined to provide always the right kind of material for reading; material which is attractive, systematic, and consistently meaningful (material in this connexion implying pictures, apparatus, reading books, work-books, and any other supplementary matter devised). Most up-to-date reading series are compiled with these principles in mind, although they vary considerably within the approved limits. Standards of presentation, also, differ widely, cost often being a limiting factor. Ideally, of course, one would choose a series that was well and colourfully illustrated, having the text suitably sized and spaced so as to avoid any confusion and encourage good phrasing, and which would appeal to its readers, not only by virtue of its superficial attractions, but also by reason of its subject matter. One should remember, also, that the older children are, the more should the criterion of subject matter influence one's choice, for such children are becoming increasingly aware of what is considered right and proper for their age (especially in the eyes of their companions), and should never be offered what they would consider to be a 'babyish' book. Indeed, it is always of high importance that a reading book should be acceptable to its reader, if a favourable climate for learning is to be preserved.

Thus, the organization of reading as a subject, always a complex matter, varying with whatever conditions prevail from class to class, and from school to school, makes two constant demands upon the teacher; one a thorough knowledge of the reading material available;

BASIC SKILLS: READING

the other a sympathetic understanding of her pupils' individual needs.

To take the question of reading material first. In most classrooms there lies a miscellany of books, the sorting of which is a formidable task. No doubt there will be a number of unsuitable books! In such a category would feature books in very small print, books drably presented, books with outmoded stories, and books written in difficult or artificial language. Such as these should be ruthlessly excluded from any teaching plan, although it is true that children (contrariwise, or so it would seem) often conceive an obstinate attachment to a certain book you wish to discard. This would be a sufficient argument for retaining an apparently unsuitable book in a 'reserve' library. Once having separated the sheep from the goats, the remaining suitable books should be classified into three main types:

(1) Basic readers.
(2) Platform readers.
(3) Library readers.

Under the heading of 'basic readers' should be grouped any graded series which would lend itself to systematic teaching at successive stages. It is customary now to have in classrooms small groups of such books at ascending levels of difficulty throughout the series. Should this not be so, and only a limited number of stages is available, access should be sought when necessary to stages other than those provided, so that children using the series may proceed steadily forward as their progress warrants it.

Again, one would hope to find that any graded series provided for use in the early stages of teaching reading would have what is termed, 'a controlled vocabulary'. This would imply that the number of new words introduced in each book was definitely restricted, and also, that once introduced, each new word would be repeated sufficiently often to ensure its absorption into the child's reading vocabulary.

The second type of book to seek, commonly known as a 'platform' reader, is one which can be related in difficulty to a certain stage in the main basic reading scheme, and which may therefore be used at that stage, to provide extra practice before anything more difficult is presented. If one is fortunate, one may find such platform readers provided as an integral part of the reading scheme, or schemes, e.g. as in the 'Happy Venture' series, but even so, it is often necessary to seek others. It would be almost impossible to make a comparison between a book with a controlled vocabulary and one which is freely written, therefore it is simplest to ignore the latter type, in one's search, and then equate the books in different basic series to one another. (A note entered within the books, stating to which others they may be compared, is a handy and effective guide for future reference.) Thus such books can function either as basic readers, or as platform readers according to requirements.

Any reading material which now remains unclassified, would fall into the miscellaneous 'library' class, and as such should be freely available to the children.

To become thoroughly acquainted with the basic reading material is of primary importance, if a correct and efficient allocation is to be made. Although experience must always be the best guide in making an ultimate judgement, it is none the less advisable at the outset to make a general appraisal of stock available for direct teaching. The range of its appeal should be estimated, after considering the scope and presentation of its subject matter, for example. The early stages of infant reading schemes with their restricted interests, are not usually acceptable to children after their second year in a junior school, although the final books of some, e.g. the *McKee Readers*, or *Janet and John Readers*, might be so, because they are more in the nature of transitional books, having a wide range of subject matter, yet retaining the highly attractive layout associated with a good infant reader. Again, the appeal of a book could be limited by its style of language, e.g. overmuch repetition can prove very wearisome, and may even sound ridiculous to a sophisticated type of child, however backward he may be.

After making some assessment then of a book's appeal, one should consider next the teaching theory embodied in it. Naturally, differing methods are advocated according to the author's convictions. Some tend to lay stress on phonic methods; for example the *Gay Way* series, while others favour the 'whole word' or 'sentence' method based on a 'Look and Say' approach, e.g. *Pilot Reading Scheme*. Many, however, prefer a mixed approach, with perhaps a

BASIC SKILLS: READING

particular bias; a method which, generally speaking, is more successful at the junior school stage, e.g. 'Happy Venture' series, *Janet and John* series, *Wide Range Readers*. Obviously an occasion might arise when either a wholly 'look and say', or a wholly phonic treatment might prove to be just the right method if one were to be guided by the individual needs of one's children, e.g. a phonic approach could be profitable with an older, slower pupil who had had little success in earlier years with the 'look and say' method.

Lastly, the teacher should determine as far as possible the intellectual demands which are likely to be made by the different books at her disposal. A general inference can be drawn from the word lists usually given in the books themselves, for they indicate the extent and quality of the vocabulary required. From them can also be ascertained the rate of introduction of new words, from page to page, and from book to book; a matter of vital importance when assessing the standard of difficulty. In a good series the rate will be gradual and often 'plateaux' will occur in the curve showing the rate of introduction, thus permitting of adequate revision and consolidation.

Once the survey of books has been carried out, the situation makes its second major demand of the teacher. Does she know sufficient about her children to enable her to allocate to them those books most suited to their individual needs? To do this successfully, she must take into account, their attainments, their maturation level and interests, and possibly their past difficulties in the subject. As time is always a pressing consideration when a teacher faces the organization of reading in a sizable class, it is imperative to make a quick assessment of individual attainments. If previous records are available, then the process is simplified, but it is still advisable to ascertain current reading ages by administering a standard word recognition test such as Schonell's or Burt's. The reading ages so obtained will provide an indication towards correct allocation of books, especially if the basic reading books are graduated according to reading age, e.g. as in the *Wide Range Readers*. It may be that some children, having made but slow progress in the past, achieve little on the word recognition tests, when it will be found more useful to examine them on the vocabulary listed at the end of the easiest reader of the series in use, and then to progress from these through the vocabulary of the next book, and so on if necessary. Some idea withthen be gained of the point at which the child in question begins to fail, this indicating approximately where he should start. It should be remembered that in all cases, it is beneficial to start a child on a book which is slightly easier than would appear to be his actual level, thus enabling him to experience initial success, which will promote confidence and pleasure in reading.

Reading levels having been ascertained, the teacher must now turn her attention to consideration of maturation levels, that is, the general development of her pupils in relation to their ages. If a child's reading age is normal, or near-normal, for his age she need not be unduly troubled by this factor, for he will be allocated automatically a book suitable in style and content for his developmental level, but if his attainment should fall considerably below what would be expected for his age, then some probing must be done, to find out what are his attitudes and interests, before starting him definitely upon a certain reader, lest he be affronted by being given a book which he despises because of its infantile subject matter and style. This latter type of child is naturally more common in the older classes in a junior school, and may constitute a real problem, unless suitable books catering for more mature interests at a simple reading level, are available.

Assuming then that books and children have been suitably matched, let us turn next to the problem of how best to organize the actual reading lessons. As the children will be grouped in the main according to attainment, the number of groups, and the number of children in a group will depend entirely upon circumstances, although some ceiling must be imposed upon both numbers if a practicable arrangement is to be maintained. The instruction of the groups so formed is a somewhat complex matter, for it is no longer considered necessary, or beneficial to restrict activities, during the official reading lesson, to 'reading' in its narrowest sense. Instead, a number of related activities might take place, which would all be calculated to improve reading skill: for example, some children would be receiving direct instruction from the teacher; others would be performing teacher-directed activities (usually written exercises) connected with their current reading material, while yet another section might quite possibly be carrying out some independent work

BASIC SKILLS: READING

arising from interests aroused in other lessons, such as making an illustrated 'topic' dictionary.

The smooth organization of these complicated activities depends partly upon the teacher adhering to some form of rota for hearing the children read. Obviously no hard and fast rule can be laid down concerning this, as so many variable factors are involved, but it could be safely stated that one should aim at giving each group one's direct attention at least once a week, and possibly twice a week where need is greatest. It will also be found both convenient and beneficial to instruct the children in the pursuit of their directed activities while they are assembled in their group to receive actual teaching. They can then be expected to proceed independently during their next lesson when the teacher will be occupied with a different group.

Simple records showing the ground covered by each group, and indicating particular difficulties will also help to facilitate organization and enable the teacher to maintain a high standard of preparedness.

Under such an arrangement, as is outlined above, the teacher's influence is exerted not only directly upon the group or groups receiving instruction during that lesson, but extends in a lessening but still effective degree over those engaged in other activities. This type of organization is infinitely preferable to one where the teacher attempts the almost impossible task of keeping all her children 'reading', either to her or to their group companions, for a period of from thirty to forty minutes. Naturally this looser arrangement of the class, advocated above, makes heavier demands upon the teacher's organizational skill than a simpler or more formal one would do, for she must ensure that all children receive direct help in turn, according to their several needs, and that they have adequate opportunities for supervised reading practice. She must also be planning ahead the various written activities necessary to consolidate teaching points as they may possibly arise, and, lastly, she must be prepared to give guidance where necessary to those pursuing independent activities related to their project or centre of interest work. No mean task!

Matters may be further complicated for the teacher of the older slow children in the junior school for amongst them one almost inevitably finds one or two children who, despite all efforts made to launch them on a course of reading, fail to make any appreciable progress in the lower classes. These we tend to classify somewhat loosely as, 'non-readers', a rather misleading term, for it is rarely found that a child is unable to read anything whatsoever. More usually a child whom we designate a 'non-reader' has a very scattered but scarcely usable vocabulary consisting mainly of: words instilled through much emphasis in early reading schemes, boy, girl, house, little; words of particular personal appeal, e.g. ice-cream, bicycle; words of striking pattern or configuration, e.g. elephant, motor-car. Very few verbs figure among the known words and as phonic response is weak, similar words, especially short ones, such as 'in' and it', 'as' and 'an', are not readily distinguishable.

Each child of this type presents a unique problem and therefore requires individual treatment whenever possible. A positive attempt must be made to assess his reading ability however limited it may be, the initial aim being to establish some point of intellectual contact with the child, yet at the same time to gather information which will help to make a preliminary general diagnosis of difficulties and more important still, of attitudes. As has been mentioned previously, the administration of a graded word reading test may produce no significant results, in which case one may have to improvise along the following lines: first ask the child (as previously suggested) to attempt the words listed at the back of one of the introductory books in any graded reading series available, carefully recording the results as he progresses, i.e. a dot for each word correctly read, and the actual error, or its nearest equivalent in phonics whenever a word is incorrectly read; next ask him to tell you any words which he knows he can read correctly and add these to the tally of known words already recorded, that is, after ascertaining that he really is able to read them. The information so gathered will serve as a starting point for one's individual teaching, which should emphasize from the very start what the child knows rather than what he does not. It will then possibly be as well to abandon the use of an orthodox reading scheme and adopt a fresh approach utilizing at first what little knowledge the child has, and later incorporating in the material devised, subject matter of genuine personal interest to him, thus compiling a first reading book, tailored more or less to his own individual needs. The vocabulary of this would only be somewhat loosely controlled

BASIC SKILLS: READING

compared with that of the usual graded reader but the advantages gained in the psychological field – the stimulation of interest through novelty – the sense of achievement gained in a personally satisfying field of activity – the bolstering effect of fairly easy success – all these considerations would far outweigh any lack of scientific vocabulary control.

Advice on the *modus operandi* is perhaps, best given by exemplification, although it is obviously up to the individual teacher to exercise her own skill and ingenuity in order to enliven the presentation of the work and at the same time direct attention to the best means of recognizing unfamiliar words. Here one can only suggest a likely sequence of work.

Let us then suppose that a child's reading vocabulary were limited to a few words such as, 'boy', 'girl', 'school', 'is'. After reviewing these for her own benefit, the teacher should decide upon a small number of additional words, likely to prove most useful in building up meaningful phrases and sentences in conjunction with the known ones. She might, for example select for immediate introduction, 'here' and 'a', thus making it possible for the following phrases and words to be constructed and read.

> Here is a boy.   A boy is here.
> Here is a girl.   A girl is here.
> Here is a school. A school is here.

These together with pictures or illustrations may be finally entered into the child's own exercise book to constitute the first page or pages of his new reading book.

It is advisable to introduce some interesting subject matter at the earliest possible opportunity. To illustrate this point we will assume that the boy in question is interested in swimming. After some preliminary discussion, the word 'swimming' could be introduced and a page or more set aside for gathering together in pictorial form ideas related to the topic of swimming. Each page so apportioned would be headed appropriately. It might also prove profitable to invite the child to make some comment about any picture worthy of particular note, which remark suitably condensed and simply phrased, could be written underneath it as a caption, e.g. Swimming in the sea; swimming under water, etc. When the teacher was satisfied that the child could read most of these phrases he could be set to make a revision page entitled:

WORDS I KNOW

Here he would set out words introduced on the various pages (which should be numbered)

Page 1	*Page 2*	*Page 3*	*Page 4*	*Page 5*	*Page 6*
Here	girl	school	swimming	in	under
is				the	water.
a				sea	
boy					

He now has twelve words which he can utilize. If these were written out a number of times on separate slips of cardboard, he might be encouraged to try his hand at forming new phrases or sentences with them. On completing the exercise satisfactorily with the cards he could be asked to transfer the results correctly to his own book, thus:

> Here is the sea.
> A boy is swimming in the sea.
> A girl is swimming under water.
> The boy is in school.
> The girl is in school.

Further revision could be devised by means of converting these statements into questions, e.g. Is the sea here? Needless to say, all these entries could and should be accompanied by suitable illustrations made by the child himself.

At this point it would obviously be necessary to begin widening the scope of vocabulary and introducing fresh facts of interest – a swimming gala – a holiday by the sea – a dramatic rescue from drowning – any avenue could be explored which promised to sustain the child's pleasure in his work, provided that the teacher sought frequent opportunities to give definite and systematic training in word recognition. Armed, as she should be by now, with detailed knowledge of this child's particular weaknesses and difficulties, this training could be tailored to suit his exact requirements.

As always, time is the main limiting factor in any enterprise of this nature, therefore it would be expedient, if at all possible, to

BASIC SKILLS: READING

encourage any interest which might satisfy more than one child. This simplifies the work of accumulating suitable material likely to stimulate further interest and reduces teaching demands somewhat as it is usual for very poor readers to have certain common needs. e.g. phonic practices related to the work in hand. And again, some children respond very satisfactorily to partnership in their work and may influence one another for the good in the carrying out of such a project as making a reading book, the keener child stimulating the less active one, or the one with wider interests contributing to the background knowledge of the one with the more limited resources and so on.

To return to the conduct of a normal lesson with any one of the number of groups within the class: procedure would follow the usual routine; namely that of reading passages in turn from the basic reader, assisted by the teacher in a variety of ways. The amount read by each child, and the general course of instruction would depend upon the number in the group, time available, and on individual needs related to those of the group as a whole; for example, there might exist a certain group whose attainments were fairly equal except that one child, although not poor enough to warrant his belonging to a less advanced group, was yet lagging behind his companions. In this instance it would be wise to give priority to group needs, and proceed at a pace suitable for the majority, asking the weaker member to read less than the others, and arranging if possible that he should read the simpler portions. By participating in the group lesson he would cover the same ground as the rest, but with less certainty. To give him an opportunity to revise and consolidate, he should be instructed alone at the end of the session for a few moments. If on the other hand the majority of the group was to be composed of slower readers while one or two members were more fluent than the rest, then it would be best to allow the more fluent readers to read first, while the rest of the group followed. The quicker ones could then be dismissed to read a designated amount to one another, while the teacher concentrated on helping the slower ones to revise and proceed further. Before the end of the session the better ones could be recalled and asked to read their prepared portions to the rest of the group. Thus, in a general sense, the whole group will again have covered the same ground.

Each child should be provided with a simple bookmark on which would be recorded the minimum of necessary information: namely, a group symbol, the title of his reader, and appropriate dates and pages. Besides acting as an orderly and accessible record, this card may prove useful to him as a pointer (especially if his directional attack is weak). He should also possess a notebook, in which the teacher may record immediately it occurs, any point of difficulty which arises during the actual reading practice. In it may also be worked any companion exercises. This book, if brought to her at least each time the child reads (oftener if possible), would serve as a valuable reminder to her of her pupil's difficulties and thus could give point to subsequent teaching. It would also show what use he was able to make of the reading skill he was gradually acquiring and would help to record satisfactorily his general progress towards competence in English.

When hearing a child read, the teacher should refrain from prompting him too easily, for by allowing him to attempt an unfamiliar word, at least until his powers of attack are expended, she will learn much about his methods; his strengths, and his weaknesses.

She might discover, for example:

(1) that one child recognized words or parts of words best by attempting to sound them. Therefore a phonic approach would always be most helpful to him, but none the less, practice in 'look and say' would be doubly necessary when words did not lend themselves to phonic treatment.
(2) that another child's attack on words was essentially erratic; that perhaps he read 'was' for 'saw', or missed out sounds and therefore needed definite help in establishing a consistent left to right attack on words.
(3) that yet another persistently confused 'b' and 'd', 'p' and 'q' and emphasis must in future be laid upon observing the essential differences between such pairs of letters.

It is apposite here to mention that there are two main methods of attacking a new word. It may be recognized, either by references to the sense expressed in the known part of the sentence, that is, by a context clue, or it may be recognized by observation of its own particular features, that is, by a word-form clue. The children should be encouraged to use both methods, actively seeking clues from all sources, even from accompanying illustrations. An attempt to recognize a word by inference from the text should not be labelled as a careless guess, and so provoke criticism; if, however, the child tends to rely too much on this form of attack, and is making a high percentage of errors, then the teacher should endeavour to strengthen his ability to use word clues by directing his attention to features likely to aid recognition.

Useful features to look for are such as these:

(1) A striking visual pattern.
    e.g. (1) 'oo'
        (2) exceptional length of a word compared to others around it – 'aeroplane'.
        (3) a preponderance of tall straight letters – 'little'.
(2) Essential differences in similar words.
    e.g. – the middle vowel in 'get' and 'got'.
        – the initial letter in 'hand' and 'band'.
(3) The presence of easily recognizable phonetic elements.
    e.g. 'th', 'ch', 'er'.
(4) The presence of known syllables and/or small words within a larger one.
    e.g. 'ing' in looking.
        'big' in bigger.
        'grand' and 'father' in grandfather.

A record of new words should be made after each lesson, and also of any outstanding difficulties met by each group which has been taught. As the number of new words encountered increases, which it well might towards the top of the junior school, then it would suffice to record only the words which seem difficult to recognize and grasp. Any words so recorded would be of great assistance to the teacher in anticipating the course of the next lesson, for they would enable her to decide upon suitable revision, and to prepare consolidatory practices (oral and written) to accompany the next passage to be attempted.

In this matter of revision, the rapid presentation of new or difficult words can be achieved by using flash cards; that is, suitably sized cards, each clearly lettered with an appropriate word, designed to be held up before the group for a short space of time. A second method of presentation is by the use of a simple tachistoscope. This is a display board, with a window cut in the centre, behind which may be slotted a card bearing any word you may wish to test. A simple shutter-like device operates at the front, whereby the teacher can expose the word for whatever length of time she may think desirable. The value of such apparatus lies in the neatness and precision of the word-exposure, which method of presentation more truly resembles the situation as met in actual reading, where almost instantaneous recognition is required, than if one were somewhat laboriously to write the word for the child.

Revision, however, should not stop at word-recognition, but should embrace the use of the new word in contexts other than the one in which it was first met, for if the slower child does not fully comprehend the meaning and use of the word in everyday speech, then he is not likely to recognize it easily when next he meets it in reading.

It should not be forgotten that time spent in discussing the content of reading matter may pay surprising dividends at a later date, when some interest or awareness aroused by a discussion, may act as a spur to further reading – and in this direction lies the true goal – that of reading to extend experience and knowledge. The testing of comprehension can also be made a lively process, if one is prepared to depart at times from the formal question and answer routine. For example:

An answer may be given in the form of a drawing or illustration;

or,

A simple crossword relating to the subject matter can be composed;

or,

Questions can be framed with a humorous twist.

Comprehension exercises of all types, formal and informal, will constitute a substantial part of the work set regularly by the teacher to occupy the children not actually reading to her.

This occupation of children not actually in contact with her is one of the most difficult, and yet most important aspects of the teacher's

BASIC SKILLS: READING

work, for in a large class so much time must, of necessity, be spent by the children beyond the teacher's direct influence. Therefore it is absolutely imperative that enough work shall be available to keep all the children (as far as is humanly possible), busy in a profitable manner. To aid the teacher in this difficulty, many reading schemes supply graded work material in various forms, as in the *Happy Venture* series, where picture and card material is available, or in the *Gay Way* series which offers useful 'work books'.

Some children, of course, will be engaged upon reading independently books which come within the range of their reading ability. These books will usually be specially selected by the teacher for this purpose from whatever 'platform' readers are provided, or will have been sought amongst the miscellaneous stock.

The question of transition from book to book in a graded scheme is always a matter deserving of serious thought, for it does not follow that because a child has finished a book, he is necessarily ready to proceed to the next one; so a quick review of the vocabulary and content of the completed book should be carried out before it is replaced by a more difficult one. As a result of this review the teacher might discover any of three possibilities: the child is competent and ready to proceed to the next book; he needs further practice at the same level; although he has managed to finish this book, his grasp of the vocabulary is but a weak and temporary one. Confirmation of the third state of affairs might be sought by studying the entries made in the child's notebook concerning difficulties he has encountered.

A quick review of the child's assimilation of words in his newly finished reader could be obtained in a variety of ways. If the vocabulary to be tested were small, as in some of the first books of a series, then the complete set of flash cards could be utilized. At a slightly later stage, the word list printed at the back of the book could be employed – until such time as it became too formidable. Then it would be preferable to rely upon making a selection of 'test' passages from various parts of the book, or upon testing only the words recorded as having presented difficulty.

Once the review has been carried out, it is a simple matter to deal with the competent children, and the semi-competent would be directed to further practice with a 'platform' reader, but what of the child who is 'floundering'? Merely setting him to 're-learn' what he has already failed to learn is not sufficient. He needs special attention if his particular difficulties are ever to be ironed out. Further explanations, and stimulating activities which will arouse in him an interest in words should be the order of the day; for example, if he shows a tendency to fail upon longer words he should be encouraged to search for recognizable elements (known sounds, syllables, and small words) within them. Further similar words to those being studied might then be sought from other sources.

It is at such a juncture that apparatus specially designed to give practice in some definite aspect of word recognition would be called for, and I propose to consider at some length, the making and use of such apparatus.

When planning and using apparatus with this remedial function in mind, certain fundamental principles require observation if satisfactory results are to ensue: the apparatus should be interesting and directed towards a definite aspect of word recognition; its use must be systematic and restricted to those children requiring practice in the skill which it demands; the children should be instructed carefully in its proper use, so that they may proceed independently; only appropriate demands should be made upon their knowledge and experience, thus allowing for a reasonable measure of success; for example, where phonetic analysis is required only words within the child's known vocabulary should be used; finally where a series of practices is devised to illustrate one point, the material should be graded to ensure progression.

In the following paragraphs are described some useful types of activity which would provide practice material for children with specific weaknesses and difficulties.

1. To Encourage a Left to Right Attack on Words
Apparatus of this type is best made in the form of duplicated expendable work sheets. On the sheets would be printed rows of symbols, designs, or pictures upon which the children would be instructed to make some definite marking or colouring, always beginning at the left, where an arrow pointing right, would be a constant reminder of the correct direction to take.
For example:

BASIC SKILLS: READING

Here the child is instructed to join together the groups of circles with a horizontal line, thus: O-O-O The first pair is joined as an example.

Secondly the child could be invited to number the triangles in each group, as shown in the left-hand margin, thus:

In this third type of exercise the child could be required to score through the vertical bars with a horizontal stroke, thus:

4 ⟶

In this example, a completed picture appears at the beginning and end of the row, while in between successive stages of construction are shown. The child is asked to complete the first one in various colours and then work along the line from left to right putting in each colour in its proper place, until finally he has at the end an exact copy of what is in the first square.

Endless variations of this type of exercise are possible, especially if the instructions relating to the prepared material are altered from time to time.

2. To Improve Skill in General Word Perception
Steeplechase Game

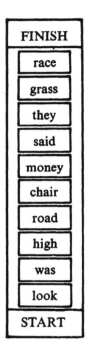

A race track is marked out on a strip of stout cardboard, the track being divided into anything from ten to twenty spaces according to requirements. Starting posts and winning posts are marked out, and the players (two) are provided with a miniature horse and jockey. The words selected for drill are printed on cards of suitable size, three cards being made for each word. Each player receives a complete set of cards which are shuffled and placed in a pack face down. The third set is then laid out along the track, one in each space, and the game begins. The first player looks to see if his first card bears the same word as the first card on the course. If it does, then his horse may move into the first space. If it does not, he may not move, and the other player tries his luck. So the game continues, the winner being he whose horse finishes first.

Word Dominoes

Cards are made resembling dominoes but with words taking the place of spots. The game follows the usual rules.

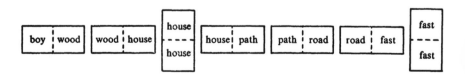

Any word you particularly wish to stress, if made a 'double', will stand out in the pattern of the game. Players might well write such words four times each in their notebooks.

BASIC SKILLS: READING

Small in Large

Certain new compound words are introduced.
  e.g. shopkeeper

    timetable   armchair   rooftop   sideboard

The child is asked to find the small words contained in each longer word and write them thus:

  shop   keeper   shopkeeper

3. Word Recognition Through Visual Clues

(1) To help in the differentiation of similar words, for example: house and horse, print the word which gives the most difficulty, probably 'horse', on tracing paper, and the other word (house) on a card using letters of identical size and pattern to those employed on the tracing paper. The child places the tracing paper over the word on the card matching the first letters carefully. The essential differences between the two words are then displayed and the teacher points them out carefully.

Now the child is given several sentences in which both words appear, either singly, or together, and he must find out by using his tracing paper where the word 'horse' appears. In order to record his result, he should copy into his notebook any sentence where the looked-for word occurs, and mark the word in some way, e.g. by a ring in colour.

```
HORSE     AND     HOUSE

1. The farmer is in his house.
2. The farmer has a horse.
3. The horse comes to the house.
4. The farmer pats the horse.
```

(2) Observation of general word pattern can be stimulated by asking the child to select a given word from a list of similar words.

bread	close	shriek	when
1. bed	1. cloth	1. ship	1. what
2. broad	2. cold	2. stroke	2. when
3. beach	3. close	3. sleep	3. while
4. bread	4. clear	4. shock	4. went
5. bride	5. clock	5. shriek	5. whether

Lists may be transcribed into the pupils' own book, and the appropriate word underlined in colour, or he may write the answer as a number, e.g. bread = No. 4.

4. Word Recognition Through Sound Clues

(1) *Cards*

Cards are made each bearing a different string of words, according to the sounds you wish to use.

The children are expected to select either those having the same initial sounds or blends, or those having the same final sounds or blends, or perhaps both, according to their progress.

e.g.

> rich, red, grow, pill, fetch, bed, fill, grip, pretty, fall

Words would be transcribed into notebooks in the required grouping or groupings.

(2) *Word Building Game*

Envelopes containing small cards on some of which are printed singly a certain number of consonants, and on others word 'endings' or 'families'.

BASIC SKILLS: READING

e.g. One envelope might contain:

b	twice	ill	3 times
c	twice	ame	3 times
s	3 times	ail	3 times
t	4 times	ool	twice

Possible Words

bill	bail
came	cool
sill	same
sail	till
tame	tail
tool	

As no spare cards are included the player knows when he has completed the game. The game may be played individually, or against one or more opponents if further sets of cards are available. Once made these cards are extremely useful as they are interchangeable from envelope to envelope. Progression is easily possible by extending the number and difficulty of the cards, e.g. double or treble consonantal blends such as 'ch' and 'spr' can be used.

(3) *Rhyming Game*

This game directs attention towards the final sounds of words being studied.

A large card is provided showing at the left-hand side a chosen list of words. The child holds a number of smaller cards each with a word printed on it. He must select from this pack a word which has the same final sound as each one on the big card. This he lays in place at the right hand side. Finally he copies the pairs of words so obtained into his workbook.

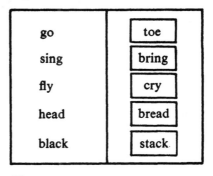

5. Word Recognition Through Context Clues

Cards are lettered out with simple sentences from which certain words are omitted. The child must be encouraged to read and re-read the rest of the sentence to see if help can be obtained in finding the unknown word.

At an early stage a choice of word may be given, e.g.

John put on his . . . . boat, coat

It was a . . . hot / cold day.

He ran all the . . . way / play to school

Later the child might be expected to find the word himself, for example:

(a) . . . . falls on a wet day.
(b) Susan plays with her doll and pram.
She likes her . . . .
(c) Our cat and dog hate each other.
They are . . . .
(d) I waited for the clock to . . . . . .
(e) Buses, cars, and lorries were held up.
There was a . . . . jam.
(f) John soon went to sleep for he was . . . . .

6. Progression in Units of Reading

(1) Reading phrases.

(a) Questions based on any story in the current reading books may be framed in such a way that they are answerable by definite phrases from the story. These are set out on a large card with a space at the right hand side for answers. The child has an assorted bundle of phrases written on slips of cards. From these he selects the correct answer and places it in position on the large card.

BASIC SKILLS: READING

e.g.
Where did Cinderella sit?	in the ashes
Who helped her?	her fairy godmother
How did she go to the ball?	in a golden coach
When did she run home?	at twelve o'clock
What did she lose?	her glass slipper
How does she live in the end?	happily ever after

After finding the correct answers, the child may, if he is capable of it, convert the phrase answers into full sentences and write them in his book.

e.g. Cinderella sat in the ashes.

(b) Dominoes. Played in the usual way but with phrases taking the place of dots.

e.g.
| round the corner | over the hills |

(2) Sentence reading.

A line picture of a house might be given accompanied by a description such as this:

> Here is a house. The door is red, and the roof grey. There are yellow curtains at the windows. A dog sits on the path. He is a black dog. There is one tree in the garden. It is as high as the house.

The child is then invited to make a complete picture which would correspond with this description exactly. The amount and complexity of the description would, of course, be suited to the attainment of the child likely to use it.

(3) Paragraph reading.

Various exercises, based on suitable paragraphs taken from the basic readers, could be devised. These would correspond very closely to what we normally call comprehension exercises. For instance, a child might be called upon to select from a given list, a suitable title for the extract, or he might be asked to answer questions relating to the sequence of events in the paragraph. On another occasion he might be expected to study a paragraph with a view to picking out detailed information.

7. To Enrich the Vocabulary

(1) *Word Pairs*

Sentences may be composed which contain one of a familiar pair of words, the child being asked to supply the missing one, helped perhaps by dots representing letters, e.g.

    John sat at table and picked up his knife and . . . . .
    Mary wore a blouse and . . . . .
    The children played with a . . . and ball.
    Horse and . . . . . fell at the fence.
    The wind blew night and . . .

(2) *Suitable Words*

Here the child is given a list of words from which he must choose those most suited to a suggested topic, e.g.

Which of these words would help to describe a windy day?
gale   roaring   calm   hungry   force
still   empty   shaking clatter   windless

Now write a sentence describing a windy day.

---

(3) *Overworked Words*

An extract, in which figure several over-worked words, is supplied and the child is asked to substitute better words in the place of these, from a list which is given.

e.g. Mr. Brown |went| in his |nice| car to a |good| shop where he |got| a |nice| cake.

BASIC SKILLS: READING

Choose from this list a better word than the one in each little box and then write out one sentence using the words you have chosen.

| fast   delicious   drove   bought   well-stocked |

(4) *Word Puzzles*
Single word puzzles rather like the separate items of a crossword puzzle can be presented in the following way.

1. To walk quietly	t - p t - e
2. To make up your mind	d - - - - -
3. Stops a car	b - - - -
4. Always busy	a - t - - e
5. A step	p - - -

The amount of help given would be varied to suit requirements.

It will be seen that games and practices of the types suggested above would provide considerable scope for written work, and in this respect would play an important part in laying a foundation for further written 'English'. It is an unquestionable fact that practice in written English of all kinds helps to improve reading skill, therefore it is incumbent upon the teacher to provide frequent opportunities for combining the activities of reading and writing in the course of the day to day instruction which she gives her children. This is but the reverse side of the coin for obversely she must remember that learning to read, and reading to learn are reciprocal activities and she must so manipulate the situations arising in her classroom that these two activities may take place concurrently.

An ideal medium for the former purpose, that is of giving daily practice in the closely related skills of reading and writing, is the recording of daily happenings and observations by means of a News

Sheet and the use of diaries. Here the teacher must perforce display some ingenuity and imagination, for although some days abound in 'big news', others are singularly lacking in it, 'hum-drum' in fact. It is then that news must be 'manufactured' out of personal and domestic events; for example, birthdays, observations about classroom pets, individual achievements of the moment must be elevated in importance. Once such a news item has been composed and read from the teacher's copy, it should be transcribed into the children's own diaries, and whenever possible they should be encouraged to add something extra of their own which might later be read out (on a selective basis) to the rest of the class.

Fortunately there is to be found in children of the junior school age an immense eagerness for learning of all kinds, which dynamic force the skilful teacher will harness to serve those ends which she deems most desirable for her pupils at any given time. It is against this background of potential mental activity that I will now examine the opportunities afforded for teaching reading through the children's desire to know more of things and people around them.

Here it would be pertinent to refer to an actual occasion when intense interest in everyday affairs could really be said to have lent impetus and meaning to the teaching of English. I propose to discuss only those developments connected with reading and written English as the wider aspects of this type of work are dealt with in Chapter X.

It so happened that groups of children amongst a class of 9-year-olds began to arrive late for school. Enquiry revealed that their lateness was due to their being fascinated by the appearance of gangs of workmen and much equipment on the arterial road which ran past the school. A major road development plan had been put in hand and was likely to last some months. Thus an opportunity was presented to the teacher to pursue the teaching of English under highly favourable conditions, for the children genuinely desired knowledge and enlightenment and the means to satisfy them was freely available. It remained for the teacher so to guide and plan activities in this connexion that the maximum amount of support was given to the teaching of reading and written English, while yet encouraging general intellectual development along lines vital and acceptable to the children.

BASIC SKILLS: READING

Lively discussions followed concerning the necessity for improvement where the road narrowed to form a dangerous bottle-neck. So ideas were formulated and expressed in simple terms, much as follows:

> The road outside is very busy.
> Most of it is wide.
> Traffic goes along it quickly.
> It gets narrow at the railway bridge.
> This holds up the traffic here.
> It is very dangerous.

Sentences of this nature were written up on a class News Sheet at suitable intervals of time. Consolidation was effected by adding captions to illustrations, using words and phrases culled from the News Sheet.

> e.g. A traffic hold up.
> A busy road.
> This road is dangerous.

In the course of their observations the children were asked to note the different kinds of vehicles passing along the road and ascertain what they were carrying. This resulted in the compilation of booklets along the following lines:

I SPY on the road
A lorry carrying bags of cement.
A tanker carrying oil.
A van carrying furniture.
A car carrying people, etc.

Other booklets made included, *People going to work*, *Tools for the job*.

Naturally many interesting questions arose and were duly answered.

> e.g. How do the workmen know where to dig?
> What is cement made from?
> Why do they put wire in the road?

Questions and answers were later transferred to slips of card and used as matching apparatus to test reading and memory.

Certain children in the class had a special contribution to make, e.g. one boy's father was a lorry driver, one girl's mother was a cleaner at the hospital situated on the main road. Each undertook to tell the class about their parents' work. This they did and the rest of the class recorded the information by means of pictures which they drew to written specification.

e.g. Mr Green drives a lorry at night.
Mrs Taylor washes the ward floor.

From the foregoing brief survey of English activities it will be obvious that the teacher did not just wait for things to happen, but played an important role in guiding and anticipating developments. In her manipulation of the activities she displayed a sound basic knowledge of the principles involved in learning to read, and an ability to order her children's learning without undue restriction, and a recognition of the importance of motivation in encouraging children to read.

Such methods of teaching are often decried on the grounds that they lack system (as they frequently do!) but it is quite within the power of the teacher to work out an underlying system whilst still allowing her children freedom to develop along lines of thought attractive to them. Witness this teacher's systematic presentation of definite reading teaching at suitable points in the overall study. At the conclusion of the activities both she and her pupils had recorded for future use and reference a number of words and phrases which would prove invaluable additions to their growing reading vocabulary.

Surely it is when the teacher sees the majority of her children engaged upon a series of activities such as these just described that she may rightfully conclude that success is imminent, for reading is beginning to have real purpose for most of her children and is gradually becoming what it ought to be – a key to knowledge and understanding in everyday life.

For a few however, the outlook is bound to be less bright. They may be entering their tenth or eleventh year and reading still not a usable skill. Where these less successful children are concerned the teacher must be prepared to accept small returns for her skill and patience, seeking always to arouse interest and maintain effort, confident that the fruits of good teaching and personal encouragement will one day mature.

Book List

Bristol University Institute of Educ., *A Survey of Books for Backward Readers*, U.L.P., 1956.

GAGG, J. C., *Teaching Children to Read*, Newnes, 1955.

GATES, A. L., *The Improvement of Reading*, Macmillan and Co., New York, 1951.

INGRAM, C. P., *Education of the Slow-Learning Child*, Ronald Press, 1953.

MCKEE, P., *McKee Readers, Teachers' Manuals* (6), Nelson, 1954.

Ministry of Education, *Reading Ability*, Pamphlet 18, H.M.S.O., 1950.

MURRAY, W. and DOWNES, L. W., *Children Learn to Read*, Harrap, 1955.

RUSSELL, D. H. and KARP, ETTA E., *Reading Aids Through the Grades*, Teacher's College, Columbia Univ., 1956.

M. F. BOOTE

Chapter V

ARITHMETIC

General Considerations
Of all the problems the teacher of backward children in ordinary schools is likely to face, that of teaching arithmetic is probably the most difficult. This is so for a large number of reasons, not the least of which are the habits and attitudes of mind of the teachers concerned. The necessity for examining one's own attitudes and habits of mind will become more apparent as the following chapter progresses, and in any case unless the concept is clear genuine aims become impossible.

Most of the references made in this chapter are to children in special classes or D and E stream groups in ordinary primary schools.

At the outset, it is necessary to say who are the children who will find themselves in backward classes and also something of the nature of their difficulties. The largest group within the class will probably be composed of dull children. Of the remainder some will be average ability children who for a number of possible reasons have failed to learn much of any of the basic skills, some will be average children who are specifically retarded in arithmetic and one or two will almost certainly be those who are not very well adjusted emotionally.

With regard to the first and largest group, the difficulty is, that most probably they have not learned because of poor capacity and in this connexion it is worth noting that inability in simple number and arithmetical processes is often one of the signs of the dull youngster. Within the second group one can expect to find those children who have had much absence from school through sickness or shifting families, and those with some slight defect of sight, hearing or physiological function, which has made learning difficult. Among these too one finds the 'little failures' who have tried once and not meeting success have lacked the stamina or right setting to

BASIC SKILLS: ARITHMETIC

have another try. And lastly, in discussing the few emotionally disturbed children let it be said plainly that seriously disturbed children are quite out of place in a backward group. Having said this one must face the fact that in most special classes children with some emotional difficulty will nearly always be found. This is very pertinent to the subject under discussion because often an emotional upset is triggered off by this very thing, that most of us consider a common place of school life, viz. arithmetic.

Most special or D and E stream classes in ordinary junior schools will tend to be comprised of children roughly divided as stated and sharing generally two important characteristics.

(1) Lack of reasoning power and little or no capacity for abstract thought.

(2) Lack of sustained curiosity coupled with marked inability to draw conclusions.

These characteristics working together or even singly often result in what may be thought to be useful arithmetical activity being nothing but pleasant make-belive. This of course extends to many other activities but especially does it seem to apply in number and arithmetic lessons.

In view of all this why do we bother to try and teach arithmetic to children who just can't do sums? The short answer is that we don't in the purely traditional sense. Instead we decide on certain essential minimum attainments and aim at these. In cases where these minima can be exceeded so much the better. Such a decision is not made, of course, just to maintain the stake that arithmetic has in our school system. The necessity for such a decision is that the general educational aim of leading the child towards responsible citizenship makes it essential, if he is to become fairly competent in adult affairs, for him to be able to cope with the 'arithmetic of everyday'. For the less able child to be adjusted to society – both present child society and later in adult life – reasonable facility in number handling is essential. This clearly does not mean being 'clever at arithmetic'. The five basic elements of this minimum seem to be:

(1) number facility – which requires: the ability to count – certainly to a hundred ultimately. Also, to employ with certainty the four rules with small numbers especially as a mental

process. Much of everyday life consists of 'in the head' or 'on the spot' calculation (the ability to record and manipulate scores in games, rows of plants, minutes on bus journeys to and from work, etc.)

(2) money proficiency – which requires: adequacy in handling everyday coins and amounts, shopping and checking bills and the growth of sound money sense.

(3) practical measurement – which requires: understanding and recognizing three main units of weight, length and capacity but involves only what would be required for everyday use in cooking, furnishing and decorating, etc.

(4) concept of time – which requires: as well as reading the time, getting to know and feel the uses of it.

(5) spatial relationship – which requires understanding of relative sizes and masses. Also big and small, distance near and far, many and few, etc.

Bearing all this in mind and having regard to individual differences and capacities and environments of children concerned, it is well to remember that some will accomplish all or most of these basic requirements, some much less and some hardly any. Keeping this in mind the aim can still be maintained as long as real adjustment is made in the face of genuine incapacity. Success will ultimately depend on the capacity of the child and the quality of teaching employed.

Having said 'why' we should teach number and arithmetic to these children and settled certain basic requirements by way of content there remains the difficult 'how' or method of teaching.

The Hadow report defined method as ' "teacher style", the personal expression of his educational faith and experience'. This seems especially true of methods involved in teaching number and arithmetic. The teacher who for twenty, thirty or forty years has been used to the fact that the symbols four and three when united become seven feels affronted and indeed embarrassed by a child who not only cannot see that this happens but cannot even make it happen. The teacher cannot remember the personal moment when such a fact passed from something learned to something automatic, let alone what was involved by way of early experience before he learned the fact. The dilemma is complete when the same child says that he has seven brothers and sisters and perhaps oddly enough questioning reveals that it is four brothers and three sisters. It is at this point that educational philosophy, tolerance and wide human experience are most necessary, otherwise rejection can so easily occur with all the trouble that rejection stores in the child. At this point too, there must be genuine readiness to go right back to real things that can be touched, picked up and *known* as numbers of things.

There is not one sure way. The gaps in a backward child's experience cannot be filled piecemeal. Each child's environment is different. An apparently rich environment can often be poor in learning possibilities. One needs to know a child for some time before one can be sure of his true attitude to numbers or the mental sensation he derives from them. From all of this one positive feature emerges and this can only be, that no method has much chance of success without close observation and understanding of each child's own difficulty. In direct sequence to this is the fact that teacher A cannot necessarily work successfully teacher B's successful method. Also of course all teachers concerned with backward children need to know as much as possible about each other's work and above all to exchange ideas freely.

It is necessary to state that henceforth in this chapter whenever and whatever connexion the word 'method' is used it implies, in the light of the preceding paragraph, merely 'possible method'.

There seems no doubt that the problem of arithmetic teaching owes much of its thorny nature to the traditional emphasis on sums and mechanical practice. It is not possible to deny that both sums and mechanical arithmetic are part of the greater whole implied by the word ARITHMETIC. So often all that it means is a dull grind with abstract and meaningless symbols. Most people are familiar now with the example of the backward child performing twenty tricks each morning with twenty 'hundreds, tens and units' sums (carefully worked to ensure no carrying) when in fact he is doing nothing but addition of digits up to ten and is often not very sure about those. The writer is of the opinion that any process being worked without understanding is wrong practice and serves only to confuse the pupil and ultimately sow seeds of future doubt and difficulty.

The more one thinks the more difficult it becomes to understand how it has come about that in schools the one subject in which there is only one right answer has been allowed to become the one subject in which we attempt to give abstraction before the concrete and indeed the generalization before the examples.

Arithmetic is not the abstraction and the clever tricks and comptometer work that some textbook writers would have us believe. There is no doubt that like reading there is a stage of mental readiness which has to be reached before any direct instruction is of much value. This is not in the writer's experience always coincident with reading readiness but in some cases as much as a year before and in some cases as much as, or more than, a year after this stage of development has been reached.

Many backward children have been encountered by the writer counting and adding in their games quite happily, but who when asked, said they could not do sums and what is much worse, said they did not like handling numbers. These children were clearly cases in which the readiness stage had been reached but had either had numbers pitched at them too soon as abstractions, or had had insufficient time given to the concrete application of number situations. Having said so much about numbers it should be stated at once that number understanding (sequential) never seems to progress in step with number understanding (quantitative). This is a real failing and seems directly attributable to unsatisfactory introductory work. (It should be remembered here that the children under discussion are backward children. The above average to very bright child, seems to gain his own application to reality with numbers and quantities irrespective of the manner and method of his introduction to arithmetic proper. There has however, recently been some misgiving among selection boards choosing civil service candidates for posts dependent on higher arithmetical qualifications, that although many of the candidates have the ability as far as standard rule of thumb processes go, they often flounder when it comes to drawing conclusions and information from results sheets poured out by modern calculating machines. In other words they can memorize the tricks but have not the wider arithmetical understanding.)

Since few of the backward children in our schools are likely to be involved in later life in large and lengthy calculations the first and most fundamental condition seems that never should a child be

BASIC SKILLS: ARITHMETIC

expected to work with numbers or quantities beyond his understanding of that moment. Every day, children are working in hundreds with only an understanding of ten, and thousands without understanding of a hundred. Relative quantity and relationship in space are essential parts of the growth of understanding. (A hundred pins will go in a small tin, a hundred books take a big space in a cupboard, a hundred children a large space in the hall and a hundred houses a large street, etc.)

At the very beginning number and quantitative understanding are very closely linked with language and particularly word meaning. One rarely hears the word multiply in everyday life but 'a dozen 3*d.* eggs is commonplace. A hundred tickets at 1*s.* for a school concert involves the process of multiplication but from such examples could arise the basic understanding that multiplication is addition. Counting the tickets, adding the tickets, making bundles of twenty and so on, are worth acres of mechanical examples.

Discussing what is possible, its scope and the influences and tendencies bearing upon this, a general principle needs to be kept in mind. Methods attempted need always to avoid the idealistic approach. The child is under no moral obligation to succeed. Having done his best, no more can reasonably be expected. He is a good boy for having done his best but he is neither good nor bad for being either right or wrong arithmetically.

Against this must be placed the tempting attitude so easily adopted of providing less able children with prolonged and extensive success potions which may have the opposite effect to that desired.

Because of the characteristics already mentioned, methods of teaching arithmetic to backward children in ordinary schools must necessarily be:

(1) concrete in nature, which implies genuine physical handling, discussion and experiment.
(2) meaningful in the sense that they are related directly to the child's own experience.
(3) adjusted to the childrens' needs. The curriculum cannot be a pacemaker with these children and it must be flexible enough to permit of imagination and vision.
(4) controlled in the sense that it is not just aimless botching.

Progression there must be and guidance equally so, but both may be quite unobtrusive.

It is worth considering for a moment the cry of those who would have arithmetic as a discipline. That there is truth in the assertion that arithmetic disciplines the mind seems undeniably true. Yet with backward children the discipline is unsuitable and a hindrance in fact, to the development of a normal quantitative understanding at however limited a level.

Marching and formation drill are undoubtedly very good discipline modes for fit and able bodied men with two legs but no one would dream of including a one legged man in a drill squad even though he badly needed discipline. The analogy is complete of course when one realizes the very adequate (in the circumstances) way the one legged man gets along the street away from the marching squad. The very exercise that is of value to the fully equipped is of harm to those not fully equipped.

This is not to say that backward children should not do sums. Of course they may if the sums are suitable and if the 'teacher freeing time' is given to individual attention where it is most needed. If it gives satisfaction and a sense of achievement (it is worth remembering here that the traditional pattern still leads children, however backward, to expect 'sums') short periods of doing sums with suitable numbers is of just as much value as many 'music and movement' or P.E. lessons.

Content and Approach
In all backward classes the teacher is immediately concerned with the wide range of ability that he will encounter in a quite small class.

The younger children just up from infants school are much the more difficult in respect of both assessment and decision about line of approach.

With the younger backward children the strategy indicated is that of a broad framework of routine tasks which establishes a network from within which individual approaches can be made. Much of the early number work is talking and handling. Many more uses could be made of number situations in day to day activities than is generally the case. (We will paint our pictures with only three colours today, has immediate and real meaning, especially so if a pattern using large figure threes is also the subject. Contrivance is necessary and with some thought can be interesting while avoiding artificiality.)

'Ideas of number and space develop early through play with the varied material that ordinary homes supply. Children hear such words as "much", "few", "long", "heavy", "full" and can generally use them correctly by the time they enter infants school. Direct teaching is undesirable during this first period. It is sufficient for children to be given ample material for "home" play, etc., dough, water, sand, bricks, beads, etc. They will then compare, measure and weigh spontaneously, thus laying a firm foundation for more formal work that follows. Some children will begin to count and will pick up the names of the first few numbers from people round them but an attempt to force this knowledge will not help a child's later progress.'

The foregoing quotation from *Arithmetic in Primary Schools* is of course talking of normal children under 5 but bearing in mind the mental level of most young backward juniors and the lack of direct experience from which they appear to suffer, it is most relevant. Because they are of reduced capacity and unable to gain quickly from experience, the background to provide this first hand experience is necessarily extensive and lengthy in use.

Problems dealt with orally can be introduced as soon as a working vocabulary is established. They can also include the use of all four of what have become known as rules.

To achieve this, of course, the classroom must perforce take on rather the look of an emporium. The variety of materials and objects that can be stored in collections is quite fantastic. It involves organization and some time in taking out and putting away – and how valuable that time is in the fields of social training, co-operation, vocabulary building, cleanliness, etc.

Variety is of supreme importance. The value of the discovery of a box with twenty-six acorns in it is soon reduced if it just becomes a familiar part of the background. Large quantities of really large, bright, highly coloured pictures are of great importance in sowing the seeds of the 'I wonder how many there are' frame of mind. Many such pictures can be obtained from old magazines – especially the rather glossy American type that are loaded with advertisements. Every child would sooner count seven strawberries in real colour on a dish of cream than the inevitable black dots and rings that so regularly are placed before them. (It is assumed that quantities involved in pictures will be selected to meet the needs of the class and only small groups of pictures will be used at one time. The classrooms one sees overhung and indeed submerged under 'do this' and 'count that' cards, apart from depriving children of space for their work, must fail because of lack of variety and stimulus and the indifference or indeed rejection that this engenders.)

The day to day administration of the class can involve many children in an infinite variety of number situations of a real and genuine kind. Here again changing the jobs round is as important as the job itself. It should always involve the co-operation of showing each other how it is done (the milk and soap tablets and P.E. shoes and workbook stock, etc.). It is always of the utmost temptation to leave the job to the child that does it best, but once expertize is reached a new job is indicated.

The classroom shop is of value possibly more so from the social development and language experience point of view, than from the number and arithmetic angle. Many elaborate shops have been seen which are of little value to either aspect, but shops created by the children themselves, from bits and pieces assume real purpose. In the majority of cases the making of bills and accounts belongs to a much later stage and although some can be achieved with normal infants a great deal is artificial and contrived. (In any case how many shopkeepers write bills now?) The most useful part of a classroom shop is the experience of the child organizers, and thought, decision and purchase of simple objects with small amounts of money, by individual children. Beyond certain limits, which experience soon indicates, the classroom shop with backward classes can become a serious time waster. Here again fairly frequent shutting down and packing away of the equipment collected, enables it to come out fresh at a later date.

All the parts of simple recording even if only involving a tick in a square have an important and immediate relationship to number approach work. The height chart on the wall illustrates that there is vertical length as well as horizontal. The familiar use of bigger and

BASIC SKILLS: ARITHMETIC

smaller, taller and shorter are major stepping-stones to understanding. All the children should have a ruler, preferably a plain piece of lath cut precisely to one foot with no end margins. Few if any of the children under discussion have the necessary skill, muscular control or even strength to make a cardboard ruler that has a very satisfactory use. It is argued by some that children should always make their own rulers in first stages. Provided children have had much practice of measuring with their own feet and have been told of the unit being that of a man's foot the connexion between reality and practical use is established. Once a proper and accurate foot has been given them then much practice can be indulged in with real materials, and the practical necessity of the smaller unit of the inch and larger one of the yard, can follow if the practical work is thought out. The practice of guessing (estimating) prior to measuring should be encouraged at all times but the actual measure with a ruler stick should be a matter of careful training and accuracy. 'Eighteen feet and a bit' is very useful measuring of the classroom in the earlier stages providing the eighteen feet is accurately achieved. From lengthy experience with this sort of young backward child it seems certain that most of the measuring activities are more satisfactorily achieved if completed in pairs with the aid of a piece of chalk and each job repeated in changed roles to see 'we have not done it wrong'. The most one can expect by way of pencil work is just the simple record of a statement regarding a given measurement.

Weighing is a necessary part of the scheme but the provision of scale weights and materials is not of much value in itself. (The unit of measure to start off with seems to be quite clearly the pound, as it is the most common everyday unit and is within the vocabulary of most of the children concerned.)

A great deal of time needs to be spent in establishing the fact that accurate weight means balance (see-saw analogy here). In fact probably the best way to start is with a made-up suspended balance fashioned from broomsticks, sticks and tin lids. This clearly establishes the principle that if both sides are the same they balance. The progression here seems to be, after one pound, two pounds and then half pounds. The emphasis all the time being placed on balance which means fairness, leads the children to be more observant in their real dealings in local shops. The story of how the Queen always puts her stamp on fair weights never fails to appeal. If they do ask the shopkeeper politely whether they can see the weights and measures crown then they are indeed progressing.

The classroom scales have another positive role in demonstrating the different natures of some materials. The enormous scale pan full of grass required to balance quite a small lump of plasticine is one of many slants on this.

Most children (even the dullest) really want to tell the time, it is an adult facility of which they seem genuinely envious. The backward class needs a great big clock face always available in the classroom and a small portable one for each child. The latter can be stuck and assembled if the faces are first duplicated and hands holed and guillotined previously. It is essential that the models look like the real things and the hands move satisfactorily (paper fastener) or loss of interest is rapid. The difference in length between hands needs to be exaggerated and numbers very clearly printed. If the models are no more than six inches in diameter and a stiffish envelope is provided the clocks can always be readily in hand. All sorts of highly coloured freaks are often recommended as introduction to time telling but this seems to be quite undesirable as well as unnecessary. The practice dials should be as near reality as possible, in other words like the clocks and watches children see outside of school. Minute markings can be omitted of course, and in any case modern clock faces are more and more being designed without them. The actual teaching can only be achieved directly and in groups at various levels. Until children can recognize and can say numbers to twelve most instruction would be useless. It seems best to begin with hours and the big hand always on twelve so that time established is precisely 'hour o'clock'. Once an 'o'clock time' can be recognized and said then appears to be the time for setting on individual clocks and drawing in workbooks – colouring, etc. Of course a 'going clock' in every classroom of this sort should be basic equipment. Continuation work should be half hours followed by a 'quarter past' and a 'quarter to' each hour. There are no short cuts and the importance of the hour hand's position in its segment can only come with close observation. This underlines the importance of having at least one genuine clock to show the small hand trailing the hour in the 'past' times and leading it in the 'to' times.

BASIC SKILLS: ARITHMETIC

(Very few adults really look at the hour hand. They have a well developed time sense which tells them what hour it is. In the classroom situation the frequent emphasis on real time for breaks, meals, milk, etc., is of great importance.) Apart from the numbers on the face of a clock it is pointless and confusing to use the clock face for any other number work. With bright able children who know the time such use is stimulating and intriguing.

Experience with money can be achieved in a variety of ways. There is no real substitute for genuine coins and as far as possible only real money should be used, at the introductory stage. When children are willing to accept cardboard coins, having had an opportunity of seeing fake and genuine side by side, they should have a small tin with a well-fitting lid in which to retain their coins. In the early stages it is thought that three pennies, six halfpennies, one threepenny piece and sixpence is the essential minimum. The combination and relationships within this group of coins are many and of everyday significance. The farthing, which ceased to be a legal coin on 31st December 1960, was always a source of confusion and worry, and, so far as the children are concerned, we may be glad that it has gone. As each child can satisfy the teacher of his ability to name and show relationship between all coins in a box so another coin can be added to increase number of relationships. The child who understands all the possibilities of two and sixpence will have no difficulty with comprehending 10s. and £1. Here again they need a number of opportunities of seeing, handling and talking about the money values.

With all learning of money, talking, handling and use are the essential steps before recording. To a child who cannot read, the funny little 'd' and 's' and strokes and lines we use for recording money are just hieroglyphics and quite meaningless. The real thing is the money and what can be done with it. Stamps, bus tickets, admission tickets to class shows, all have immediate value as a way of introducing the symbols without the premature burden of written evidence.

The value of games as aids to notation is very great providing the game is simple and created for the children rather than the children being fitted to the games. Clear, simple rules are necessary and some time must be spent on using them as a pastime so that mastery is obtained before any second use is made of them. A few games are best used with the whole class like Lotto and Blackboard Roulette but the main and most valuable purpose is in games involving two or four children.

No consideration is being given here to the details of the individual games and activities. They are all available in a variety of books on method and techniques, many of which appear in the list at the end of the chapter. By far the most useful games are those created by the teacher for use with his own class. He is the only one who knows the limitations involved and just what he is trying to get understood by his class.

As was stated at the beginning of this chapter the biggest single difficulty with dull and backward children is that of obtaining the recognition, feeling and understanding of the symbols in number use. When one remembers that a large number of children know the early numbers before they ever go to school at all and then a comparison is made with the children in backward classes in junior schools, the nature of this problem becomes clearer. The children have had five years growing up in the house and two in the infants department and still some of them do not know and cannot recognize number symbols above five or six. How can this be rectified without undue stress or strain? In some cases even dull children seem to recognize the failing in themselves and resent it. In others, the lack of ability is caused clearly by an early rejection (for almost any reason) and persistence in the rejection.

Everyone is familiar with the number cards and matching cards. Dominoes and picture counting cards all have their place. With the hard core of inability, however, even this very early pre-arithmetic work is premature. The small group of children involved (and they have appeared in most intakes over a number of years) needs to be led into number situations which give pleasure to them. To be asked to bring four of a special sort of container (previously ascertained) from home, involves a child in a real situation. To go and get three of this and five of that means that he and the number are directly involved. No opportunity should be lost of involving these children in number tasks which they can see and recognize as immediately useful.

One oddly successful game with a small group was devised with a

BASIC SKILLS: ARITHMETIC

tin and glass and a bell in an open-ended box facing the teacher. The children sat round the desk with hands hidden. At intervals the teacher struck different numbers on the different objects in the box which the children couldn't see. After each object a small pause was given for children to arrange their fingers. On the word 'go' hands were raised showing number of times the funny clock struck. Even the wrong ones could say nearly always what object had been struck. (Incidentally this simple piece of apparatus, costing nothing, provided the first clue to what was a long standing case of poor hearing.)

For all the children in the backward class the most important realization is that numbers mean something real. The complete abstraction is as out of place in such a class as is the child who can cope with it.

'The basic ideas of geometry, viz. shape, symmetry, size and position are as important as counting and serve as a means of mental development particularly stimulating to children who find difficulty in work with abstract foundation for logical thinking. . . .' *Arithmetic in Primary Schools.*

Right from the early days much can be done to establish interest and realization along these lines. The ordinary classroom is full of examples which will remain unseen unless attention is drawn to them. Bricks, mosaics, jigsaws are enjoyed by most of the children and enable them to perceive differences in shape, size and position.

No backward junior class is complete without at least two large sackfuls of regular smooth blocks and the same quantity of wood pieces cut into every conceivable shape, size, width and dimension. A carpenter's or furniture maker's offcuts are cheap and invaluable.

Paper folding, pattern making and cutting, further the process of understanding shape and dimension, interest in which is ageless.

The connexion between this and practical measurement mentioned earlier is clear and a one foot cube, a one foot square and a one foot equilateral triangle are useful objects to have readily available and occasionally on display.

A great amount of space has been devoted to many aspects of pre-arithmetic teaching. Where does this stage end? It should again be emphasized that we are dealing with essentials and not ideals. If any of the children in the class can go much beyond these minima then the child is misplaced and needs a class more suited to its capacity.

The completely traditional pattern of number and arithmetic work is of little use to the less able child. On the other hand however, all the approach work and understanding gained by the methods indicated are of little value unless put to real use.

Two quotations from R. K. Robertson are worth recording: 'If a child cannot use his arithmetic in simple problems, it is useless to teach it to him' and 'Most books contain entirely stupid problems'.[1]

Both these statements are rather blunt, over-simplified and not completely true but the attitude towards backward children implicit in them is entirely sound. The very word *problem* has in normal arithmetical parlance, a connotation of difficulty and indeed trickery.

The same author advocates a clean break from informal to formal stages of arithmetic. In this way a start is made on teaching rather large numbers (e.g. five and four), which it is said discourages counting. The writer goes on to say: '... use flash cards and work sheets, teaching say, twenty combinations until you get an instant response. Then immediately use these known combinations until you get an instant response. Again immediately use these known combinations in problems of a simple type. Keep a constant rhythm, teaching more combinations revising the old ones, then using all-in problems. Do the same with subtraction, multiplication and division combinations. Go back constantly to problems ...'[2]

The intention here is quite clear. If you can get the number combinations and bonds thoroughly learned with instant response and recall, then all the early processes in formal arithmetic become possible. That this is *not* possible in fact, is soon apparent to anyone who makes a genuine experiment along these lines. There are two major stumbling blocks to this sort of teaching. The first of course is the poor remembering capacity of these children, and secondly, fitting problems to the combinations becomes artificial. A few combinations can certainly be learned by rote but this suffers from the same difficulties as learning tables by rote. If the facts are learned and sometimes remembered they become just abstractions, and of course practically meaningless to the children. Like all the earlier

---

[1] *The Treatment of the Backward Child*, p. 21. [2] Op. cit., p. 21.

BASIC SKILLS: ARITHMETIC

stages the combinations to twenty seem best tackled by continuation of earlier work rather than clear breaks. The children need to grow into using numbers with which they are familiar in situations which are real and have immediate purpose but most of all with numbers of which they have the feeling and understanding. If this work is continued through the stages of plus and minus combinations much can be accomplished by way of more formal work. Subsequently multiplication and division can follow on apparatus and activity lines.

John Dewey said that 'all that a school can and need do for a child is to develop his ability to think' . . . 'the essentials are that the pupil have a continuous activity in which he is interested for its own sake, secondly that a genuine problem develop within this situation as a stimulus to thought, third, that he possess the information and make the observations needed to deal with it, fourth, that suggested solutions occur to him which he shall be responsible for developing in an ordinary way, fifth, that he have opportunity and occasion to test his ideas by application, to make their meaning clear, and to discover himself their validity.'

Hours spent in purely mechanical and abstract arithmetic situations do not fulfil any of these essentials. Worse still, when a problem presents itself in real life which could be solved by one of the known processes failure usually results because real understanding is not present and there is no immediate connexion between the problems and the process that has been learned. It may be necessary to wait a very long time for this understanding to develop, in fact it may never come at all.

When the children in a backward class have had the experience outlined and have accumulated a body of number knowledge that is real to them they are ready to move on to manipulation of numbers in the more traditional sense. This involves abstraction to some extent but always it is necessary to have the problem based firmly on reality and not just a problem for its own sake.

The decision still rests with the teacher. Is a method or approach suitable? Can I operate it? These perhaps are the two most critical questions which only the teacher concerned can solve. There is no royal road to success and whatever is done is best done slowly. It is necessary to observe results. Not always do children gain the concept from a process or activity that we had anticipated. Progression is vital and width of experience of paramount importance. If the aim is kept constantly in sight that experience and language must come before comprehension, that concrete visual experience (including kinaesthetic) come before abstraction and that qualitative notions should precede quantitative ones the stage has been properly set. Not all children will achieve all that we aim at and some will achieve hardly any. These are justifications for such lines of approach and not reasons against them. The fundamental is progress and not attainment. Certainly the aim must not be to drive children to a preconceived artificial standard by means of tricks and dodges. The differences in individuals even within a small group are quite often extremely wide. This alone dictates what is done. 'Is it suitable?' must be the decisive question followed by 'what will it achieve?' and subsequently 'what has it achieved?'

Suitable activities can only be organized and arranged providing the teacher really knows his children. This of course demands accurate records of what the child can do. Accurate records do not mean those of the glossy, beautifully printed kind so much liked by certain college authorities. A book ruled with manifold analysis columns containing a scribbled note on each phase of number experience thought to have been passed with understanding, is of much more value. In many cases the result will not be first indicated in a period nominally called Arithmetic. Records of this must be completely and absolutely the tool of the teacher. They are solely to keep before him a picture of the experience so far provided and as a guide to the next stage. A more formal record card is required for internal school use when the child moves to another class or department, and suggestions for this will be found in Chapter XI.

It is at this stage that a number of difficulties are likely to be experienced which are brought home by the consideration of record and progress cards. In backward classes in ordinary schools care should be taken to see that no child is moved into ordinary classes without careful thought. Much depends on the pattern of the school as a whole and a great deal on the relationship that exists between the special classes and the rest of the school. The whole child must be considered and in no way is this more important than in his 'ability in' and in 'his attitude to' arithmetic. A child will be at no

BASIC SKILLS: ARITHMETIC

disadvantage for having had experience on the lines outlined and given time and sympathetic handling will, if he is really suitable material for promotion soon cope with a more formal course in arithmetic just because of such experience. But if the arithmetical scheme in the rest of the school and in particular in the class to which he is going is extremely mechanical then he needs at least two more terms preparation on individual lines within his present class.

(It is necessary to state this because, as was said at the beginning of the chapter, not all children who find themselves in a backward class are there because of inferior mental capacity.)

It is not the job of the teacher of a special class in an ordinary school to call the tune for the whole of the school. All that has been argued here is what is considered necessary and suitable for backward children in a special class in an ordinary school. That most of the techniques involved could be equally employed with bright children (more speedily and extended in content) is probably true but beside the point for the purpose here.

Finally a word about apparatus. The teacher of a backward class will find over the years he will construct, invent and improvise apparatus in connexion with number and arithmetic work. This always involves much thought and very often much physical effort. If it was worth making once it is worth storing and preserving. If it can, it should be packed in a box and labelled briefly with an indication of its point and use. Fresh clean apparatus is as stimulating to children as a shower on a hot day. In any case apparatus not in immediate use becomes over-familiar, boring and *en masse* overpowering to the class. A full discussion of the use, construction, and storage of apparatus will be found in Chapter XII, so I will say no more here.

In conclusion, no excuse is offered for the concentration on fundamentals and beginnings and thus by implication on the early years in junior schools. By the very nature of the problem it is at this stage that most of the work will be done. All large junior schools need at least two special classes and in the second class work will be concentration upon but expansion of, what has been done in the earlier stage. In some respects the problem is more straightforward in the second stage because the pattern (educational and emotional) of each child has emerged more clearly and any that are suitable for transfer to ordinary streams will probably have gone. Children of very low (but educable) I.Q. should by this time have been transferred to special schools. This leaves the not inconsiderable group of below average and dull normal children who will be the main constituent of most special classes at the top end of the junior school.

Organization

It is inevitable that organization should have been touched upon in the first two sections of this chapter. There is a place however, for a more detailed consideration of this much misunderstood and overworked word in an arithmetic teaching context.

Many apparently highly organized classes in arithmetic seem to achieve very little by way of real progress by the children whereas some apparent shambles achieve wonders in this respect. The first principle is still therefore 'what is each child doing?' irrespective of what the whole appears to be.

It was many years before even the traditional arithmetic period was organized into ability groups of any real meaning. Streaming and vertical sets in large primary schools have gone a long way toward improving matters but a lot more is necessary when dealing with classes for dull and backward children.

In the wide sense organization primarily depends on the school. It was said earlier that most large primary schools needed at least two special classes. In certain cases a D or E stream class is necessary for each year of the school. Certainly D and E stream and special classes need to be outside and separate from any 'vertical setting' or 'cross classification' arrangement that applies to the rest of the school – this is necessary because with the less able children arithmetic cannot be dealt with on separate and subject lines.

Ideally, a suitable and specially responsible teacher should act as leader for the group of teachers concerned with D, E and special classes. The word leader is deliberately chosen in this connexion because the responsible person can have no other useful function. Great value can be obtained from the co-ordination, continuity and progression that such an organizational set-up implies, as Mr Bannister pointed out in Chapter I.

At the class level only the teacher can decide. A great deal depends

BASIC SKILLS: ARITHMETIC

on the limitations of space and equipment but most depends on the teacher himself. It is a highly individual matter. Constantly changing patterns of organization is just a muddle, organization that never changes just becomes stagnation. In between these two extremes lies the real thing. The less able children need to see the clear simple lines of an established régime and in most cases respond well to it. The teacher too, needs the framework from which to push out but to which he can always return if his reconnaisance fails or results are not forthcoming. No teacher can work somebody else's organization but this makes more, not less, important the necessity of knowing and considering what other people do. A teacher who knows his children's needs, has a clear aim in mind and organizes his time and activity so that each child gets his just proportion of teacher time, is doing all that can be reasonably expected of him.

There are, of course, many ways of achieving this. One way – which on paper would appear to result in giving only a much reduced amount of time to each child but in fact doubled it – was dependent for its success on the careful grouping into four groups with a colour name for each rather than the more conventional grade or letter name system. The groups were in fact as nearly as possible composed of children of like arithmetical capabilities and contained five, six or seven children in each. This particular system was worked only three mornings a week in the period 10 a.m. – 11 a.m. before break. It was firmly established that this period was a 'quiet' period and the teacher was directly concerned with only one group. On Tuesday morning, for example the teacher would be working with Yellow group

while Blue group were – with individual sum cards on mechanical practice and self marking.
and Red Group – jigsaw puzzles or other desk fitting apparatus
and Green Group – number scrap books
word and picture tracing books
but for those above this level news picture and sentence work.

The groups working apart from the teacher were limited to desk work but of course knew where to find and had access to the things they needed. At first sight the period may seem lengthy but ten minutes or so at each end for 'getting out' and 'putting away' reduced it to little more than half an hour. Yellow group is thus able to have the complete attention of the teacher for the whole of this time. On Wednesday each group changes one place round and again on Thursday. This sort of thing takes a little time and a lot of forethought to get going and it has the danger of course that the same group can be missed too many times if school closures, nurses' visits and other interruptions happen too frequently on the 'same day'. Friday or Monday mornings can of course be used to make adjustment when necessary.

Regarding the small group that the teacher has been at such pains to get quietly to himself, let it be said at once that it is out of the question to give examples of all the possibilities of work with such a group. With some of the children direct application to the difficulty is clearly the best way, with others a more circumspect approach is preferable. (A child who does not know the symbol two and who may not even be able to write the figure will not gain by being confronted with the bald injunction to keep on trying.) Whatever else is attempted the immediate and concrete use of each glimmering of understanding is now possible for each child in such a small and closely related group and is the most important part of the activity. With really dull children even the vocabulary of number and spatial relationship is best dealt with in this way. With the more able groups, which can usually have one or two more children in them than the others, more ambitious work can be attempted.

All this of course is only a possibility. It worked quite well with one class, but it certainly might not work with others. The other two mornings were used for longer and more informal number activities along lines mentioned in the previous section. (To anyone, with experience with backward children, it will be obvious that for such a plan to have any chance of success the teacher must know his children very well indeed. Such knowledge might be gained by an experienced teacher within a few weeks of taking over a new class. With someone just beginning this work, a whole term would probably not be long enough.)

It cannot be said too often that the work that is possible with dull and backward children depends on the teacher. Similarly all

BASIC SKILLS: ARITHMETIC

organization depends fairly and squarely on the teacher's personal organization. The old style 'lesson notes' of training college days are clearly out of the question because very rarely is a lesson in the 'class' sense possible. In spite of this, however, preparation is necessary and to begin a number period without a clear idea of what one is going to attempt is just inviting disappointment and weariness for the teacher and continued failure and frustration for the children. The aim, of course, must always be simple but it may still be clear. Furthermore, unless the teacher has a quite out of the ordinary memory system, jotted notes are very necessary. Having done this and with the same courage involved in making a note of his simple targets, the teacher must be prepared to abandon his plan and grasp boldly that occasional moment, when an unexpected incident reveals new understanding on the part of one child and really help that child to capture and enjoy it.

Finally, organization is not only the physical arrangement of events as has been briefly outlined here. It is seriously suggested that a most useful part of the teacher's personal organization is the quiet reflective session in physical comfort away from the class and away from the school. In this way objectivity is more easily achieved and one's scribbled notes take on real meaning. After such a period in which notes written and mental are safely recorded, the whole thing should be put firmly from one's mind.

The Last Word

For convenience and easy reference for discussion purposes, the teaching of arithmetic to backward children has been given a chapter of its own. As will readily be seen elsewhere in this book, the problem is part of a greater whole applicable to 'whole children' in the primary school setting. There is a danger that as a subject arithmetic tends to assume a special importance which it does not merit. An attempt has been made to indicate fairly where its importance lies in relation to the child's social, emotional and educational development. It is hoped that any enthusiasm visible in this chapter will not be misunderstood as asking for special status for arithmetic teaching for backward children as possessing special value itself.

In conclusion it must be said that the criticisms that have been stated or implied of the traditional and formal arithmetic teaching methods are not intentionally destructive. Many thousands of children have fared well on them and will continue to do so; but as far as backward children are concerned such methods are in the main 'unsuitable' and must be replaced on this account.

Suggestions for Reading

Assoc. of Maths Teachers, *Arithmetic in Primary Schools*, Longmans.

BRIDEOAKE, E. and GROVES, I. D., *Arithmetic in Action*, U.L.P., 1950.

BRUECKNER and GROSSNICKLE, *Making Arithmetic Meaningful*, Winston.

FLAVELL, I. S., *Mathematics in the Junior School*, National Union of Teachers, 1960.

FLAVELL, J. S. and WAKELAM, B. B., *Primary Mathematics*, Methuen, 1960.

KIRK, S. and JOHNSON, G. O., *Educating the Retarded Child*, Houghton Mifflin, 1951.

ROBERTSON, R. K., *The Treatment of the Backward Child*, Methuen, 1950.

SCHONELL, F. J. and E. F., *Diagnosis and Remedial Teaching in Arithmetic*, Oliver and Boyd, 1957.

STERN, C., *Children Discover Arithmetic*, Harrap, 1953.

D. A. RAY

Chapter VI

ART

In the present emphasis upon the use of the practical subjects of the curriculum as a means whereby the slow learner is expected to find an easier path to the understanding of the three R's, art, or rather that aspect of art which deals with picture and pattern making, has an honoured place. This chapter, whilst dealing in part with such teaching, is mainly devoted to the teaching of art as a subject. Therefore the term 'the slow learner' need not have the same meaning as regards art teaching as it has in, say, the teaching of reading; for is it not a fact that the normal or supernormal child could be found who is below average in art ability? Specifically this chapter concerns the slow learner in the basic subjects, although it could be of use in the teaching of all children retarded in art performance.

Teachers of the backward whose previous experience has been mainly with children in the normal streams are so often conscious of the disparity between the art-work of their present class with those they have previously taught. These teachers may react to this fact in one of two ways. They may accept what they find, or they may attempt to raise the standard.

Acceptance could have many implications. It could mean that the position is regarded as hopeless, or that the teacher feels that he is technically unable to remedy the situation. It could mean that he has yet to find his children's wavelength, or, again, that he just could not care less.

On the other hand there can be no unhappier person than the teacher who has conscientiously set out to raise the standard of his children's work through his own interest in the subject, only to find all his attempts unavailing. With backward children any attempt to raise the standard of work is doomed to failure unless certain factors within the child are taken into account and the work the child is called upon to do is planned accordingly. The following points are introduced as an attempt to put the teacher in the picture and also as a basis for the make-up of this chapter.

(1) The teacher must be aware of the children's limitations and work within them.
(2) He must have a knowledge of the variability of performance expected from average children of similar ages so that he has a basis for comparison with the work of his own children.
(3) He must be clear in his own mind as to the value to backward children of free expression in art; its use and misuse; its comparison with the so-called traditional methods. He should also consider the possibilities of a combination of the two methods and decide for himself whether he should provide the materials and the inspiration and let the children take over from there; or whether his help should take a more practical form.
(4) He so organizes the materials that the possibility for misuse is cut to the minimum.
(5) He must provide exercises aimed at developing a facility with tools and materials.
(6) He includes in any scheme opportunities for experiment in colour and form.
(7) He has a well-defined scheme geared to the children's limitations yet aimed at maximum progression.
(8) He is aware of the possibilities in the correlation of art with other subjects.
(9) In all the above he bears in mind the value of art to slow children.

Limitations

Just as it is unwise to expect too high a standard from backward children it is equally unwise to accept anything on the basis that these children are incapable of better work. There are certain generalities that can be borne in mind which will help in making a better estimate of what to expect.

It should be remembered that if a child be backward because of dullness it should not be expected that his paintings will be of equal merit with those of brighter children, but it is possible that he may do

EXPRESSIVE WORK: ART

better in art than he does in the basic subjects. Again, a child who is backward but not dull will, in general, do less well than the more intelligent child who is average, or above average, in art, although exceptions to this will be found. It often happens that a child of normal or above normal intelligence, produces pictures that are not so good as those done by backward children who, compared with their performance in other subjects, excel in art. Therefore, if the teacher should not expect that the range of art ability will be as wide in a special class as it can be in a class of brighter children, he should also not be predisposed to considering that the limitations of his class should be set very low. In all, the maximum expectation for his best children will at best not much exceed the average standard of a normal class.

A moment's thought will bring the realization that there is a greater possibility of inability through physical causes in a class of backward children than in any other class. Therefore in his provision of special educational treatment the teacher will base his methods on his knowledge of the child including, in particular, any physical or psychological defects the child may have.

Limitations cannot be adequately assessed without a knowledge of the normal performance to be expected at any stage in the life of the child. In art assessment it is more common than in any other subject for the teacher to apply a subjective estimate based upon his own standards and prejudices. Yet it is quite possible to make an objective estimate based upon a knowledge of the stages in the art development of the average child. Many investigations have been made in this field including those carried out in America and called the Cleveland Studies. An account of these studies will be found in the American book *Art Education – its Philosophy and Psychology* by T. Munro. Here it is sufficient to mention the five stages that have been confirmed.

They are as follows:

(1) The Primitive schematic stage.
(2) The Full, or developed, schematic stage.
(3) The Mixed stage, between 2 and 4.
(4) The True-to-appearance stage.
(5) The Perspective stage.

So near to the early development in the history of art are these stages that it would seem reasonable to subscribe to the Atavistic Theory of Education, if it were not that the theory has been, to some extent, disproved.

Development in child art does not necessarily run through the five stages. Witness the fact that many adults, educated and intelligent ones at that, are unable to draw anything in stages four and five. Regression caused by disuse of the ability is one factor to be considered and there are many more. Whatever the reason, Munro states that the evidence points to the fact that no individual can advance without going through the order named. It is, however, Bühler's theory that the artistically gifted child does not necessarily pass through the schematic stage.

In his book, *The Mental Development of the Child*, Karl Bühler states that in his early drawings the child forms a simple mental pattern of objects that interest him, which forms his *schema*; and it is from this concept that he draws, not from concrete images. This *schema* tends to become habitual and may persist throughout the early stages of the child's art, and even to a later stage with educationally sub-normal children. Rouma thinks this tendency towards automatism is responsible for the queer effects in some drawings by children, such as two eyes to a profile, where the child is obviously drawing what he knows and not what he sees. This is of course acceptable in drawings by children below, say, the age of 7, and no teacher should go out of his way to force the children on to a further stage for which they are not ready. For the backward this matter is tied up with their mental ages, therefore the teacher of such children will accept automatism to a much later age than will the teacher of normal children.

It is important that the teacher should not interfere with the child's first efforts at painting from his *schema*, although help can be given should the child ask for it. The courageous attitude with which the child attacks his painting can produce pictures of great beauty and it is no part of the teacher's role to spoil this and engender a lack of confidence by the introduction of adult concepts.

Hilda Eng, in her book *The Psychology of Children's Drawings*, has put forward a theory of the eight steps in art development. She imagines a continual spiral of growth beginning at step one and progressing to step eight; then beginning again at step three at a later stage in the spiral.

Her steps are:

(1) The Scribble. Usually pre-school but often found in school.
(2) Formalized drawing.
(3) Automatism.
(4) Orientation. This is the first sign of an advance. The child covers his paper by cataloguing those parts of the subject that are related in his mind.
(5) Perspective. Not the final perspective of the Cleveland Studies, which cannot be expected to appear before the age of 12, but a demonstration of depth by placing objects above others in the drawing.
(6) Proportion. A definite stage which is not very important to the child in his early years.
(7) Colour. In the early stages savage, bright colour. The subtleties come much later in the continuing spiral.
(8) Ornament. Textures and patterns upon areas, i.e. leaves, bricks, etc.

How should the teacher help the child?

It seems that the term 'free expression' has as many definitions as there are teachers to define it. It is within the experience of many to find the term used as an excuse for the teacher to provide materials for the art lesson, see that the children have started, and then to concern himself no more with the lesson until it ends. Such teachers find the art lesson a convenient time for getting on with their marking, or some other task, whilst the children are seemingly engaged.

The greatest exponent of free expression in art, Dr Franz Cizek of Vienna, had no such conception. His art lessons were as much full of activity for the teacher as they were for the child. To Cizek more than to any other man do we owe the emancipation of the child from the restrictive academic approach of 'Do this!', or 'Copy that!' Unfortunately it can be suspected that Cizek was far more interested in Child Art than in the child artists. His plan holds that Child Art is sacred and should not be influenced by outside factors such as photographs, pictures, and exhibitions. Cizek's biographer quotes Cizek's friend, Geo. E. Mackley, as saying: 'The new art appears not to recognize the tendency of a growth in art knowledge but is a fostering of artistic Peter Pans who will not grow up.' The teacher has to decide whether the art produced by the child is of the greater importance, or whether it is the child and his continuing satisfaction through his increasing facility and dexterity that matters. With the slow learner there is no doubt that satisfaction in achievement is the most important consideration.

The old academic approach that stripped the art lesson of its glamour and appeal to the child by making him work through interminable and uninteresting exercises, is also to be condemned as being calculated to do away with all originality and experimentation. In fact both the academic approach and the Cizek method fail because they are equally restrictive, although in different directions, and both fail to aid the growth of creativeness through a lack of the presentation of techniques and a lack of variety in artistic forms.

To bring about a growth in art performance the needs of the child must be met by providing him with adequate opportunities for self-expression and with some freedom in the choice of his subject. At the same time there should be constant vigilance on the part of the teacher to detect those occasions on which the child is seeking for further technical knowledge. That is not to state categorically that advice should only be given when asked for, but that the teacher should be aware of the children's needs so that he can plan his lessons accordingly. Therefore, instead of just giving the children art materials and telling them to get on with it, a better idea would be to organize the lesson, or series of lessons, in the following manner:

(1) The subject is discussed.
(2) The teacher demonstrates any particular technique that is required.
(3) The children work under individual supervision where the teacher endeavours to bring out the best interpretation of the children's ideas.
(4) The finished paintings are discussed.

It is also a good plan to consider that whilst a painting is complete in itself, and as such has merit, it is also but a stage towards the next picture in a continual growth of technique.

EXPRESSIVE WORK: ART

Materials and Organization

Very early in his career a teacher realizes the necessity for careful planning. He learns, too, how expert is the child in intentional, or unintentional, sabotage. He endeavours to counter this tendency by compiling certain rules that govern most of the contingencies that may arise. The art lesson is a perfect example of when the children must know exactly where they stand. To devise rules to ensure the smooth passage of the lesson the teacher must bear in mind the following factors:

(1) That the children are slow learners. So his rules must be few and within the comprehension of the children.
(2) That the children must know the reasons for these rules and also be aware that they cannot be put aside lightly without the express permission of the teacher.
(3) That some of the rules must be aimed at the preservation of the children's safety and the protection of property, both personal and communal.
(4) That those rules dealing with technique are explicit and are expected to be observed, although the teacher may allow deviations to suit any physical or psychological disability in particular children.
(5) That there are two conditions that govern the conduct of the lesson. Firstly, that the children must find satisfaction. Secondly, that each child must grow to some measure in art concept. It must be remembered that over a short period the second condition may not be measurable.

Consideration can now be given to the materials of the art lesson such as paint, paper, brushes, etc.

It is rarely seen now that expensive cartridge paper is used for the lesson. The so-called kitchen paper is very popular both for its cheapness and for its suitability. Its cheapness enables the children to paint on larger areas with beneficial results to their paintings, but false economy must be guarded against. There are some kitchen papers so thin that normal use causes them to disintegrate, and others have a shiny surface that is unsuitable for painting. Others are so many tones off-white as to be almost muddy-coloured. This is not to state that coloured papers other than white should not be used when required, but that when white is wanted white should be used.

Sugar paper is admirable for art work, particularly in the choice of colour and surface that is offered. But, compared with kitchen paper, it is expensive, too expensive to allow of its sole use in the art room. The reasonable teacher is well aware that his Head teacher does not conjure the money for school stock out of the air, therefore he should proportion his art requisition accordingly, whilst bearing in mind his responsibility to the children to see that they are equipped with materials adequate in size and durability for the job in hand.

These last remarks apply equally well to the supply of paint, which should be adequate; but all possible steps must be taken to see that wastage is cut to the minimum. In this respect it might be thought that solid blocks of tempera colour are superior to the powdered variety. This is true up to a point, but it is a difficult matter to ensure that the blocks retain a clean, pure hue once the children have been let loose amongst them. It is said that the blocks may be cleaned easily by holding them under a tap, but this can cause a colossal waste of paint, not to mention the time factor involved and the multi-coloured staining of a sink. The writer confesses to a predilection in favour of powder colour and this chapter is continued with powder colour in mind although the suggestions will apply equally to solid blocks. (A discussion of the use of solid blocks for *special* purposes at the top end of the junior school can be found in Chapter XII.)

It must be rare in these enlightened days to find water-colour boxes used in the junior school. The water-colour technique is considered to be the most difficult to teach and is suitable only to the most gifted of the older juniors. The secondary school is the place for it to be taught, for misuse in the junior school may lead to the development of bad habits which will be found too difficult to eradicate later.

So far as the actual colours he uses are concerned the slow learner will find the manipulation of the Ostwald Colour Range well within his comprehension. There is no other range so compact. These eight colours and two neutrals, the use of which will be hinted at in a later section of this chapter, may all be contained in a

EXPRESSIVE WORK: ART

nine-hole bun tray. That is if the teacher does not provide purple which can be kept in a tin under his eagle eye; for purple has a great attraction for children, especially the less intelligent, and many good pictures are spoilt by an excessive use of this colour.

As for brushes, the teacher who has used squirrel-hair brushes in the junior school will have learnt through experience how unsuitable for tempera painting these are both in size and fragility. Bristle brushes are essential and it is suggested that a complete set of size seven or size eight are acquired, together with a few of each size from one to twelve for any particular task that may be undertaken.

The supply of water is probably the greatest problem with which the art teacher has to deal. To have water piped to the classroom is of course ideal, but how many classrooms are so equipped? Buckets of water have to be used in most cases and their use must be carefully organized. The distance from the tap, which in some instances can be far, and the number of steps up which the buckets must be carried, can cause the nervous teacher many qualms when dealing with the slow learner. As it is better to be safe than sorry it will pay individual teachers to consider this problem carefully.

The best water containers to be placed on each set of tables are those cone-shaped paste jars, the broad bases of which make them difficult to overturn. Two buckets of water are required, one for the refilling of these jars and the other for the occasional washing of tools. The buckets must not be more than two-thirds full as it is obvious that full buckets are more likely to lead to wet floors. As one of the buckets must contain clean water and the other will soon contain dirty water, they should be placed at opposite ends of the room to ensure that their different functions will not be confused. They should be stood upon old tarpaulins, or raincoats, or, if nothing more suitable is available, on pads of newspapers.

The children should be allowed to use the buckets freely but should the water-tap be distant a limit might have to be placed upon the number of times the water containers may be refilled. It is advisable to have a rag box available in case of accidents.

In addition to the paint trays previously mentioned clean trays are provided, preferably one between two children, to be used for mixing the paint with water. These mixing trays can be made from tin lids nailed in a cluster upon a square of wood if expense is to be avoided. The children will be taught that water must not find its way into the paint trays and with the slow learner it might be advisable to provide a means of transferring the paint to the mixing trays. Wooden ice-cream spoons are useful for this.

Ancillary aids with which to equip the art corner are reference charts such as the Ostwald Colour Wheels; pictures of the subject under review, which must be out of sight during the actual lesson; a collection of sprays; colour scraps; tooth-brushes for spatter work; stick prints and any other media for the occasional art lesson.

A reference box should also be provided, with suitable pictures catalogued alphabetically. Backward children need to refresh their memories occasionally about even the most commonplace things and they should be allowed the freedom of the reference box which they will help to build. On no account, however, should the pictures be removed from the box for the purpose of copying. The box is for reference only.

Lastly, a supply of card strips cut to one-inch, two-inch, and three-inch thicknesses should be provided so that the children may use them to make the different sized squares needed in their pattern-making.

Experiments with Colour

Backward children should have the opportunity of experimenting with colour on a much wider scale than with the traditional three primaries of the Brewster theory. Also they should not have to deal with unassociated colours that have exotic names, such as ultramarine, viridian, magenta, and so on. As mentioned in a previous section the Ostwald range of colours give greater scope than can be obtained than by just using the three primaries and their derivatives; and it limits the uncontrollable span of the usual colour range which is so unintelligible to these children.

There is no room here to more than mention the Ostwald Theory and its use with backward children but it would pay the reader to obtain those excellent books by A. B. Allen: *Colour Mixing for Beginners* and *Art in the Junior School*, where he will find a simple exposition of the theory and suggestions for its use with children. Suffice to mention here that as colour plays so great a part in the lives of these children more should be made of colour by the teacher

EXPRESSIVE WORK: ART

in telling colour stories, letting the children make colour books, letting them become familiar with the Ostwald Colour Circles and the ladder of neutrals. The child should be encouraged to mix his colours with black or white, or even grey, if he so desires or if circumstances make it necessary. He will soon discover that some familiar colours are not obtainable in the Ostwald range without mixing. He has to be taught that orange and black mixed will give him the brown he wants. He will be faced with such problems as how one gets the colour for faces. The steps to the discovery of flesh colour will not hurt him provided he records his discovery in his colour book.

One word of caution when dealing with colour mixing. The child should not over-mix, for the brilliance of the colour that results from mixing is less than that of its components. Therefore the teacher should hesitate before allowing more than the mixture of two colours.

Use of Tools

Backward children are more likely than their brighter brethren to produce messy, almost indecipherable pictures. There are a variety of reasons for this, not the least of which is the impatience of the slow learner to finish his painting which over-rides all caution and restraint. That a child should attack his task with zest is an admirable quality and in a brighter child to be encouraged, for such a child is painting not only with his brush but also with his mind. He composes, compromises, and solves difficulties as his brush moves over his picture with a sure touch. On the other hand the backward child soon forgets the original intention for his picture and resorts to mere space-filling which can result in an untidy mess.

Some slow learners produce insipid, lifeless, automatic pictures that are rarely finished. Such children are, beside being backward, usually slow, finicky and ultra-careful. To provide suitable training to embrace both the impatient and the finicky is a difficult matter, but if certain rules are formulated for the average situation, and if these rules are few and their observance enforced in a sensible manner, the child will advance in manual dexterity, he will produce reasonable pictures, and his satisfaction in his task will be thereby increased.

To produce better work from the children the teacher must be very conscious of his own example. When illustrating a lesson he should not draw at speed, that is if he is capable of so doing, but with care, for the backward child will associate the good drawing with the speed with which it was executed and will attempt to emulate his teacher with disastrous results. If care in drawing is to be impressed upon the children then the teacher must curb his own impetuosity. To issue hastily torn paper to such children is not conducive to good work. Remember that carelessness communicates itself to the children.

It pays to demonstrate the proper use of materials so as to cut down as far as possible the chances of messy drawings; and, what is more, the teacher himself should always use the materials in the manner he has prescribed for the children. He may get better results in his own paintings by using other methods but he may be sure that if he does not adhere to his own rules when teaching then neither will the children.

Examples of some of the rules that backward children can be expected to observe are as follows:

(1) Draw large. Small details and tiny figures are not easily seen.
(2) Simple instructions for mixing paint and water.
(3) Clean brushes in the desk water container after using one colour and before using the next.
(4) Carry out the correct method of holding the brush and making brush-strokes. Ban the careless backwards and forwards brush-stroke common to most slow-learners.
(5) Paint carefully up to the line of the drawing so that a neat edge to all figures, etc., is obtained.
(6) Do not paint adjacent colours until the first is dry enough not to cause the paint to run.
(7) Rules for general tidiness during the art lesson.
(8) Concise instructions to the art monitors on the changing of water in the buckets and in the washing of tools after the lesson.
(9) Haphazard mixing of colours is forbidden.
(10) Do not leave brushes head downwards in the water-pots.

Obviously the teacher will not commence his teaching by reading out a list of rules to be learnt by heart. He will introduce them gradually when and how it seems to him that they are needed. To reiterate, he must bear in mind that any rules for backward children must be few in number and that the reason for any particular rule is well known by the children through explanation and demonstration by the teacher.

Methods

Paintings in school usually alternate between patterns and picture-making. Of these the slow learner will usually produce better work in his pattern-making, perhaps for the reason that the patterns, at least the simple ones he is called upon to do, call for little imagination beyond the building-up of the pattern and an automatic repetition. As children love patterns the wise teacher knows that besides the finished pattern itself here is a heaven-sent opportunity to teach the children colour manipulation, brush-work, or any other technique he desires the children to learn. So then an important secondary function of the pattern is its use as a medium for practice in the skills required for picture-making.

There are two types of patterns, space-filling and repetitive. As the repetitive side of pattern-making needs some understanding it is easier to commence by teaching the space-filling variety. To undertake such a pattern the child is told to divide his paper into irregularly shaped areas and to paint-in these areas with as attractive an arrangement of colour as he can manage. Later he can be introduced to textures to decorate his pattern. Examples of space-filling patterns and other patterns and pictures will be given in the Appendix at the end of this chapter.

The repetitive pattern can become as complex as the children's understanding and ability allow. For early patterns, and indeed the majority of patterns undertaken in the junior school, the processes can be reduced to two basic rules which, if always observed by the children, can render an apparently difficult pattern to something near simplicity. Firstly, the child is told to paint the first motif in the first square and to repeat it in exactly the same position in each square before commencing the second motif in the first square. This is continued until the last motif is completed in the last square. Secondly he is taught that one colour is used at a time until all the motifs in that colour are completed.

In this manner repetition is being carried out as regards colour, size, and position; so that if care is taken no square is appreciably different from any of the others.

Of course there are some patterns which are not based on squares, such as patterns made from templates where the joining of the pattern is made at fixed points on the template, but to some measure the afore-mentioned rules still apply.

The discriminating use of textures enhances the beauty of a pattern, but the slow learner, once his enthusiasm has been aroused, will allow himself to be completely carried away so that he will often ruin a perfectly good pattern. The teacher must be well aware of this tendency and also be prepared to intervene with a gentle restraint.

Textures are not limited to patterns. There are very few things in everyday life that have no textures and it is not often that a picture will be found that has none. Hence another example of pattern work used as practice for the techniques of picture-making. Such textures as leaves on a tree, brickwork, pebbles on a path are rarely represented by the artist in their entirety. He merely places his textures in the appropriate position on his picture so that the least amount of strokes suggest the most. To emulate the artist the child must learn to curb his enthusiasm in whatever manner the teacher finds expedient so that he places his textures only where they are needed.

Examples of textures to use for pattern making are hatching and cross-hatching; dashes representing rain; spots and circles; repetition of shapes such as letters, figures, or abstracts; lines, whether horizontal, vertical, oblique, dog-toothed, wavy, or any combination, etc.

Picture making can be carried out in a variety of media. It is not necessary to adhere to the most common medium of paint to produce attractive pictures. Indeed much pleasure can be found and much knowledge gained in making pictures from coloured paper, from materials, by printing, or by montage of newspapers, etc. Deviations from the more normal method of painting should not be considered as stunts. Instead an attempt should be made to evaluate the benefits accruing to the child from these unorthodox methods.

In the main, picture work, in whatever medium it is carried out, is of the following types. Interpretations of things seen at the time

EXPRESSIVE WORK: ART

of painting; objects or situations remembered; imaginary situations either dictated by the teacher or by the child himself; flights into fancy; abstracts or semi-abstracts involving emotions or situations; cataloguing and montage, where the various objects associated with the subject of the picture are arranged in the most pleasing manner; interpretations of ideas with a utilitarian purpose, such as posters and stained-glass pictures.

It is not to be thought that the backward child can be expected to undertake the whole range of picture work, but, within his limitations of thought, he can be brought to an understanding of his materials and gain some little ability in the overcoming of technical problems. With this in mind the teacher may safely expect him to execute reasonable pictures from imagination and from known and unknown situations. He can also be expected to follow dictated instructions regarding the subject of his picture so long as the instructions come within his comprehension.

Whilst the teacher will endeavour to make the utmost of whatever imagination the child possesses, he must know that the slow learner may have little imagination, and what little he has needs constant stirring to keep it alive. To give such a child free choice of subject and method is to expect little return. The slow learner prefers to be directed rather than to be left to his own devices, and it is by discussion, suggestion, description, and example that the skilful teacher can draw from him more than he will normally give. On the other hand there is a possibility of good work being done by him if he is taught to execute his work mechanically; but here the teacher should consider well whether or not he, the teacher, is justified in teaching this method, and whether, in so doing, he is thinking more of the child's painting than of the child himself.

When deciding on subjects for the pictures the teacher should not stray too far outside the bounds imposed by the children's comprehension. He should also be prepared to spend much time in stage-setting and in using all his persuasiveness and dramatic ability in painting the subject in the minds of the children.

When the work is finished he should attempt to evaluate the pictures in three ways. On the basis of the efficacy of his teaching; on what standards he expects from each individual, whilst bearing in mind the child's limitations; on the progress made.

Correlation with the other Subjects of the Curriculum

With the exception of the craft lesson there is no subject in the curriculum so useful in the teaching of the others as art. This the teacher of the backward must acknowledge, but he must also see that the standards he imposes during the art lesson proper are not dissipated when art is being used for another purpose. Consistency in teaching is one of the keys to success when dealing with the slow learner. The child should know what is expected of him as an individual and should not be allowed to fall from this standard, however low, without enquiry.

It is not the purpose of this chapter to deal with such topics as projects and centres of interest. To the teacher it is obvious what an important part art can play in these methods. What is not so well known is the value of art in the teaching of reading and arithmetic, or if it is how little it is used! When one considers how much both reading and recorded arithmetic, as well as writing, owe to their pictorial ancestry, is the teacher wise in ignoring art when teaching these subjects?

Writing is itself an art form and these mystic symbols to which we are expected to provide the child with the means of translating can, in the education of backward children, be better understood by the use of art. By this it is not implied that all readers should be translated into pictographic script for the purpose of teaching backward readers to read, but that drawing, picture association, word-matching, free expression in art forms, etc., must help in the understanding of a writing which is based on these very things.

The Value of Art to the Slow Learner

'Far more than with ordinary children, painting or drawing can be for them (backward children) an extension or even a substitute for language, its symbolic nature enabling them to give form to ideas and emotions which they may be unable to express in any other way.' (*The Teaching of Art*, L. de C. Bucher.) Many avenues of communication are almost closed to the slow learner in the junior school. His verbal ability is practically non-existent and his number sense is woefully inadequate. Yet in art he can find a measure of success. A word must be recognizable and be recognized to be read, a sum has only one correct answer, and elaborate oral communication needs a vocabulary above the attainment of the slow learner; but in art there is no such absolute demarcation line between right and wrong, for he can be correct to his own satisfaction within his present stage of art development. He finds that his ideas flow more readily as he draws and that there is greater facility in his conversation when he discusses what he draws. He is even prepared to argue his case in the face of skilful and gentle opposition when rapport has been established between himself and his teacher. There is within him a capacity for deep feeling seemingly incompatible with his paucity of intellect. These emotions can be intensified by an inability to understand the situations that foster them. As he may be unable to give vent to these emotions in any other positive way, art gives him his chance to express himself and to work out graphically those things that disturb him.

In conclusion then, art has for the slow learner many of the elements conducive to his happiness and well-being. It can give him success; allow him an outlet for his emotions; give him an easier means of communication; provide opportunities for developing his kinaesthetic sense and the finer muscular co-ordinations; and be a means whereby he may be taught more easily to read and to write as well as to converse.

Appendix

Art exercises which the slow learner in the junior school can be reasonably expected to undertake.

Space-filling Patterns

The Scribble. Basically a matter of scribbling with large loops all over the paper and then painting the spaces thus formed with flat colour and textures.

Space Division. As mentioned earlier in the chapter.

Cobblestones. Draw overlapping circles using a template. Then colour in the circles.

Tartan Pattern. Paint irregularly spaced lines downwards and across. Colour spaces thus formed.

Scattered Shapes (hands, objects, figures, etc.). If hand shape used the child draws round his own hand on the paper in as many positions as possible. He paints the hand shapes in different colours. The background is painted in one colour. Lastly, textures are painted on the background.

Large Motif (i.e. Leaf). Leaf shape drawn from corner to opposite corner with main vein lines drawn. The spaces between the veins are painted in different colours. The background in one colour. Textures are painted in appropriate places.

Symmetrical. Fold paper lengthwise. Draw half the pattern in charcoal on one half of the paper. Fold over to obtain impression on the other half. Colour.

Crazy Paving. As name implies. Draw line by line.

Wavy Lines. As for tartan pattern but lines going one way only.

Repetitive Patterns

The following patterns should be within the ability of the slow learner. They should be taken in the order given which is the order of difficulty.

Linear Border Pattern.

Linear All-over Repeat.

All-over Repeat with some spaces filled in.

Tram Lines. Use three-inch card to produce three sets of tram-lines down the paper. Pattern with wallpaper motifs.

All-over Repeat (using recognizable motif). As for all-over repeat except that object such as a man is used as the main motif.

Drop Repeat. Where two designs are used which are placed as are the black and white squares of a draughtboard.

Half-drop Repeat. The framework is set out as the bonds in brickwork.

Counterchange Pattern. An all-over repeat where the design is the same in each square but where the two colours that are used alternate in their position in each square.

Edge-stencil Pattern.

Stencilled Pattern.

Potato-cut Pattern.

Stick-print Pattern.

Pictures

From Imagination. The Haunted House; The Monster; My Dream; Space Travel; Scenes from stories, i.e. Robin Hood, *Black*

EXPRESSIVE WORK: ART

Beauty, The Wind in the Willows, King Arthur, etc.; The Three Witches; The Gypsies; Santa's Workshop; Under the Sea; The Battle; Never-never Land; 'I am Tom Thumb'; The Treasure; Black Magic, etc.

From Known Situations. Scenes from home and school; The Family at Dinner; Bath Night; Washing Day; My Party; Playground Games; Sports; Shopping; The Cinema; The Boxing Match; Gardening; Road-up; Safety First; Jobs, i.e. The Postman, The Policeman, etc.; The Fair; Topical Events; pictures needed for projects.

From Description. A short description is read to the children and also written on the blackboard. The children make their own interpretations of the description. The children can deal with good descriptive passages from poems and books, such as extracts from Belloc's *Cautionary Tales for Children, Gulliver's Travels, King of the Golden River,* and 'The Highwayman', by Alfred Noyes.

Other Methods

The slow learner should receive plenty of opportunity for practice with still-life as well as with drawing from life when he may use his friends as models.

Poster work should prove very rewarding and, when working in a group, wall panels, friezes, and scenery for puppet plays should not be beyond his capabilities.

Book List

ADAM, L., *Primitive Art,* Penguin.
ALLEN, A. B., *Art in the Junior School,* Warnes.
— *Art in the Senior School,* Warnes.
— *Colour Harmony for Beginners,* Warnes Information Series.
— *The Teaching of Colour in Schools,* Winsor and Newton.
BUCHER, L. de C., *The Teaching of Art,* Blackie.
DUNNETT, R., *Art and Child Personality,* Methuen, 1948.
GOODENOUGH, F., *Measurement of Intelligence from Drawings,* World Book Co., New York.
LEMOS, PEDRO DE, *The Art Teacher,* Batsford.
LOWENFELD, VICTOR, *Creative and Mental Growth,* Macmillan.

TEACHING THE SLOW LEARNER IN THE PRIMARY SCHOOL

Ministry of Education, *Art Education*, Pamphlet 6, H.M.S.O.
MUNRO, T., *Art Education – its Philosophy and Psychology*, Liberal Arts Press, New York, 1956.
ORPEN and RUTTER, *The Outline of Art*, Newnes.
RICHARDSON, M., *Art and the Child*, U.L.P., 1954.
VIOLA, W., *Child Art and Franz Cizek*, U.L.P., 1942.

G. A. EDMONDS

Chapter VII

MUSIC

The teaching of music to children has, for most teachers, been a difficult problem. The reasons for this are I think as follows:

(1) Being non-musicians they have felt that they have nothing to give to their children through music and

(2) Having a complacent attitude towards, or a dislike for music, they have not felt that they wanted to take part in any music in the school, and have left this to the pianist or the interested person on the staff.

If we consider only singing and the reading and writing of music then these feelings have some point, but I hope that through considering the other aspects of music and pointing out the values they can and do contribute to human development, I will convince the non-musician that he must attempt to change his attitude and bring music in a fruitful way to children in school. Before I go on to discuss the benefits that humanity derives from music, I would like to state quite clearly that it is not understanding the fundamentals of music that will help us to pass these benefits on to children, but it is the understanding of slow children and their needs that must be foremost in our minds when we are arranging our programme of musical activities in school.

The problem seems to be that having considered our children's needs we want music to help in meeting them. I will attempt to solve this problem in two parts. In the first place it will be as well to consider some of the human values that we can pass on to our children through the sensible and thoughtful use of music in school.

Secondly we can examine how this can best be done in school.

The first part of our problem can be considered for the sake of convenience under the three main headings applicable to child development (i) physical; (ii) intellectual; (iii) emotional.

Physical

All children and especially backward children, will benefit by responding to music, by movements. These movements in general are as follows (*a*) the fundamental movements that are characteristic of the different stages in a child's development: rocking, swaying, jumping, running and then skipping.

(*b*) Older backward children will use a combination of these which will be more boisterous or more refined as the temperament of the child makes itself manifest. Later we shall see how this physical activity can be used in creative activities, impersonations and dramatization all enhanced by the use of music.

Intellectual and cultural

Music as an art has always been closely related to human development. Therefore through music children can study more intimately and gain a greater understanding of a period of history; they can enjoy and respond to the music to which their forefathers listened. Children can make contact with people overseas through enjoying their music and so on. Can we deny that this is a particularly attractive way in which to broaden our children's cultural horizons? It may be as well to add here that all this music can be enjoyed and these benefits derived without attempting to build up the technical knowledge of music in backward children and without the aid of a trained musician.

Emotional

There is no doubt that when music is presented to children effectively they get much enjoyment and satisfaction from it. Our aim then must be to provide musical experiences that backward children will enjoy and that will satisfy them. When we observe children responding freely to music through some childlike activity what we see is an expression of happiness. These activities may appear to some people to have no educational value. 'They do not appear to be learning anything' is quite a usual remark made, but the children are moving

EXPRESSIVE WORK: MUSIC

towards the enjoyment of music, in fact they are learning to enjoy music. We have already seen that this enjoyment of and interest in music will not only benefit them at the present but it augurs well for their future afterschool life. Music has so many sides to it, as we shall see later, that it is possible for everyone to succeed in some aspect of it. Thus, it is not dominated as are so many school subjects by the 'success-failure' complex.

Up to this point I have only discussed some of the benefits that our children will get through having music presented to them in a satisfying and fruitful way. But, I think that a teacher can derive much benefit himself through enjoying music with his children. He will perhaps see himself as a person who is not only responsible for putting over a quota of knowledge to his children, but one who I think is largely responsible for shaping and guiding the lives of young people.

Of course a little more thought can produce many more ways by which backward children in particular can benefit from responding to music. More thought in this direction will, I am sure, convince the non-musician that he can and must give music to backward children in school.

I have now come to the point where we can consider *how* these benefits can be given to children. Teachers may well ask at this point 'Are we to requisition a few dozen records, a gramophone, push back all the desks in the room, put on a record and "let t'battle commence"?' It is not quite like this, you certainly need a record player and records, and space is desirable, and in the first place you may get something akin to 'battle'. But remember that it is the music that you are trying to get your children to enjoy and not the opportunity to break all the school rules. The approach to presenting music is the next thing that I would like to discuss. You will remember that I said that through music we wanted to satisfy some of our children's needs in their development, and I have also mentioned enjoyment. I think then that this should be our first aim. We should get our children to enjoy the period set aside for music. In this respect I think that we have a point that will help us in the very first place towards getting enjoyment. Music can come as a pleasant change in the school programme, but in my experience this will not be so if children (especially those who are backward) are sat down in a classroom to learn by rote from a piano, songs that are not appropriate to their needs, or ability to learn. They will attempt to sing them if they have to, but the relationship between class and teacher will often become strained and the beauty in the music will be lost. You will gather from this that I certainly do not advocate rigid control during music lessons. The music itself will, if you let it, make your children behave in a reasonable manner. Of course it is no good using music which backward children cannot respond to and enjoy. It is most difficult to state clearly what sort of music will be enjoyed by children of different ages and abilities, but my experience has taught me that it is good and well tried music that always 'catches on' in the end. One may reasonably ask 'what is good music?' To this I have no answer, but I have heard bad music used for children when some point in music reading or voice production was being put over, and have observed the result in the children. It may be added here that much time has been spent by teachers in preparing reading and voice exercises that are designed to practise some melodic phrase or rhythm – this is not good music. To illustrate more clearly; if you went to a concert and heard nothing else but Czerny's piano studies played you would know what I mean. There would be plenty of gymnastics and flourishes but there would be no beauty. There is no doubt that it is the beauty in music that the children find so pleasing and satisfying. Backward children will in the first instance respond by movements to the rhythm of the music, the way that it rocks along, sways along, jumps along, runs along and then skips along. Here then is the first thing to look for, some shortish piece of music that has a definite rhythm, that does not chop and change about. You will yourself, no doubt, feel what the music tells you to do in this respect, and no harm will be done by your mixing with those children who, in the first place, are forward enough to want to express their feelings in this way. The second thing that they will notice is the tune and this will help them to vary their movement, for instance, a soft skipping tune will help them to skip lightly, a louder skipping tune will make them want to skip more heavily, and so on. From these two points then, it appears that the best music to begin with is a piece that is not too long, that has a definite rhythm and that has a simple and pleasing tune to which to listen. This sort of music is found among

EXPRESSIVE WORK: MUSIC

folk music, i.e. country dance tunes, folk songs of many lands and of course excerpts from ballet music. Some very good ideas in this direction can be gleaned from radio programmes that are specially designed for young children, and often the children themselves will have many suggestions. I have pointed out that we must be aware of our children's needs and then partially try to satisfy them through music. I venture to suggest here that in observing and participating in our children's activities during the music lesson we will get to know them more soundly. I do not think that there are many subjects on the time-table that lend themselves so admirably to this end. We are too often occupied with the subject matter of a lesson rather than the child itself. This is what I meant when I said that music offers opportunities for us to introduce human benefits to our children. We all know the children that come in for most treatment in the three-R lessons, they are the ones who are boisterous and have to be kept quiet and the abler ones. My experience is that teachers know quite a lot about these two types of children mainly perhaps, because they judge their own capabilities as 'disciplinarians' by their influence over the first and their success as 'teachers' on the results obtained by the second.

To sum up then this section on approach. When considering our work in music we must prepare experiences that will make available to the greatest number of children those benefits we have been considering and which will suggest themselves as the individual needs of our children become known to us. The music lesson must be enjoyable (this can be obtained by presenting the right kind of music). It must come as a pleasant and therefore refreshing change from normal school work. Opportunities must be given to the children to reveal themselves so that a greater understanding of them may be gained by the teacher who can then more fully cater for their individual needs. Of course these points can be added to and no doubt this will be done when the teacher gains more experience in choosing and presenting music to children and closely observing their reactions to it. It is very improbable that a teacher will be satisfied with his first attempts at presenting music to a class. There is no doubt that many backward children will not respond. For instance (i) requests to listen to the music may be awkwardly received, (ii) older children especially, will not want to express themselves in movement, and so on. It takes time to establish the correct attitude in children especially if they have been used only to singing activities and following a piano. But patience and persistence must prevail and the teacher must think and plan in terms of enjoyable musical experiences rather than in getting across a certain amount of musical knowledge.

I mentioned some way back that music has many sides to it and it may be as well now to consider how the human race has used music either as a means of expression or enjoyment. Briefly these uses can be summarized in the following activities.

(1) Through song.
(2) Through improvising rhythms and tunes on simple instruments. To appreciate this point more clearly a study of the apparatus and musical instruments used by primitive peoples may help.
(3) Through movements of the body which when organized are known to us as dancing and/or dramatization.
(4) Through listening.
(5) Lastly through composing.

It is obvious that if we are to use music in schools to its fullest effect we must organize for our pupils most of all of these activities. Naturally it will not be possible to include all of these activities in one lesson nor will it be possible for the untrained musician to deal effectively with voice training, or (on the rare occasions when a backward child is musically gifted) the elements of music leading to composition; but there is no reason at all why he should not, with the advice of experts, organize some work in these directions. It must be remembered that it is the children's attitude to this work that is essential. Successful music teaching must depend upon the attitude of the staff to the subject; it cannot be confined in a little compartment of its own and conversely good music experiences will spread themselves through the school. Perhaps now it would be as well to consider each of the five points mentioned above, but I would like to stress that they are not five separate departments of music to be treated individually. They are just separated here for convenience.

(1) Let us then begin with singing. By placing singing first I do

EXPRESSIVE WORK: MUSIC

hope that I have not given the impression that it is the most important thing in music, although you should do everything that you can to help and encourage backward children to sing. I have found that they will do this under almost any circumstances, for it comes just as naturally to children as talking. If you observe them closely when they are not under your supervision you will find that there will be lots of humming and singing. The rise and fall of their voices when playing naturally is very musical, and I have often noticed the so-called school 'groaners' (often in the C stream) using quite pleasant voices on the playground when they are trying to get someone to chase after them. For instance I once heard a child who had never been known to sing a note in school singing out in quite a nice voice whilst playing on the playground 'old Fatty Spencer, old Fatty Spencer' in an attempt to get old Fatty Spencer to chase him. There is no doubt that there is a lesson to be learned from this. In ninety-nine cases out of one hundred the groaner's trouble is not in his physical make-up but is a personal one. Some people of course will sing better than others, just as some have better speaking voices than others, but this is not only due to training. Nature has equipped them more adequately with the means to make pleasant sounds, but almost everybody who is not dumb has adequate physical equipment for singing. It is our task as teachers to create situations which will make the backward children want to sing. They must feel free to sing and we must give them the opportunity to develop confidence in their ability to sing and the opportunity to find pleasure in the use of their voices. Of course this means that their singing must be spontaneous, happy and the expression of something which is beautiful. The song must be meaningful to them, they must know and feel what they are singing about, otherwise there will be no true interpretation of the song. This latter point is limiting when selecting a song for backward children but to neglect it is fatal.

It follows then that you should not necessarily aim in your singing lessons at getting backward children to sing correct notes or even to produce a good tone. These will come when they understand better what they are trying to express. Remember, it is the whole child that sings and not just his bellows, his throat, his tongue and his teeth. When planning a programme of singing keep in mind the times when people have enjoyed singing, these we know are times when people have been deeply moved into happiness or even sadness. Of course we cannot expect backward children always to interpret such music but it is well worth stimulating their imaginations by getting them to suggest under what circumstances a certain song would have been sung. Let them, if they will, accompany their singing by actions much as one does when dramatizing a poem. Sea shanties, folk songs, etc., lend themselves admirably to this treatment. In country dancing let them hum and sing the tunes and conversely let them wander about while singing a song if they are so inclined. Some children can be given apparatus during the singing lesson with which to assist in the accompaniment. Obviously the use of this has to be carefully watched especially if children are not used to this. I have found it an advantage to give a shy retiring child these pieces of equipment and have often noted especially in a song with a chorus that he will join in whole-heartedly with the singing when he has got something else to think about. In other words he forgets what he is there for, the music takes charge of him and the nature of the chorus makes him join in, which of course was exactly what the composer intended it to do. One could go on for a long time giving examples of this type, but the success of a singing lesson must be determined by the social climate prevailing in the music room. The sort of apparatus that I have in mind here, and have used, will be found at the end of the section which deals with the expression of music through movement.

(2) Next we can consider the improvization of rhythms and tunes on simple instruments and apparatus. I have already said that children will respond to rhythm first and I think that it is true to say that they will create rhythms before tunes. I have not a great deal of sympathy with the orthodox percussion bands, where children are taught to thump, tinkle or crash at certain places in a tune that is thumped out on the piano over and over again by some well-meaning person. Not only does this sort of thing lack beauty but backward children especially are being asked to do a very difficult thing, i.e. to conform to a very intricate pattern. If you have watched this sort of thing closely you will have noticed the automatic actions of the children who have been thoroughly drilled in their parts, accompanied by the anxious nods of the pianist or the frantic actions of the person in front who is conducting this little scene. I much prefer to

EXPRESSIVE WORK: MUSIC

see children using percussion band instruments individually and in response to the sort of tune that makes them want to put in a cymbal crash, a drum beat, the tinkle of a triangle, etc. Here again success does not come at once, for backward children have got to be led towards listening to the music and then suggesting themselves where these different instruments will fit in, and of course no two children will think alike about this. But that does not matter, the children will eventually surprise you with their ingenuity, and though the result may not be very beautiful, at least the children will have listened to the music and in their own way have contributed to its making. It is worth remembering that the conventional percussion instruments as we know them in schools today form only a very small part of the apparatus that is available for making rhythms. Small stones, etc., in tins, pieces of wood knocked together, large shells and of course the hands, are just the beginning of a very long list of apparatus that can be used for rhythm making. As a start I would suggest different material in different sized tins, e.g. rice, marbles, sand, larger stones, pieces of wood – these different media make different sounds and sharper or less defined rhythms. If allowed to, children will experiment with these and become quite expert in their use. Rhythm making, as Mr Ablewhite suggested in Chapter II, is very useful in P.E. lessons and I always bring music into my P.E. lessons in some way or another. This can be done by the children themselves who will use triangles, cymbals, drums, etc., to induce gliding movements, jerky movements, silent movements, loud and boisterous movements. After some work with rhythm children may want to create their own tunes. Their first attempts of course will again be very unmusical but with encouragement and guidance they will gain confidence in this activity and their work will improve. It is not necessary for backward children to record their tunes and in fact I have found that most of them do not want to. However there may come a time when this becomes necessary if they express a desire to do so. Of course this would be the time to introduce the elements of music reading and writing, but, I always feel that there is a step before this akin to the scribbling age through which a child passes before he expresses himself in writing. Before I go on to explain this process I will mention some of the tune making apparatus that I have used. The school piano is the first thing if the children are allowed to touch it, and musically gifted children will soon find their way about the piano and pick out pleasing little tunes. If this is a sacred possession in your school then other apparatus must be supplied and made by the children. There are many music making toys of quite high efficiency on sale in the stores but to facilitate the easy recording of tunes such instruments as the dulcimer will be found most useful. Bottles of approximately the same size (beer bottles or something of this nature are best) can be filled to appropriate levels to make different notes when tapped, the fuller the bottle the deeper the note. These are hung by a piece of string round their necks, suspended from a bar at an appropriate height to the size of the children who are to use them. They are tapped lightly with a hard stick like a drum stick and notes will ensue. These bottles or the note bars on instruments like the dulcimer can be numbered; I have found that it is best to begin numbering at the lowest note. Children can then pick out their tune and write down the numbers of the notes which they have played. At first there will be much 'fiddling about' but I have been agreeably surprised at the way in which some backward children will persevere, experiment and then create quite good little tunes. In the first instance it is a good plan to give them some simple rhyme for which to write a tune, it can be a nursery rhyme, a piece of poetry, or the words of a song that they know for which they are encouraged to write a better tune. This numbering deals with the recording of the tune but not of the rhythm, we must turn to music 'shorthand' for that. This can be explained briefly as follows.

Walking steps of equal length and duration can be illustrated thus: | | | | Running steps, two of which are equal to one walking step are illustrated thus: V V V V . Faster running steps four of which are equal to one walking step are illustrated thus: W W W W . A step and a limp which is equal to two walking steps is illustrated thus: ♩ ♩ . The more complicated rhythms are shown in this way: ♩ ♪   ♫   ♩ ♫

Children will make up rhythms that conform to no pattern and here is your chance to introduce phrasing, which is not at all difficult if you get them to listen to what they have created, for they will soon spot the unbalanced nature of a tune that is badly constructed. But here again it is not wise to expect an adult standard any more than it

EXPRESSIVE WORK: MUSIC

would be wise to look for perfection in the child's paintings or drawings. The main thing is to give them opportunities to create and experiment. This activity is not suitable for class work, and is best suited as an extra, i.e. the tune making material can be left in some corner of the room where children can experiment at odd times, but the system of recording can be explained during the normal music period. In fact children like to write down little tunes that have been played to them or sung to them. Rhythms can be tapped out with a pencil on the desk and the children can write these down in a rhythmic way, for instance, taa taa taa or ♩ ♩ ♩ will be recorded by the children like this: | | | . It is as well here to get them to write rhythmically, i.e. to draw their strokes rhythmically to imitate exactly the pattern given to them, e.g. | | | regularly and not | wait | | .

(3) I would now like to turn to that aspect of music which I consider offers most opportunities to the non-musician to present music to children of all ages in an advantageous way. In fact, movement to music comes even more naturally to children than singing. Children soon enjoy simple rhythms, the normal child will 'pat-a-cake' with his mother quite well by the time that he is 2, and the 3-year-old will romp and dance about merrily to tunes and rhythms that will move along sympathetically with the large physical movements characteristic of that age. You will note that I have mentioned that the music will move along with the child, and I think that this is how it should be introduced to him. We all know that the normal child of about 3 years has reached a stage in his development where he is more sure of himself, is less dependent on his parents and is ready to mix more freely with other children for short periods, but of course his interests are mainly centred on himself. It would be impossible under these circumstances to get the 3-year-old to conform to any pattern in a dance, but he will become aware of music and it will help him to enjoy his new physical skills, jumping, rocking and swaying. I think that it is most important at this age that he should hear good tunes but rhythm is much more important for him. However, music should not be forced upon him, he should as I have said become aware of it and be able to enjoy it as he does so many things in his widening horizons of experience. He will enjoy the same tune over and over again and on the whole will enjoy the

gramophone more than the radio. Let it become for him even at this age, a normal part of normal living. I think that the next age we might consider briefly is 5 because this is the age when most of our children enter school. I have found that these new entrants as in everything else differ greatly in their response to music, but it is most important that their first musical experiences in school should be happy ones. I think that there is some value in continuing the 'Listen with Mother' series in school but most normal 5-year-olds are ready to stride ahead and expect to meet new experiences. This was forcibly brought home to me the other day when a quite bright little 5-year-old remarked to her mother that now she was 5 and went to school she didn't want to 'listen with mother' any more. I think perhaps that the time to use the radio programmes such as 'Listen with Mother' comes when the child has been in school for a few months, finds that he is not quite sure of himself and then a link with home may be useful. Of course this is all in passing, but I mention it because it is something that has happened to me and I have been led, from it, to believe that infants are better catered for by live music, i.e. without the use of a gramophone or a radio. A non-musician is not handicapped in this direction because as I have already stated rhythm is the main thing to which children will respond at this age. Here, such apparatus as I have already mentioned (stones in tins as well as the percussion band instruments) can be used by the teacher to make up rhythms. These can be jumpy rhythms, swaying rhythms, walking rhythms, etc. After a few short periods on these lines the children will readily respond to wireless programmes and even more to appropriate music played on the gramophone, folk dances, etc. But I feel strongly that in all these lessons the teacher must be the central figure, must react to the music in a positive way and join in with the children's activities.

If the music makes you pretend to cry, then pretend to cry, if it says rock baby to sleep then do it. The happy relationship between class and teacher will no doubt spread to all the other lessons. I have found that this kind of attitude on the teacher's part gains much more respect from the children than scolding and grumbling. It may be as well to point out here that music not only induces movement but it also establishes a mood. This latter is done mainly through the tune: note for instance the mood created by a funeral march as compared with the 'Blue Danube Waltz'. Although it is wrong to expect infants always to react to the mood of a piece of music, they will very often imitate movements that have impressed them. For instance, on questioning a child about a swaying movement that he was making recently, he answered that he was a tree swaying in the breeze. Other answers to similar questions have led me to believe that juniors like to imitate sailing clouds, flowing water, the dart and swoop of birds and of course dancing people whom they have seen on the television and cinema screens. With reference to this, as a step forward from using shortish pieces of music of the folk dance type, try short excerpts from pieces of music that contain plenty of flourishes, momentary pauses, loud pieces and soft parts; in fact music that has plenty of climax in it. Such music will be found among well-known ballet music by Tchaikowsky, Delibes and Chopin. In the first instance when introducing this music don't be frightened to stop in the middle of a piece if you find that the children are becoming weary of it, remember that it is enjoyment of the music that is your aim, not boredom. Obviously it is an advantage for a teacher to know what the music is going to say before he introduces it to the children. She should have some idea of the way it moves along, what beauty of melody it contains, and whether these two things will come within the interest and therefore comprehension of her pupils. Any remark that you have to make during an interval between pieces played should draw attention to the music and not be confined to suggestions about what the children could have done in response to some curve, flourish or climax in the music. For instance don't say 'let's have this again and notice what John does when those running notes suddenly stop before the end'. It is much better to say 'those little running notes suddenly stopped just before the end, some children noticed it and that was nice'. You can of course use several devices in this lesson to help the children to express themselves more adequately: P.E. hoops can be decorated with ribbons, etc., and given to the children with which to make rocking and sweeping movements. Some music such as Tchaikowsky's '1812' overture, or the Polovtsian dances from *Prince Igor* will induce the use of percussion instruments. Ribbons and streamers used by individual children or in combinations are very effective and so on. But there is one word of warning here – encourage the children to use these devices as a means of expression and not as implements to waggle or flick about. I have found it useful to suggest that they can use these things as paint brushes to paint in what the music says. Here again your own activities with, say, a floating piece of ribbon waved through the air in response to a waltz tune will quickly be imitated by the children and built upon. There will be many individual differences in behaviour portrayed in this activity; many of the children may not be responding to the rhythm of the music in the manner that you would like to see, others will no doubt take advantage and 'try you out'. Of course there is no answer to the latter behaviour except a firm hand and an appeal to their better nature for more reasonable behaviour. This is an opportunity for social training applicable to the age and ability of the group with which you are dealing. My experience of this sort of activity has convinced me that it is the shy and retiring child who needs the most attention. He may not be responding to the rhythm of the music in any visible way but a word or two with him during the playing of the music or at some quiet moment after the music, may reveal that even if his body is not responding to the rhythm, nevertheless he may be responding to the appeal of the music in some other way. I have noticed, for instance, that these children succeed particularly well in expressing pictorially in a later art lesson what the music has said to them. The brighter sensitive child will often liken some tune to a colour, they will answer that it sounds like 'red' or 'green' music. Perhaps one or two words about a lesson like this should be issued here. Help children, especially the slowest ones by example to express themselves in their own individual ways, e.g. from just finger wagging to leaping and bounding. Choose a variety of pieces in each lesson and include at least one with a constant rhythm such as a march or a waltz tune. Avoid at all costs the practice of using one stimulating piece of music throughout the whole lesson and then trying to get a group of children to emulate Margot Fonteyn while the rest of the children act as spectators. As in all lessons, you will find the gifted ones, also those who are learning ballet dancing; these children will undoubtedly take the lead but they are best dealt with by confining all your remarks to the music. The other children will soon respond to their leadership and accept it and benefit from it. Never force a hesitating and unco-operating child. My experience

EXPRESSIVE WORK: MUSIC

is that ultimately the music will induce them to take part in some movement. Those very few who are obviously bored by such a period of music, often respond readily in a lesson where movements are organized for them, such as in country dancing. In this respect I have found the *Folk Dances of Many Lands*, Series 1, 2 and 3, published by the Ling Physical Culture Association to be very useful. Of course some of our own country dances are useful too. It may be as well here for me to outline a music and movement lesson that I have found useful.

Play a well-known record like 'The Teddy Bears' Picnic'. Say nothing about the music before you start but allow your children to do anything that they like provided that they do not rush around and make a noise. They can move about quietly, tap out a rhythm with their finger or just sit and stare. Boisterousness as I have already stated can be controlled by suggesting that the offender sits quietly and listens to what the music has to say. After the record has finished playing question the children and ask them to suggest what could have been done in response to the music, ask them what kind of music it was, was it fast or was it slow? was it loud or was it soft? was it sad or was it happy? Some children may be able to tell you how they felt when they heard the music, some may even suggest a title for the piece. After this questioning the record can be played again and modifications in response will be observed. Remember at this point make no attempt to get a reluctant child to join in. If it is felt that more discussion is necessary allow this to go on. At first I have found that responses are a long way removed from what you desire, but gradually, as the children begin to listen more intently, their answers become more adequate. Of course the choice of music at this point is most important. I would suggest shortish excerpts from ballet music and tunes that the children know themselves. The point here is to get the children to talk about the music and to express what they feel about it, not only in movement but in drawing, etc. Before ending this section, I will examine two common faults in so-called musical appreciation lessons, which I think can spoil them.

(*a*) Before the music is played the children could have been asked to beat out the beats of the music thus drawing their attention to one part of the music only, being led towards thinking technically about the music rather than experiencing its beauty. In this respect it may be noted that it is the beauty of the spider's web with the dew drops on it that attracts a child first rather than the intricacies of the construction of the web. I cannot stress this point too much where school music is concerned. We must allow our children to experience it, respond in their own way to it, enjoy it, talk about it, be enthralled by it and *then* become inquisitive about it.

(*b*) After the record has been played a piece can be picked out for the children to imitate as a form of voice production exercise.

Further to this point it may be observed that it is the feeling behind a voice like Kathleen Ferrier's that is just as important as the training that she has received in the past to make her voice so beautiful, and it is that feeling in our children that we must engender.

(4) I now move on to listening. This of course is very closely linked with the last section, but there are times when children of all ages and abilities should be encouraged to sit down and just listen to the music. In general let the children listen for a little while and then encourage them to talk about what they have heard. With very backward and younger children it is worth making up a story of the music where this is applicable and displaying figures in flannelgraph, etc., to depict the story as it proceeds. There are many pieces of music other than 'Peter and the Wolf', with which this procedure can be adopted, for instance the 'Peer Gynt' suite, excerpts from opera music and of course all of the ballets have stories. Let children of all ages make up their own record programmes and present them to the class (they will use their own records as well as those that may be in the school); some guidance will be needed here but this should not be difficult.

Another listening musical experience that you may be able to organize is to induce one of your musical friends to come to the school to play to the children or perhaps one of the children may have a parent or friend who would be willing to do so. These latter activities are examples of how you can extend and keep your eyes on the children's horizons outside the school. This of course must be your ultimate aim in all of your teaching.

(5) With regard to composing, it is not beyond the scope of a non-musician to give opportunities to his pupils to compose. I have already referred to a method of recording tunes and rhythms that

EXPRESSIVE WORK: MUSIC

children will make up. The non-musician will naturally not be technically capable of helping his pupil beyond this point, but he can show a positive attitude and give encouragement.

In concluding this chapter I wish to point out that I do not consider music to be the 'be-all' and 'end-all' of education. It should not dominate in a school, but it should be a part of every child's education. As I have already said, it should be a normal part of everyday life, and there are many values to be derived from its intelligent introduction into our children's education in school.

After having carried out some of this work for some time, how can you judge the worthwhileness and success of it? I think that you should seek answers to questions like these. Are my music lessons helping the children towards better personal development? are those in need of help getting the right sort of help? e.g. is the withdrawn child gaining more confidence? are my class as a whole or groups within the class working happily together? and perhaps most important of all am I enjoying the music with the children? It is obvious that the answers to these questions are all connected with human development. Perhaps you will be concerned that evidence of the work that you have done with your children cannot be shown by written tests, and your class may not be able to take part successfully in music festivals, but I leave you with the question: are these last two things really necessary?

D. H. CLEIFE

Chapter VIII

DRAMA

Before you condemn these suggestions as being the uninformed outpourings of a drama enthusiast, it may be well to make my own background clear so that you may know I can and do appreciate some of the difficulties that confront anyone beginning such work.

My first efforts were with a class of sixty juniors in a rigid Glasgow school. They were tough and unstreamed; the room had a raked floor and there were badly fitting glass partitions on either side. The head teacher bracketed any speech, other than a direct reply to a question, with vice and any sort of liberty with licence. But even he could not expect poetry repetition to be silent, so we managed to get a modicum of dramatic work, unblessed and unproductive perhaps, but better than nothing and worth the effort for the integrating effect it had on the class.

During this time I tried producing plays and concerts with a team of Lifeboys in a very strict Presbyterian church. We needed to raise money for camp funds, but our choice of plays, etc., was limited by the fact that girls' parts had to be taken by boys, and susceptibilities were tender. We lost a much-needed annual donation of £5 because we acted a scene from *Treasure Island* and the wealthy benefactor was a rabid teetotaller. The 'Fifteen men on the dead man's chest' were more than he could stomach! I learned to be selective in my choice of plays.

Later work was done in a one-teacher school, age range 5—14, roll thirty. Later still I had to devise dramatic activities with subnormal children in a classroom that was only a passage less than ten feet wide. Here I used puppets. I have never had a proper platform or a stage with two exits, and generally I have had no platform at all.

EXPRESSIVE WORK: DRAMA

And, finally, I am no enthusiast. From my earliest days I have had to brace myself to tackle the extra work involved in even the simplest of dramatic efforts. As I have grown older and more experienced I have devised ways of lessening the initial strain, and means of simplifying problems of dressing and production, but nothing alters the fact that dramatic work *means* work for the teacher concerned. The more successful you are, the harder it becomes – for you get caught up in the children's enthusiasm. As you find them throwing themselves into whatever you are doing, inevitably you think of some property or bit of costume that would just make all the difference to their performance. All too seldom are the children able to make it unaided – and away goes the leisure from another weekend!

It is naught for my comfort, either, that I always feel slightly guilty at taking valuable time for what is, in fact, pure fun. No doubt my early days are partly to blame for this, but the fact remains that although I *know* dramatic work to be as basic a need as bread (and especially so for the slow, inept and inarticulate members of the class) another part of my silly self grudges the time spent on it, and feels it should be in the nature of a frill, an extra, a rewarding cake.

If you, for your particular reasons find yourself about to start dramatic work with an unfamiliar class, how do you begin?

First of all, forget about performances for special occasions and try to establish classroom conditions where dramatic activities are (*a*) enjoyable; (*b*) natural and (*c*) genuine communal efforts. This may not be easy. They may be a 'sticky' class who have 'done' plays before and been sickened thereby, they may not be sure of your sincerity, and there are almost certain to be one or two children who are scared stiff of acting in any form, even though at the same time they most genuinely want to join it. It will help your patience if at some time you have suffered from the constriction of the throat and the clammy hands which go with unsuccessful theatrical endeavour. If you can recollect in comparative tranquillity the emotions then engendered you will be less likely just to tell members of the class to act some story they have read. Even if they comply they will probably be wooden – as wooden as you would once have been. But you are older now, and able to let yourself go. Perhaps you could read a really dramatic poem, very dramatically – even over-dramatizing at first. They will enjoy the experience, if you do not – it makes a change – and at the end of your effort some of them will have gathered that speech need not always be tepid or monotonous. Possibly you could tell a short story in the course of which a blood-curdling yell is called for. Ask for volunteers to scream. You will find probably that your loudest-voiced barbarian will only produce an ineffectual squeak. If this muted music is all that is forthcoming then yell yourself. Done without warning it will at least make the class sit up and laugh and you can usually go on profitably from there.

You might like to read a narrative poem – say 'The Barring of the Door' or 'The Highwayman'. (Both these are actable.) They usually enjoy slinking round the quiet house at midnight looking villainous, while the good man smokes a pipe of cinnamon stick and the good wife nearly bursts with indignation in the 'Barring of the Door'.

'The Highwayman' is more theatrically intense. Older juniors ought to like it. In any case they enjoy hearing Teacher swearing in the line 'I'll come to thee by moonlight, though Hell should bar the way'.

As soon as possible, get as many children as possible really acting. On your next drama day you might arrive with a miscellaneous bag of 'props', e.g. a stethoscope, an umbrella, a rope, gun, dagger, ear-rings, cloak, fan, spanner, wad of money, policeman's helmet, large baby doll, sealed envelope, etc., and tell three or four children to choose one article each and work them into a short play. Allow them a few minutes to go into a huddle outside the door before they start, and the class can suggest a title for the 'play' when it is over. Limit the show to five minutes and let one of your reluctant participants time them with a stop-watch or the classroom clock. Then let another batch have a go, either with different properties – or, for purposes of comparison – with the same ones. If you are wise, you will keep a notebook and jot down the plots and business that develops, and also the players. You will probably find the germ of a longer play in one of these pieces of spontaneous acting.

If their ideas are sparse and inclined to be repetitive a change of properties will generally stimulate them to fresh efforts and a new approach. Alternatively, you can tell a story up to a point and let the children act 'what happened next'. Try to have several versions.

Almost any class will enjoy playing at Parent with-complaint-against-the-school. They will also give an interesting impression of yourself or the Head handling an irate mother or a recalcitrant child if they trust you enough to do so. Do take this one step further and let the 'Mother' or 'Child' give an account of 'What-I-said-to-Him' over the family tea on the evening of the incident. You will gain insight into home conditions.

Ready made plays that are suitable for backward children are not easy to find, but the ideas in such plays may give you a starting point for adaptation and play-writing with specific children in mind. It is always easier to trim the play to fit a particular child than to try to squeeze him into an inappropriate part. For example a big spluttering backward boy with flickering eyes was a 'natural' for the mayor in the Pied Piper, though he could not remember all that gentleman's words. With a little help from the chorus, he was perfectly able to bring out the key words of the speeches on his own. The chorus is invaluable. Almost anybody can manage to write rhymed couplets either in the style of 'Hiawatha', or on the old pantomime level and the class as a whole can keep the words going while each individual is responsible for his or her own particular couplet.

This type of play lends itself well to use on the floor of a hall, where the class is sitting in a semi-circle after the style of an old-fashioned Pierrot show. It can come as the finale after an itemized concert announced by a compère. If some of the children can play mouth-organs or guitars, let them supply overture or interval music, and keep the rhythm going in the choruses. Modified skiffle is much pleasanter to listen to than inept squeaking on recorders and far more fun to do.

Mime is often advocated for backward children, who may have difficulty in reading, or in speaking, or in both: and Mr Ablewhite in Chapter II gave suggestions for mimes which may be useful in physical education. At the same time, it should be remembered that mime is not easy to do, nor is it easy to 'put over' with the average boy in the juniors – whether backward or not. He regards it as 'sissy' and anyone who has seen Joyce Grenfell's wicked interpretation of an enthusiastic folk-lorist and dancer may find it difficult to teach dramatic movement ever again. This is all to the good where general dramatic work with a class is concerned – dramatic movement should not be 'taught' but rather caught from the synthesis of imagination and material. If your play situation is a group of suspects in a foreign land with no common language, then mime is the only means of conveying what is happening and what has happened before the play opened. Have both men and women in your group of suspects, possibly a grandmother and a bad child for comic relief. Other situations where mime is natural: A family in a burning house trying to open a window, neighbours are gathered below; The back view of a row of people watching a football match, supporters of both sides present; The class humorist showing off unaware that the school martinet is behind him, while children try to convey a warning.

There are some excellent suggestions to be found in *Practical Miming* by Gertrude Pickersgill (Pitman, 17s. 6d.). The second edition gives photographs of hefty males in costume in *Robin Hood* and the *Beggar's Daughter* which should reassure shy junior boys.

When you feel easy with your class, you might like to put on some fairly 'pictorial' records and let the children move to the music, as was suggested in the previous chapter, but for my purpose it is the *dramatic* element I wish to stress in my example. I have used, e.g. 'Ritual Fire Dance' and 'Night on the Bare Mountain' with infants of 5 to 5½ with surprising results. I told them the name of the record but gave absolutely no 'programme notes' or any other suggestions. They evolved an exciting Indian scene with tom-toms beating round the fire, squaws lifting and lowering arms to the music and an enemy tribe attacking and being driven off. In the 'Bare Mountain' they 'saw' and danced witches and remarked of their own accord as the music changed, 'The witches have gone.' One child said, 'Are these fairies coming?' another replied before I could speak, 'No, they are angels.' Finally the dance developed into a quite dramatic conflict between witches and angels, with good triumphant and evil driven away. I found it very exciting to watch, especially as I am myself deficient in musical appreciation and knowledge. Since then I have experimented with a wide variety of records and the results have been surprising and extremely interesting. I have not had the chance to do this with older children but with infants it produced most expressive

EXPRESSIVE WORK: DRAMA

mime. Admittedly they were an ordinary class but the most vivid interpretations came from two of the most poorly endowed children. They fairly came alive for the first time since they had joined the class and their joy at finding something at which they could excel convinced me that this work was of value especially for the backward children.

It is better to avoid pretty-pretty fairy plays, though your girls will quite possibly produce one when they start inventing their own plays. This is not necessarily evidence that such plays are appropriate to their development, it may merely show the poverty of their ideas and the meagre dramatic fare they have previously been given. Usually they will find it easier to throw themselves into far stronger dramatic parts (e.g. an old woman, a bad-tempered young one, a hep-cat, or a demure miss) if given the opportunity. There is no need for you to show them 'where to put in the expression' – give them something real to express and they will do it, provided that the emotional content is within their scope, and understanding. Domestic drama is not to be despised. Often scenes from home life are very well observed and their expression can provide considerable emotional release for the children as well as giving valuable pointers to their teacher of problems in their lives or in those of their parents.

Puppetry is not everybody's fancy, and far too much time tends to be wasted on the handwork of *making* the puppets and not enough spent on using them. However, very satisfying puppets can be made from fibre flower pots or old tennis balls which can be completed in one afternoon. They will stand up to any amount of hard use and are most valuable for encouraging free work and expression especially among the children who may feel shy about performing in the exposed conditions of an ordinary play. Shadow puppets are within the scope of quite inept children and only old cereal boxes, match boxes and a piece of paper nylon costing 2*s*. 6*d*. are needed to make a start.

Leaflets on how to make and use these puppets and also one on making a really workable stage may be obtained from the Educational Puppetry Association, 23a Southampton Place, London, W.C.1. They cost 9*d*. each post free. The most valuable and comprehensive book on puppetry is *The Complete Puppet Book* edited by Wall and White (Faber, 25*s*.). This can be got from any library, but

TEACHING THE SLOW LEARNER IN THE PRIMARY SCHOOL
is worth buying for the general suggestions it gives in devising and producing plays, suggestions which are equally applicable to plays without puppets. Macmillans publish a series of 'Puppet Plays for Schools' – *The Magic Tower, Silly Willy, King John and the Abbot, Brer Rabbit Plays, Lazy Jack, Mumbo-Jumbo*, etc., priced about 1*s*. 9*d*. each. These are attractive and simple to read, excellent material for backward readers and supremely actable. They have been written by practising puppeteers who have proved their unfailing appeal to children, and are virtually foolproof. Full, though simple, production notes are included and directions and diagrams given for the making of the simple 'props' required.

Your own feelings will decide whether or not you dramatize Bible stories. Be cautious in your choice of scenes (if any) from the New Testament. There are many dramatic scenes, however, in the Old Testament and your language difficulty may be solved. Whole chapters of Exodus are actable with Moses and Aaron at the court of Pharaoh and the class as a whole beating the refrain of 'Let my people go'! In this context remember Negro spirituals. There are some fine and unhackneyed ones in *The Fireside Book of Folk Songs* (Simon and Schuster, U.S.A., 40*s*.). The early life of David is packed with good dramatic material – more suitable for children than that of his later years! The whole story of his friendship with Jonathan and his conflict with Saul is thrilling, while his lament over Jonathan may easily give a new conception of poetry to some of your pupils.

The story of Baal – 'Perhaps he sleepeth!' gives good crowd scenes, so does the story of Esther. You can always hang Hamaan off-stage or use a shadow. Both Esther and parts of Ruth give the girls a chance to star.

Nativity plays produced by juniors are risky, unless the urge to do one comes from the children. Certainly they give opportunities for using up poorish actors as angels or shepherds, but the result must be sincerely felt or such a play is better left alone. If you do have a Nativity play, spare the husky shepherd the indignity of carrying a stuffed lamb and give him a pull-on mop – sold by Woolworth's – and fitted over his forearm. Give it two black ears and a black nose and let him carry it in the folds of his cloak. Manipulated puppet-fashion it looks most realistic.

Whatever form your dramatic work takes you will sooner or later find yourself trying to improve or polish up either your general standard, or a particular play. Many helpful ideas will be found in Peter Slade's writings and in old copies of the 'Theatre in Education Series'. These invaluable little books are now not on general sale but odd copies may be found in Foyles, price 6d. *Magic and Makebelieve* by Robert Newton is one of these and is very stimulating, especially at the stage when you are becoming slightly stale and weary. At this juncture the use of a tape-recorder may be helpful. Never record a performance without warning (in the early stages) and be sure to record your own voice too, *and* play it back to the class. Let the children make critical suggestions. Act on these – even if you don't think they are sound – and the class will probably be of your way of thinking if, in fact, the suggestions were not good. Only by developing their judgement can you really improve the quality of their work.

Among all your enthusiasts – and, make no mistake – the bulk of the class *will* be enthusiastic – you are almost sure to have one or two children who don't want to act. For goodness sake, avoid forcing them, but *do* include them in the production. There are endless things for them to do. Put one in charge of the gramophone or effects, make another property-mistress, or – if they can read – continuity man. If need be let them possess a labelled chair after the fashion of film producers, but keep them in the show. And when another play is being produced, give them another chance of a speaking part, for they very often are only too anxious to join in.

Properties, etc.

These are important or not, according to the view you take of the work being done, but they are a delight to most of the children. If you are working in a poor district do try to get some bits of colourful finery – for the girls especially, though even a 10-year-old boy likes to ruffle it occasionally in a doublet and hose! Collect sheets, rugs, old dressing-gowns, scarves for turbans, discarded hats and caps, at least one 'topper'. Make wigs from plumber's tow, wool or nylon stockings or chiropodists' wool for grey hair (avoid *crêpe* hair, it is expensive and never looks convincing). Try to get a moustache and beard (clip-on variety) and do get some make-up and cold cream – this is really important.

On the question of make-up and character acting generally, you may find, as I have done, that both boys and girls enjoy looking through books with pictures of actors and actresses. Macqueen Pope has compiled a whole series of such books. The children will ignore the reading matter, but your heroes and villains will develop some new attitudes.

Jewellery is an outward and visible sign of the glory within and your king's daughter will act royally in a gym tunic provided she has a diamond tiara, rings on her fingers, and dangling ear-rings which make it essential for the head to be held proudly. But if you *can* get hold of a few discarded evening frocks or fancy dresses and one or two pairs of high heeled shoes it is well worth doing so. Very often friends are only too glad to get rid of out-dated garments and accessories, nylon nightgowns and so on, and it is wonderful what effects can be produced with a collection of what looks like rubbish. Patterns can be stencilled on sheets and canvas, cut-out cretonne flowers may be pasted on with Bateman's Rubber Paste or 'Copydex' and wonderfully rich effects obtained by the judicious use of coloured 'glitter' that is sold for Christmas decoration.

Old underwear – especially interlock – dyes beautifully for tights or short-hose with cold water dye and 'Dylon' dyes will 'take' on both nylon or wool. An unpromising looking blanket dipped in 'Drummer' old rose shade becomes a rich peach colour and makes a handsome cloak. Hats, domino masks, fans, a stage dagger and a bag of gold are stimulating 'props'. Odds and ends of chain and a few nuts and bolts make a weighty bag with a convincing jingle. You can equip an expedition for outer space with head-dresses made from polythene bags over lampshade frames and diving goggles can transform a boy into an inhabitant of Mars. You will also need shawls, scarves, crowns, blunt-tipped swords, at least one lethal weapon – preferably a Colt – a telescope and binoculars. Many of these 'props' can be made by the children. Hats and animal masks that are too difficult to make can be bought quite cheaply in Ellisdons, High Holborn, London, W.C.1.

For sound effects, try to get a large triangle or tubular chimes for bells or a clock striking. Records of fanfares, crowds, trains, cars, etc., may usually be obtained through the school record library.

Storage of all this equipment can be a real problem. Probably the

EXPRESSIVE WORK: DRAMA

easiest way is to fix a clothes line between two hooks along a wall and hang up the cloaks and dresses on hangers, covering the whole with a plastic curtain. Keep small props in plastic bags, also hung up, and see that each bag and hanger has its appointed place. Try to give them the clothes in as good condition as possible and do try not to let things get crumpled or 'tatty'. There is often an iron in school for the needlework classes. Borrow it and train both girls and boys to use it in order to keep the costumes fresh. It takes time and patience to get the class to feel a responsibility for keeping dressing-up clothes in good order, but they finally come to accept it.

In the foregoing hints and suggestions it may seem to you that I have been diffuse and that have not tied my argument to backward classes. I deliberately made the remarks cover as wide a ground as possible so that however your interests lie you may possibly feel 'I might try *that*'. However backward your class may be, I feel that they will surprise you in their response. I remember the zest with which a group of ascertained sub-normal children threw themselves into making puppets. I was actually learning the technique along with them, but they soon outstripped me in modelling, and no one was better pleased than myself when one of the children took away the cat I was trying to make saying, 'Give it to me, and I'll do it properly.' He did, too! There was considerable uplift to their morale in the fact that they could make and use puppets that were really good by any standards. It compensated, perhaps, a little for all their failures, as well as providing a manageable world in which they were supreme instead of being the misfits some of them felt themselves to be.

Repeatedly I have found that it is the lumpish, the dull, the awkward child who benefits most from having an excursion into make-believe. There are many by-products of dramatic work, handwork, sewing, designing of posters, writing of programmes and invitations, looking up pictures of costumes, etc., but all these are subsidiary. The prime purpose should be enjoyment, and the other desirables shall be added unto you in the measure in which enjoyment is achieved.

You may not appreciate how much this experience means to the children till much later. It surprised me very much that the pupils in an E.S.N. school where I taught six years ago, not only remembered the puppets they made with me, but also each step of the fairly intricate process involved, though they had not made any similar puppets in the interval. I should not have expected this from subnormal children with their short memory span, though normal or backward former pupils regularly say, 'Do you remember that play we did?' or 'Do you still make puppets?' usually adding 'I've still got mine.' Not one has yet remembered the day I taught him to read or get his equal additions right! Still that may happen, too, if I wait long enough, and I shall be as overcome as I was in 1945 when I found one of the quietest and least noteworthy of the Lifeboys I mentioned earlier still carrying tattered snapshots of himself in costume some twenty years later, when, a veteran of the Guards Armoured Division, he sought me out in London. In the meantime he had become a compositor on a Glasgow paper and a married man, but those odd Thespian interludes still mattered.

Dramatic work is wearing, wearying, and results are not measurable even on a five-point scale. But neither can one number the sands of the sea, nor need one try.

Appendix
Some suggestions for poems, scenes for plays and other sources of dramatic material:
   'The Highwayman'.
   'Sherwood in the Twilight'.
   'Barring of the Door'.
   Ballads with a refrain.
   Parts of the 'Bab Ballads'.
   Some of Bret Harte's poems.
   'Songs of a Sourdough'.
   'Santa Fé Trail'.
   Bliss Carmen's travel poems.
   'Eddi of Manhood End'.
   Kipling's poems with refrains and good rhythm, e.g. 'We haven't a camelty tune of our own'. 'There runs a road by Merrow Down'. 'Davis'. 'Four ducks on a pond'. 'I hear leaves drinking rain'. 'Ducks'.

Stories and Scenes
   Jim Hawkins in the apple barrel.

EXPRESSIVE WORK: DRAMA

Ferdinand the Bull (use a mask with eye piece and horns only, but do not forget his tail!).
Parts of the *Just So Stories*.
East o' the Sun, West o' the Moon.
Peter and Wendy Nursery Scene.
Peter and Wendy Pirate Ship.
Peter and Wendy Rescue of Tiger Lily.
Stories from Robin Hood.
Parts of Heidi.
Pocahontas.
Brer Rabbit.

Book List
BATCHELDER and COMER, *Puppets and Plays*, Faber.
CHESMAN and WILES, *Mime for Schools*, Nelson.
COBBY and NEWTON, *The Playmakers*, Pitman.
COLLINS, F., *Acting Games*, U.L.P.
LANGDON, E. M., *Dramatic Work with Children* (Dobson, Theatre in Education Series). Available at Foyles (N. 824 price 2s. 6.) not now on general sale.
MCCREA, L., *Puppets and Puppet Plays*, O.U.P.
— *Stories to play in the Infant School*, O.U.P., 7s. 6d.
MILLS and DUNN, *Shadow Plays and How to Produce Them*, Doubleday, Dunn and Co., New York, 1935. This book is in Kent County Council Library No. 4810644 and gives most interesting plays for Human Shadows including a Nativity Play.
PICKERSGILL, *Mimed Ballads and Stories*, Pitman.
— *Practical Miming*, Pitman.
STONE, A. R., *Story of a School*, H.M.S.O., 1949.
Teachers Omnibus of Plays, O.U.P., 9s. 6d.
WALL, L. V. and WHITE, *Complete Puppet Book*, Educational Puppetry Association, Faber.

A. F. HARRIS

Chapter IX

HANDICRAFT

> Children at this stage begin to show a real interest in the traditional crafts; Needlework, Pottery, Weaving, Bookcrafts and the simple woodwork involved in making toys. It is the teacher's task to see that the work that is undertaken is well within the power of the children and while there should be no over-emphasis in the matter of technique, children must not be left to flounder aimlessly for lack of guidance, nor should slovenly work be tolerated.
>
> Board of Education, *Suggestions*, 1937

It may perhaps be considered that suggestions for teaching handwork compiled more than twenty years ago will not be relevant today but, basically, the aims underlying the work have not changed for many years. After all, handwork may be interpreted as work done with the hands, and the word tends to be charged with overtones of craftsmanship, whatever one may think of the results achieved by some of our pupils. Everyone has to make a beginning and great care must be taken not to belittle the first feeble attempts of backward children.

The majority of children can be persuaded to have a splash at handwork, one is tempted to write 'bash' to contrast with the bashful, or bold, admissions of quite a number of teachers who claim to dislike teaching the subject in any form. These people put forward a number of reasons for this antipathy including (*a*) can't do it myself; (*b*) can't think what to do; (*c*) can't stand the mess; (*d*) never do it until after the 11 + Examination because English and Arithmetic are more important. None of these considerations need trouble the teachers of dull children in the primary school if they bear in mind a few fairly straightforward, common-sense aims. These are necessary to have at the back of one's mind in order to prevent the aimless floundering referred to above, but, just as in point-to-point races where one must go to the finish via certain clearly defined landmarks there is plenty of scope for deviation in the actual courses taken.

With that thought in mind some of the following ideas may be considered as forming the basis for a sound scheme, although, for reasons which may become apparent later, it is asking the impossible to outline a specific scheme which would suit even a small majority of teachers. Nevertheless, it might be generally agreed that at some points in the chosen scheme we should come near to the following aims.

(1) To satisfy the children's need for activity by providing means for expression.
(2) To give them power and experience in manipulating tools and media of all kinds.
(3) To teach a series of progressive craft skills with materials.
(4) To grade the materials in texture to enable controlled work to be done by the different age groups.
(5) To encourage individual work and design.
(6) To train the children to appreciate sound construction and to be dissatisfied with slovenly work.
(7) To encourage neat and faultless execution of the work.

Many of these aims can be covered very simply by saying,
   (*a*) Let the children do the work;
   (*b*) Only the best work of each child is good enough.

In case there are some people who are rather anxious about the demand for work of a high standard from slow children, the criterion should be the best work which one thinks each child can produce. It is worth while to aim a little higher than seems possible, otherwise the lazy ones will be content to jog along quite happily, filling in time without really being extended to the limit of their ability.

Sometimes people come up to one and say, 'I like so and so, how did you do it?'

This can be a very difficult question to answer because so many factors may be involved. One can reply by giving a factual account of how the job was done but no matter how skilful an explanation is given, one simply cannot transfer to another person the feeling for tools and materials which may have taken years of practice and application to acquire. No amount of money paid can buy this 'know-how'. It has been said that experience is, 'That which I do myself', and no amount of time spent in watching a process being done will be as valuable as actually tackling the job oneself. Thus, from the start, one must allow the children scope for experimenting with different media. Town children, for example, may have less opportunity out of school than country children for handling such things as straw or clay. Handwork lessons may provide both lots of children with opportunities for handling materials which they normally have little chance to use.

It is very important to be aware of the tremendous range of abilities to be found in most backward classes, and one is frequently meeting children who, having unsuccessfully attempted a process, are about to give up in despair. One should be ready to spot children who have reached such a barrier and assist them by giving advice and encouragement. The most useful teaching can often be done when such situations arise.

One must, however, firmly resist the ever present temptation to do the work for the child. Obviously that is the line of least resistance but, on a future occasion, when the same problem arises, one will only have to repeat the performance. The best way in the long run is to let the child make an attempt and, in the event of failure, let him try again. Before long, certain results will be found. If the child is ready to progress he will do so, but if the work has been badly graded it will become clear that he needs to do much more preliminary work before he is capable of advancing in that kind of work. A change of craft may prove beneficial.

One must always be on the alert so as to build on the unexpected accomplishments which are occasionally revealed in casual conversations, e.g. whilst one is on playground duty. In one backward class there was a girl who proved to be unusually skilled in the use of a screwdriver and other tools which her father had taught her to use. In spite of the fact that she seemed most refined and feminine in her manner she was superior to many of the boys in her handling of these tools. The group accepted her readily because of this skill and the resulting gain in confidence led to a considerable advance in reading at which she had been rather retarded.

In contrast to this case one sometimes meets boys who appear at a superficial acquaintance to have all the potentialities for doing excellent craftwork, but who, in practice, do not seem to have the least idea of how to tackle the simplest operation. Home environment may hold the key to the mystery, for, in some flats, children may have to keep very quiet to avoid neighbours' complaints and so are unable to delight in hammering or other play creating noise.

In other homes, the very idea of children cutting up paper, using glue, paint or even ink, and experimenting with those materials would be frowned upon from a great height. It is sometimes most puzzling when one pays an unexpected visit to homes where there are two or three children to find how spick and span everything looks. There are no toys in sight, no books lying around, everything is so perfect as to be unnatural. One can only be thankful that one's own family escaped being born into such a house-proud place. It is an excellent idea to get children to put away their things when they have finished with them, but sometimes one gets the impression that the children in certain homes never handle their toys after Christmas Day.

Environment includes the whole atmosphere in which the children exist, so that links with the homes should be made wherever possible, always bearing in mind that the best time for a teacher to see a parent is when there is something to discuss. The parent-teacher-child relationships need nurturing because better understanding will exist all round if ideas can be exchanged. Mutual interests and tact usually prevent any unnecessary friction between school and home and so enable both groups to steer the children in the same direction. With backward children this co-operation is probably even more than ever necessary.

Parents can help to see that every child starts the day looking neat and tidy, with brushed hair and clean shoes. Attention to these details, as well as to posture and carriage, usually leads on to a feeling of confidence which has been known to express itself further in the form of tidy desks and neat manipulations. Parental co-operation can be extended still more if they contribute old newspapers and other material for handwork lessons.

Schoolkeepers too, as a rule, readily assist by supplying polish and dusters to enable children to polish their desk lids. Children who become accustomed to shining desk tops rarely need telling to spread out newspapers for a handwork or pasting session.

Many Head teachers greatly simplify the teaching of handwork by the way in which they organize their requisitions. Each child should be able to have responsibility for the care of his own pen, pencil, ruler, rubber and so on. If children do not have to share this type of stock with those in other classes they can more readily be taught to realize that carelessness with property cannot be tolerated. Life not only becomes much easier for all concerned but, because of better tools, e.g. rulers without notched edges caused by being banged on the desks, completed work usually reaches a higher standard.

Many schools have rotary pencil sharpeners which when used properly are very useful. However, when children become so fascinated by the machines that the lives of pencils are shortened too quickly it is time to prohibit the use of the sharpeners and to have handy a sharp knife or a razor blade in a holder.

We have found that pencils last longer if the names of the children, or alternatively, numbers corresponding to the names, are put on the pencils. We also made a chart using a sheet of graph paper on which, every Friday, the children used to place their pencils in the column above their names and mark off where the pencil tips came. By filling in the alterations in length each week, using a different coloured wax crayon each time to mark the length of pencil used, it was easy to see at a glance which children were using reasonable care in the use of pencils. One or two children thought it very amusing to use a pencil brought from home so that there was nothing for them to record on the chart.

We made another rule that new pencils would only be issued if the old stub was produced in exchange with the name or number clearly visible. This was an indirect approach to the stopping of pencil chewing. A few old pencils were kept in reserve in case of mishap but, with the weekly marking on the chart, losses were very rare. Once a tradition of good habits is formed it is possible, eventually, to omit this regular checking, but there can be no hard and fast rule as to when this stage will be reached. Everything depends on the children themselves and on their earlier training, for in some schools even the smallest infants seem to be reasonably careful of equipment from the very beginning. In other words, the home environment plays its part for good or ill. Undoubtedly there are other influences too, and an old colleague used to sum these up by remarking, 'What's in the well comes up in the bucket.'

HANDICRAFT

Rubbers caused us a lot of trouble until one lad made a small hole through his, fixed on a length of string and fastened the other end inside his desk. This scheme worked so well that we formally adopted it and have lost no more rubbers. Various modifications have been introduced by some of the lads, including the fixing of the string to buttons or metal washers which are then attached inside the desk. It is necessary, by the way, to have the string long enough to allow the rubber to be used with the desk lid closed.

Although there is plenty of scope for giving children responsibility for personal equipment, the larger items should be arranged so that everyone knows where to return them after use. It is useful to paint on the board where they hang, or perhaps inside the cupboard, the shapes of hammers, leather punches, etc., so that one can see at a glance which tools are in use, or missing at the end of the lesson.

From the very beginning attention should be given to the correct use of tools, e.g. cutting knives must not be used for prising open the lids of paint tins. The names of tools should be learned even though much repetition of names may be necessary. Mistakes will occur, such as 'brilliantine' for guillotine, but the use of correct names not only saves time eventually but employs the language familiar to craftsmen. Handwork lessons can be made easier from the teacher's point of view and more enjoyable for the children if enough attention is given to their preparation. During the dinner time or at playtime the materials likely to be required can be set out in front of the class. At this point I would like to refer back to the detailed suggestions for organization of materials given in Chapter VI, which are equally relevant here.

Each child must become thoroughly used to going out sensibly to the front of the class to collect his own materials. Better work seems to result under these conditions and also if some choosing of work to be done is permitted.

Collisions and subsequent messes may be prevented if one insists on one-way traffic similar to that in 'serve yourself' shops or restaurants. Some helpers show considerable initiative and forethought in setting out the goods on display. Occasionally one can introduce a 'cashier', price the articles, issue cardboard money and give practice in shopping.

Dull children, having met failure, are sometimes rather slow in coming forward but most children like being made responsible for a classroom job. Lists should be displayed in the room so that everyone knows what is expected of him. Arrangements can easily be made for replacing absentee helpers.

This giving of responsibility according to the capabilities of the children is often very necessary because so many backward children have not only met repeated failure, but have been so hurried and fussed over when doing tasks like dressing, that they sometimes seem hopelessly incompetent and nervous when given the seemingly simplest thing to do. This state of affairs should be recognized and tackled. It would often be much easier and far quicker to do the operation oneself but that is not helping to overcome the child's problem. One must be prepared to do a certain amount of waiting – to relax.

Plenty of newspapers should be spread out on tables and floors where one anticipates that a child in this condition is likely to spill things. It is useful to let children pour out their own ink, etc. We have met some who were almost terrified to try this at first, but after being encouraged (particularly by the teacher taking no notice if at first they spilt some on the paper ready for such mishaps) they became quite competent eventually. The secret of success lies in allowing these children plenty of room, without fear of being bumped into, to give them time, but above all, not to show displeasure at their rather weak first efforts. Very often one has to suffer for the sins committed by the parents in over coddling, or in other ways interfering with the child's welfare, frequently under the mistaken impression that they were helping him.

At the beginning of the school year with a new class one should take the trouble to let the children know exactly how one wants things to be done. Slow learners and younger children need taking along at a steadier pace than older and quicker ones, and with the backward children particularly, it may be necessary to give fairly frequent repetitions, bearing in mind that in backward classes attendance is usually more irregular and so earlier announcements may have been missed by absentees. The teacher must learn to 'hurry slowly' and be more prepared to wait for results. This requires confidence, a firm understanding of what one is trying to do coupled with the determination to try to achieve it. There may be lurking at

HANDICRAFT

the back of one's mind the thought, 'I am doing this job to the best of my ability, and if anyone else feels that he can do better I am perfectly willing to step aside to let him try.' This attitude must never close one's ears to the reception of advice or helpful suggestions of any sort but, as already suggested, it is impossible to transfer experience or 'know how' from one person to another just like a Christmas present. One can adapt ideas to one's own use but to be fully effective they must be welded to one's own philosophy of teaching.

A flexible approach to the teaching of children of different ages and attainment levels is certainly required, but there should be no toleration of slackness in the care and use of tools, or in the clearing up after each lesson. Good habits are best taught by example and it is important to see that children are forewarned of the approaching end of a lesson in sufficient time to allow them to complete the task in hand, or to store away carefully the unfinished model or whatever it is, for if it was worth starting in the first place it ought to be worth finishing. If it is possible to extend the lesson so as to complete the job it may ultimately lead to a saving of time because when one is warmed up to a task it takes less time, in aggregate, than it does when one has to stop and restart again in the future.

At this point it should be stressed that all articles made ought to serve a purpose and not be given merely for the sake of having something to do. For example, puppets, if made, need to be used in English, history or geography lessons, etc., in order to illustrate some aspect of teaching in those subjects. Masks, on the other hand, may perhaps be used merely for play, e.g. on November 5th.

With dull children one must avoid having projects which drag on interminably to the point of boredom. As a rule, when children are allowed a certain amount of latitude in choosing what to do even dull ones seem to show a remarkable amount of persistence and staying power, not to mention ingenuity in solving their problems. It is when difficulties are encountered that the teacher can give advice or help that is most valuable and likely to be remembered when a similar situation is met on another occasion. One must not rush in with advice at too early a stage, but remain in the background (unless of course one bright spark decides to experiment with a sharp instrument on either the furniture, or his fellows).

Experienced teachers may be able and willing to have more than one craft going on in a room at the same time quite happily, but younger teachers may have to achieve this state of affairs gradually by empiric means. Yet it is hard to generalize because there are some young teachers, who because of special attributes, seem to be at home in a handwork group from the beginning. Where there is confidence allied to careful preparation and a knowledge of the craft in hand, a happy atmosphere free from disciplinary worries seems to follow.

There are several viewpoints concerning the choice of activities. Some people advocate that all children in a class should be doing the same thing at the same time, more or less on the lines to be found in textbooks of sixty years ago, i.e. 'At the command one, take the pencil between the thumb and forefinger'. At the other extreme are those who seem to suggest releasing the children into a classroom provided with various media and letting nature take its course.

The generally accepted approach lies somewhere between the two, but it is impossible to be dogmatic and pretend that there is only one perfect line to take because that simply is not so. Purposeful disorder may be permissible but chaos alone is not.

The choice of activity must be based on several considerations. Obviously one of these is governed by the materials available, for even the most expert cane basket maker cannot pursue his craft if provided solely with a pile of clay.

Secondly one must allow for the capabilities and interests of the teacher, for some teachers are very skilful in certain crafts and much less keen on others and this is bound to have some influence on the type of work undertaken. Some children too, even backward ones, may be reasonably skilful in some activities and it usually pays to take advantage of this skill. It does seem too, that opportunities should be taken of linking home hobbies with school handwork. Model aeroplanes and similar things can help to form a common ground between the two.

The classroom can be a type of workshop, organized so that no useless rubbish is harboured anywhere in it. Useful junk can be stored in boxes so as to keep it free from dust and at the same time allowing the school cleaners to do a thorough job. It is sound training in handwork to leave the workshop reasonably tidy. A little bending to gather up fallen oddments helps with Physical Education,

HANDICRAFT

while Health Education reminds us that, 'Where there's dirt, there's danger.'

Earlier it was suggested that with dull juniors the time-table should allow for a flexible approach and it is a further advantage if the children can remain for as many lessons as possible with the class teacher. Not only does this system permit the teacher to have better facilities for observing the all-round development of the children, but it enables lessons to be extended if it is thought desirable for this to be done. With a lot of specialization in operation this overlapping is usually quite out of the question. If extensions cannot be managed, then work must be planned in smaller units so that they can be completed in the time available.

In considering the choice of activities it seems to me that if one meets a child who is keen to do sums in a handwork lesson, and it is not unknown, there is no reason why he should not be given permission. He will be happy and more time will be available to give to others. Whether the same child should always act in this way is an entirely different matter. It may be that the child feels a sense of security in getting pages of ticks. This is another sort of problem to be faced but one can sometimes entice such a child into the group as a whole by choosing him as a helper, taking care that at first he is given tasks likely to bring success.

It goes without saying that very large classes for handwork are to be deplored, for although near miracles are sometimes performed by junior school teachers in very awkward conditions, nobody has ever given a convincing explanation of why they should have to give repeated encores.

We are told that some subjects are 'caught rather than taught', and it is undoubtedly true that an enthusiastic teacher in handwork can arouse interest in children who at first seem very apathetic in their attitudes. This interest, once roused, can be very infectious because a small group taught to do an operation are often able to pass on their knowledge quite well. They sometimes have a particular advantage over the teacher where nervous children are concerned, for the latter will pluck up courage to ask another child but remain too timid to ask the teacher to repeat a demonstration. There is nothing new in the idea of children showing one another. One has come across boys who have been able to show friends how to write legibly quite quickly. There has to be the right motivation, and maturation certainly enters into the field. When a child is ready to learn a process it can be taught easily and that is one reason why it is so important to learn just how far our pupils have progressed if we are to gain the maximum benefits from our efforts.

Handwork, as has been said above, should serve a purpose and it may be used to supplement the ordinary teaching in any subject. It can be made to serve in history, geography, English and indeed in any lesson. Various models, e.g. of harbours, contours, stage properties such as crowns, shields, swords, puppets, etc., can all be worked in handwork lessons and used as required.

One thing which adults can often learn from children is that it is not always the most expensive materials which produce the most satisfying results. It is a sure sign of progress when a boy or girl tells one in a most pitying tone of voice, 'Cor, you don't want to spend money on that, what you want to do is to get so and so, they throw 'em away at such and such a shop.'

When this stage is reached the appropriate action to take is to apologize for one's ignorance, lay all one's cards on the table and say, 'Now that you know what we want, do you think that you could make such and such a thing, by whatever time it is you require it?' The chances are that a first class result will ensue. Very often, friends are co-opted to help and these groups not only set themselves a very high standard of workmanship, but they are also likely to put in quite a lot of free time in order to get on with the job.

Much work can be done in connexion with the annual festivals of Easter, Christmas, etc., as well as seasonal and occasional activities. On one occasion some of our boys made an Easter garden, in an old sink, complete with growing plants. When these plants were watered, the cardboard tomb incorporated in the plan tended to become soggy and shapeless. On his own initiative, Philip spent two shillings of his pocket-money in order to buy waterproof material. Some of our boys and girls made up a play and quite spontaneously they collected money and arranged for three girls to visit the market on a Saturday morning to buy material out of which they made aprons needed for the play. The class was a fourth year E class in a junior school. The school funds happened, at the time, to be in such a sound state that a gesture of this kind was unnecessary, but the incident illustrates the heights of enthusiasm which can be reached by some dull children if they are allowed to feel that what they do is sincerely valued. Recognition of work done can be acknowledged by posting notices near completed models, giving the names of all who contributed to their making. School visitors can also help the children to feel important by asking them to explain how they coped with certain phases of the work.

When it comes to offering suggestions for handwork schemes one is in trouble, for it is difficult to generalize. This is very easily demonstrated if one picks up practically any book on handwork, because there are bound to be some chapters which are of great interest to the reader while other chapters get hardly a glance. Another person may be absorbed in the very chapters which one has skipped and vice versa.

If one asked point blank, 'What would you take with this class?' then, even assuming that one knows enough about the class to be competent to answer, one can only reply, 'I would do so and so.' The answer may or may not satisfy the questioner because so much depends on whether or not you have similar craft interests.

Some firms, e.g. Evans Brothers, publish schemes of work for handwork, but again one will tend to extract from the schemes those items which appeal to oneself. There are some excellent books dealing with specific crafts and it may be useful to select a number of books and leaflets for the school reference library. One cannot do better than make a choice from the books and leaflets offered by Dryads of Leicester.

An ideal scheme would fit both the children and the teacher and there would be progression from the lower classes to those at the top end of the school. For instance there might be paper tearing at one end of the scale but eventually this should give way to accurate cutting with scissors or knives. If children are to become interested in craft work in general so that they are able in later years to find interesting hobbies it is especially important that their creative abilities should not be stifled in the junior school because of a too rigid syllabus. There must be discipline in the way in which they use tools, and insistence on the use of craftsmen's language, but allied to these there should be flexibility of approach, controlled freedom to experiment and opportunities for the use of initiative.

TEACHING THE SLOW LEARNER IN THE PRIMARY SCHOOL
Book List
General Works
ARREIL, I. S., *Infant Handwork*, Nelson, 1954.
BENNETT, C. M. and JACKSON, C. V., *Read and Make Books*, 1-4, Murray.
BLANDFORD, *Handicraft in Scrap Materials*, Hutchinson, 1943.
BUCHER, *The Teaching of Art*, Blackie.
CARNER and STOWASSER, *Measuring and Making*, O.U.P.
CRICHTON, S., *Blackboard Drawing*, Nelson.
CROFTON, C. and DENTY, P., *Creative Work in the Junior School: Sources of Information*, E.S.A.
GLENISTER, S. H., *The Technique of Handicraft Teaching*, Harrap, 1953.
HORTH, L. B., *101 Things for Children to Make*, Batsford.
MCLEISH and MOODY, E., *Beginnings: Teaching Art to Children*, Studio Publications.
MACKENZIE, *The Why and How of Child Art*, Angus and Robertson.
MARKS, W., *Lively Drawing with Pencil and Brush*, Macmillan.
MOORE, E. C., *Handicrafts for Elementary Schools*, Harrap, 1953.
ROBERTSON, S. M., *Creative Crafts in Education*, Routledge, 1952.
STIMSON, W., and others, *Crafts for School and Home*, Harrap, 1951.
STOWE, E. J., *Crafts for Rural Schools*, Longmans, 1939.
WEATHERILL, *A Pattern Making Workbook*, Blackie.

Woodwork
HAYWARD, C. H. (ed.), *Hammer and Nails Carpentry*, Evans, 1943.

Gardening
COPLEY, *School Gardening*, Crowther, 1947.

Cardboard and Paper Crafts
BREDA, *Pleasure with Paper*, Faber, 1954.
CAMPBELL, *Paper Toy Making*, Pitman,
DAY, *Coloured Paper Craft for Infant Schools*, Pearson, 1950.
— *Gummed Strip and Paper Modelling*, Pearson, 1955.
HOPKINS, M. and ELLIOT, L., *Paper Folding for Schools*, Charles.
KITSON, E., *Paper Craft*, Foyles, 1951.

HANDICRAFT

PAVIERE, *Paper Twisting and Crumpling*, Pitman.
THORNE, J., *Model Making in Cardboard*, Charles.
TONKS, *Scissor Crafts*, Warne, 1938.
WOOD, A. B., *Paper Modelling*, Charles.

Pottery
HALL, M., *Terracotta Modelling for Schools*, Tiranti, 1954.
PARRY, *Pottery for Schools*, Pitman, 1952.
POUNTNEY, *Modelling a Figure in Clay*, Tiranti, 1951.
TYLER, K., *Pottery without a Wheel*, Dryad Press, 1955.

Canework
CRAMPTON, *The Junior Basket Maker*, Dryad Press, 1940.
LEE, *Basketry and Related Crafts*, Macmillan, 1948.
ORMAN, *Basketry and Weaving*, Pitman, 1954.
ROFFEY, *Simple Basketry for Homes and Schools*, Pitman, 1953.

Bookcrafts
COLLINS, *Book Crafts for Juniors*, Dryad Press.
DAVENPORT, *Binding Crafts for the Primary School*, Pitman, 1948.
GATTON, *A.B.C. of Bookcraft*, Gatton, 1950.
LARGE, *Steps to Bookcrafts for Young Children*, Warne, 1939.
LEWIS, *Basic Bookbinding*, Batsford, 1952.
MATTHEWS, W. S., *Simple Bookbinding for Junior Schools*, Pitman.

Weaving
DAVENPORT, E. G., *Your Hand Weaving*, Sylvan Press, 1948.
MAIRET, E., *Hand Weaving Notes for Teachers*, Faber, 1949.
MOCHRIE and GOBEY, *Simple Weaving*, Dryad Press, 1939.
WADSWORTH, *Easy Weaving for Little Fingers*.

Leatherwork
ROSEAMAN, *Leather Work*, Dryad Press, 1939.
THOMPSON, *Leathercraft*, Macmillan, 1948.

Other Crafts
BARKER, *Progressive Lino Cuts*, Pitman,
CHIDE, *The First Book of Model Aircraft*, Studio, 1944.
KING, *Toy Making for Infants and Juniors*, Charles,
GALLOWAY, *Model Furniture*, Pitman.

MILLER, *Toy Making*, Pitman, 1952.
NELSON, *Block Prints for Beginners*, Pitman.
PEARCE, *Toys and Models*, Batsford, 1947.
SERGEANT, *Simple Puppetry for Children*, Pitman.
SHORT, *Plastics for Schools*, Pitman, 1948.
TANNER, *Children's Work in Block Printing*, Dryad.
THORBURN, M., *Toy Making from Odds and Ends*, Charles.

J. B. HAWKINS

Chapter X

ENVIRONMENTAL STUDIES

A centre of interest is particularly suitable in a class of slower junior children as it provides a common interest in which children of different abilities can contribute to the group project according to their capabilities and interests. Although the basic skills of number, reading, writing and spelling are used in most projects it is necessary to give ample time during the day for teaching these skills to the slower children. The basic skills must be mastered in set lessons and then given interesting application and expansion in the centre of interest. It is unwise to expect a project to teach the techniques of the skills, but it will provide a vital stimulus in the whole range of teaching methods.

Before a teacher starts a unit of study it is necessary for her to prepare thoroughly beforehand. The current interests of the children have to be studied carefully. She should be familiar with their school records; have knowledge of their problems both in and out of the classroom; have an understanding of their parents and home background.

The abilities and disabilities of the children have to be known. The quality of their intelligence and their attainments in the basic skills can be obtained from records of tests. In work on local studies the teacher has to judge whether the individual child is being stretched to the limit of his capabilities. The emphasis should be positive; the stress should always be on what the child is able to accomplish rather than what he is unable to do.

The teacher must make herself aware of the interests and activities of the parents, especially those that affect the children in the class. This is often reflected in the local newspaper. Other ways of finding out include class discussions of local events and outside activities carried out in the children's leisure time.

TEACHING THE SLOW LEARNER IN THE PRIMARY SCHOOL

A study of the environment is essential in preparation for a scheme in local studies. A teacher who lives near the school will almost certainly be aware of the attributes of the neighbourhood. A preliminary survey of the area is important. A study of large and small scale maps of the area is necessary. The map on a small scale will enable the teacher to fit the immediate surroundings into the pattern of the district; it will enable her to see the direction taken by roads, railways and rivers, as well as to note the bordering towns and villages. The larger scale map will help to identify the school, the roads, the church, public buildings and so on. Contacts should be made with the local librarian on the library resources and local sources of information. Similarly, a visit to the local museum will be worth while and when at a later date the children visit these places, the librarian and curator will have a sympathetic understanding. In towns use will be made of the park and here it is useful to make the acquaintance of the park superintendent or keeper. Knowledge of the public buildings and their history should be known, including the position of the bus station, railway station, fire station, electricity and gas-works and waterworks.

When the teacher has become familiar with the interest, abilities, aptitudes of the children and the environment outside school, the facilities of the school itself can be surveyed and where necessary adapted to meet the needs of this method. A classroom arranged in a formal manner is unsuited to work which involves considerable activity. Easily moved and easily stored furniture which can be grouped together is ideal.

In order that children may have access to material of all kinds adequate storage space must be available (see Chapter XII). When the children are working the room will have material in use, but when clearing up time comes the room should be made tidy. Social training is brought in here, as each child can be allotted a clearing up job. All these tidying assignments can be outlined on a work sheet which sets out all the details clearly and which is posted on the main notice board. Frequent change of job will ensure that children get experience in carrying out a variety of tasks which will stimulate them to retain interest.

For outside work with older backward juniors, tape measures and a surveyor's chain or a string knotted at foot intervals, together

ENVIRONMENTAL STUDIES

with a measuring wheel, either equipped with a clicker, or cyclometer, are useful. Note pads mounted on stiff board or three-ply to which is attached a pencil on a string, can be used for outdoor note-taking and drawing. A magnetic compass creates interest with the children. Collecting apparatus should include pond dipping nets, carrying jars and tins, adequately stringed for carrying. Tins in which insects are to be carried should have small ventilation holes.

When expeditions have been carried out the problem arises where to exhibit and store the things which have been collected. The classroom can be divided into areas and corners. In local studies the nature table is an essential part of the classroom. It provides for both communal and individual activities and interests. A strong table is best which can be easily reached and seen by all children in the class. Makeshifts can be made by grouping spare desks together and covering the tops with oil cloth or some similar material. A wheeled trolley is ideal because it can be moved to that part of the room where it is required. If floor space is limited shelves or wide window ledges can be used. Small meat paste jars wired to a piece of three-ply can be hung or fixed to the wall in which flowers can be exhibited.

Whatever type of table is used it is essential that it should have a strong visual appeal, be constantly changed and cleaned down at frequent intervals. Labels should be made by the children with the help of the teacher. In the early stages it will be necessary to give unobtrusive supervision and possibly deal with the removal of faded specimens, but later monitors for the nature table can be selected from a list of names placed on the general notice board.

Other apparatus for the nature study corner are the simple cold water aquarium, vivarium and homes for pets. Flat enamel dishes are useful to to hold creatures which have been collected whilst pond-dipping. Nature identification books and pictures should be kept near the table. To enable children to find the place the teacher can insert marked cards in the books. Other illustrations should be available to supplement the children's offerings. The keeping of pets as part of the nature corner will depend on the facilities available, not only in the classroom but also in the school grounds and the homes of the children. Considerations will be the amount of space there is; opportunities for obtaining food for the animals and the care and cleaning of animals at weekends and during the longer holidays.

For displays of other materials, shelves, tables, desks and wall spaces can be used. Specimens, models, charts, booklets and pamphlets can be grouped and displayed, all adequately labelled. Having served its purpose, individual and group work should be removed from display so that its place can be taken by something else. Items can often be stored for future use and display. Any lettering used should be of a high standard and illustrations should be well mounted. Many original ideas can be gained by looking at displays in shop windows.

Books form an important part of the reference section. Books for reference with slower junior children should be well illustrated with fairly easy reading material. A small list is given at the end of the chapter. The best storage for books is a trolley which can be moved and used where required. One-inch and six-inch maps should be available for use as well as local guide books and road maps.

Series of pictures will be supplied by the teacher and supplemented by the children. Collections of pictures by the children should be put into envelopes, labelled in order that they may be found easily when wanted. Discarded textbooks can often be cut up and articles and pictures from them made into thin booklets.

Audio-visual aids can be used if the subject is suitable and providing the teacher has made thorough preparation beforehand. Films and broadcast lessons are normally designed for the brighter children and may be unsuitable for use with the slower classes because of the speed and manner of presentation. With these two aids the teacher has lost the teaching control of the class. It is impossible to stop a broadcast to elaborate or simplify a particular point which the teacher can see has failed to be understood by the children. It may be possible by cutting out the commentary in a sound film for the teacher to add her own commentary adapted to the needs of the class. The teacher has full control over the medium of film strips. Single pictures can be used in a way which will bring the utmost value to the children. (See also the comments on mechanical aids made by Mr Purt in Chapter III.)

A notice board should be placed in a prominent position. Whatever the board is made from it should be easy for the children to stick pins in. On it will be put class and group notices concerning the work in hand; lists of monitors for the nature table; duties and names for clearing up; a forecast of work to be done and a diary of what has been accomplished. Notices asking for information and materials can be displayed here. The life histories of animals and plants, which are being studied, can be kept in diary form. A well kept notice board is a valuable incentive to reading and to the production of a legible style of writing or printing.

A work table, on which materials and equipment in constant use can be kept, should be large enough to carry all the apparatus. Where sets of equipment are in constant use a daily check should be made to see that the sets are complete. Labels showing complete number should be fixed on the outside of every container.

A dramatic corner as suggested by Mrs Harris in Chapter VIII can be used in the dramatization of stories and events. In this corner will be puppets and a puppet theatre. A model TV set can be made by the children to take rolls of pictures which can show a series of activities.

The school site will be used to a varying degree in local studies, much depending on the playground and grounds (if any). In the older type of school it may be possible to have flower and shrub boxes in which to grow things outside. In any playground it should be possible to place apparatus for weather study. A shadow pole can be fixed in position together with a wind vane or wind sleeves (well clear of surrounding buildings) and a thermometer. Bird baths and feeding tables can be used, and simple nesting boxes put in suitable places provide fascinating objects for the children. If there is a school garden much can be done with the slower junior children to provide them with the opportunity for some training in simple gardening operations and in the correct use, cleaning and putting away of tools. The more important tools (suitable size) are light spades, rakes, hoes, some trowels and handforks and watering-cans. Oil and rags should be kept and used for cleaning.

When the preliminaries have been finished the teacher has to decide on a line of action to adopt in introducing a local study to the class. If the study is to succeed the subject must be chosen by the children with suggestions and guidance by the teacher. A teacher-planned unit seldom does any good. If the class is allowed to select, plan and organize the necessary work as far as they are able, it will remain within their capabilities and thus retain their interest. At the same time the subject must be broad enough in scope to enable the whole class to participate. In a class for slower junior children there will be a large range of ability, therefore the subject should be wide enough for each child to be able to contribute irrespective of their ability. If the class has a wide age range the overall plan must contain something to interest the younger as well as the older children.

Another consideration the teacher must make is what the children are going to gain by taking part in the work. Will it give opportunities for the tool subjects to be used and enlarged? Will it bring in other related studies, history, geography, nature study, art, handwork and drama? Will it bring into play various factors involved in social training and co-operation? Will it help children to overcome or show them how to adjust themselves to their environment? Finally the study has to be so selected that each child can contribute something worthwhile and that all children will have a feeling of achievement and accomplishment when the work has been finished. The project should continue as long as the aims of it are being carried out and the children retain their interest and enthusiasm. The best starting point for a project on local studies is the immediate neighbourhood, where the children can explore, discover and find out for themselves. Subjects chosen should be within or close to the children's experience. They will at first be closely connected with things which are domestic and personal. The aim should be for the class to go from the known to discover the unknown.

The account of a local study which follows gives some idea of the activities which were carried out. It is necessary to stress that no two environments can be similar, no two classes or teachers alike. The children in any special class will have different backgrounds and experiences. The undertaking of any procedure because somebody else has done it defeats the whole purpose of project work – finding out for oneself. On the other hand the children's reactions and the teacher's role can be shown in a concrete example if an actual experiment is shown.

The school in which this project took place was a three-stream junior mixed school, with a special class composed of thirty-six children from the third and fourth years. The class was nearly equally divided in ages and sex. The school was situated on the outskirts of an industrial town with good communications including a river. The children were from a variety of homes with miscellaneous backgrounds. The I.Q. range was from 75 to 90. The class had kept a fairly rigid time-table, with subjects kept strictly in the compartments. Generally the basic subjects were taken in the morning and art and handwork in the afternoon. The school building was old, there was a large playground but no garden or field. There was a park nearby with a large pond in it.

The teacher realized that there was a need to introduce something into classroom life which would get away from the more formal type of work, which did not appear to be getting very good results. Although the children knew something of their immediate surroundings, very little was known outside it. The topic was introduced in a class discussion and a simple aim thought out. The centre was to be the home, the parents and the children. The teacher found it necessary by suggestion to give the class ideas on how to set down their information. The work in its first stages was individual. Simple zigzag books were made as a class lesson involving simple measuring, folding and decorating the covers. Names and titles were added. In this book the children drew pictures, wrote simple sentences about their houses, families and furnishings. The teacher found it necessary to give help in varying amounts, especially to the poor and non-readers.

In one of the A classes in the school a model had been made of a medieval town and the children wanted to make a similar model of their own district but in modern times. A map was drawn on sheets of large paper covering the area where the children lived. Here group work commenced, each group being responsible for enlarging a section of the map. Co-operation was seen to be essential when it was found that due to inaccuracies the sections did not join up properly. The less able children were able to copy down the names of the roads from the master copy and transfer them to their section. The names could be checked from the actual name boards. Queries arose from the class as to the naming and numbering of new roads. On the estate on which the school was situated the roads had been named after parts of the British Empire as it was in the 1920's. An interesting piece of research was carried out later on by a group of children who wanted to find out more about the place names.

When the large map had been completed it was stuck together and spread out on the floor and each child made a model of his house, garden and family. As the houses were of one type it was easy for the teacher to make templets of strong card which the less able children were able to use as a guide. Other children made their houses from work cards on which the instructions had been duplicated by the teacher. The outsides of the houses were decorated in the actual colours. Figures representing the families were made from pipe-cleaners and were dressed from pieces of material. Both boys and girls made the clothes and original designs were produced using unusual materials. Miniature gardens were made from a variety of materials, including moss and twigs.

When the model was finished this far the class formed into three groups and with the help of the teacher decided to find out about the main services which served their estate – the gas, electricity and water supplies. This time the facts and pictures were recorded in big group books made from folded sheets of sugar paper sewn together.

From this the class looked at the necessities used in the home. Food, drink and clothes. Three groups again emerged but with different children in each. The teacher found it necessary to help group the children by tactful suggestion, in order that each contained a fair cross section of ability. The clothes group worked in pairs and produced work on wool, silk, cotton and man-made fibres. The illustrations and writing were this time made into a frieze. The groups studying food and drink, included topics on bread, milk, tea, breakfast cereals, meat and fruit. One model was made by a group of children showing a Canadian wheat farmer's year. Another frieze was made but with machines and figures which were slightly raised off the background giving a three dimensional effect of a meat packing station. Refrigeration came into the meat study. Several of the parents of the children in the class worked in a local factory which made ship's refrigeration plant and a good deal of technical information was supplied to the children by their parents. During a periodic visit to the school kitchen the local Health Inspector gave a short talk on his duties in connexion with food inspection and cleanliness.

Whenever the class was split into groups it was the duty of each group to prepare talks about their subject and thus pass on information to the other children, so that each child obtained an all-round picture on the topic. At first the teacher found it necessary to give a good deal of help with the presentation of these talks. It was desirable that the important facts were stressed.

From here the study led on to the people the children met in everyday life, the milkman, postman, baker and policeman. The routes these people took were marked on the model. The children also prepared questions which were put to the men by chosen children. The teacher had talked to the men beforehand so they were prepared. Interest was brought to bear upon writing because the children chosen as questioners insisted on having written questions given to them. They also had to write the answers down which were given to the class during an oral lesson.

During this time a new housing estate was being built not far from the children's homes and the interest of the class centred around the building operations. As the previous work was nearly finished the teacher decided to use this new interest and develop it into another group topic. The building operations could be divided into three sections which could be used: cement, bricks and tiles and timber. Groups were again formed and each worked on one of the topics. As the information and specimens were collected it was decided to exhibit the information on tables, similar to a museum collection, suitably labelled. The children who were studying cement had an easy and interesting task because cement-making was a local industry and some of the children's fathers worked in the factory. The cement firms were generous in supplying information and literature. Although a good deal of it was too advanced it could be used with the help of the teacher. To obtain this information letters had to be written. This gave an incentive to written work and the children were pleased to receive replies to their letters. The brick and tile group found out where the bricks were made, what materials they were made from; the different types and uses; types of bricklaying patterns. The children working on the timber topic found out that the wood and timber fittings came from a shipyard in the West Country. This was explained when it was discovered that the building contractors were a subsidiary of a shipping company. The countries of origin of the timber were also found out.

At a later date it was found possible to organize a class visit to the cement works; this connected up with the river and two visits were really made in one journey. Although the journey had been very carefully prepared the teacher decided two separate journeys would have been better. The ships at the quayside were also seen and their cargoes were seen during the unloading.

Various forms of transport kept coming into the picture and as a new activity it was decided to find out more about the local systems. In taking a survey of the work so far covered during the year it was evident to the teacher that little history had been brought into any of the studies. To counteract this she suggested that besides studying the present systems of local transport it might be possible to go back and see how the various forms of transport had come into being. Use was made of the local museum which had a good display of local historical items. The groups each made models showing development from early to present day of their form of transport, road, rail and water. The models were made from a variety of materials including cardboard and balsa wood. Reference books were used more and the teacher found the children wanted more help than previously. Dolls were made from pipe cleaners to go with the models and they were dressed in the style of the time.

Puppets which had been made during the year were re-dressed in historical dress and short impromptu plays were made up of real and imaginary historical happenings. At first the teacher told the story which was afterwards adapted by the children. In miming the children started off with stories of the press gang and Dick Turpin. Following on from this, speech was gradually introduced and playlets became more advanced; eventually some of the better efforts came to be written down.

Although the children kept in one group whilst studying transport the dramatic activities included a cross section of each group. Often a play or puppet play would start and gather characters as it progressed. When a play was under way it was often necessary for the teacher to give advice on the characters and to see that they were in their proper period.

As a result of this combined history and geography study which took nearly a term to work through, the children gained an amount of local history, and what is more interesting, understood the importance of the local transport system and its relationship between the town and the outside world. Amongst the activities carried out were traffic counts of types and numbers of vehicles (bringing in time, counting and classification of motors and lorries); passengers passing through the local station at various hours during the day (graphs were made from these figures obtained from the stationmaster); the policeman who gave road safety talks to the school came in and spoke about the Traffic Section of the Police and how traffic was controlled; the goods unloaded at the quayside were listed and their countries of origin were marked on a world map and the raw materials were followed through to see what the finished article would be; the weights which goods lorries were able to carry brought in discussion and demonstration of the weights table, this also came in when the children had seen a weigh-bridge just inside a factory gate.

During the year that all these local studies had been going on the teacher had set definite times aside for planned trips in the local park as a contribution to nature study.

This subject was considered to be part of environmental studies but it could not be combined with the other activities which were being carried out. During the visits to the park the park keeper became interested in the children's activities and not only was a lot learned from him about the trees and plants but he knew a good deal about the town's history and development in the past fifty years.

Weather observations were made every day from instruments set up in the playground. Pets were brought from home including canaries, a pair of hamsters and a guinea-pig. Social training was helped when the children took turns in looking after the pets. A strict feeding routine had to be laid down otherwise the pets would have been overfed. The routine of feeding and cleaning was made out on paper, stuck on to a board, varnished and hung by the cage. Before looking after a pet the children had to be able to read the instructions. The instructions also included diagrams to help the poor reader. All pets were taken home at weekends and longer holidays.

A small cold water aquarium was kept in the classroom. This was added to on subsequent pond-dipping expeditions. Other activities which took place were making plaster casts of twigs and leaves, keeping charts of birds seen in the park, tree studies (bark rubbings, leaf collections, drawings of shape and use of timber), measuring of distances (distance between cricket wickets, length of sports pitches) and a weather chart. The children kept nature notebooks in diary form. A nature table was maintained, which reflected the work of the class and various groups. The class teacher kept check on the exhibits, gave advice, supplied supplementary pictures and helped with setting out the lettering. Monitors were appointed to look after the nature table.

Throughout the year the teacher found out that she had to give varying amounts of help with preparation of written work as well as with the seeking for information in books. To the less able children simple verbal instructions were given where to find pictures and information. Book-markers were placed in position by the teacher. Help was also given to the children who were able to read a little by making up simple instruction cards with written instructions and directions. The teacher found it necessary to give the children some spare time activity to do, so that if they had to wait for help they were occupied.

Progress records were kept by the children either in diary form or on a chart. These showed what the children had done during the day. The teacher also kept her own records of the children and their work as the project progressed. From these observations the teacher was able to assess the worth of the project as a whole and a check was kept on the actual learnings and experiences as they occurred and any deficiencies were remedied by change of plan. The teacher made a daily plan of work for each group or child, so that she knew exactly what each child was doing. This plan helped to spread out the use of equipment so that not everybody was wanting to use a certain item at the same time. It also enabled the teacher to see that each child had a variety of work during the period and used various methods and materials in presenting facts, making models and writing up information.

At the conclusion of these local studies at the end of the year it was evident that besides obtaining extra knowledge and use of the basic skills the children had learned to work together and could see the advantages of taking part in a joint effort. They acquired a sense of care and accuracy made evident by the work they were engaged upon. The standards which the children set themselves for exhibition work was high, higher in fact than the teacher would have expected from a formal lesson. They had gradually developed the ability of expressing themselves and to work from directions. They learned to plan their work and to find out things for themselves. Their initiative was constantly being challenged by being brought into contact with ideas and experiences which were new to them. Each child was able to work at something within the limits of his capabilities. Achievement was felt by the children in accomplishing tasks which by the results were satisfying and worthwhile. The children were able to become familiar with their physical surroundings, to be able to place certain local areas in relation to one another, to the neighbourhood and local community. The social training was incidental but nevertheless important. The desirable social habits which were included in group work and mutual help included cleanliness, tolerance, self-reliance and respect for others' property.

Handwork materials which can be used in model making and are suitable for slower junior children include balsa wood which is soft, inexpensive and easy to work. It can be cut and sandpapered. For cutting a small, fine toothed hacksaw is recommended. For more precise work a razor blade may be used, or a sharp knife, but this is not recommended unless it is closely supervised. Various types of glue which should be strong, quick drying and easy to use are needed. Clothes-pegs or bulldog clips are useful to keep parts in position whilst sticking. Boxes should be kept in which materials can be stored. The materials can be used in constructive work and can include: raffia, milk straws, plaster of Paris (best kept separately and in the dry), cotton-reels, sand, sawdust, granulated cork, soft wire, plastic-covered flex, string, twine, rope, coloured cotton, thread, cotton-wool, crêpe paper, corks, dowelling, cardboard from boxes, date boxes (useful for barges and ships), cellophane paper, silver paper, offcuts of thin leather and wood and coloured feathers.

A plastic bowl in which papier mâché is kept should be replenished from time to time. To keep it sweet smelling a little disinfectant should be mixed with the water. Models of foodstuffs can be made from a mixture of flour and salt in equal proportions; water is added and the contents mixed until the mixture is firm but workable. The mixture is then modelled into shapes and baked in a warm oven or kiln for about thirty minutes. When the models have cooled they can be painted with powder colour and clear varnish.

For nature study activities, besides apparatus and material already mentioned, the following are desirable. Cobbler's heel-ball for bark rubbings, containers in which to take plaster casts of twigs and leaves (vaseline is required in the process). A bird table or bird bath either to stand in the playground or be fixed to the wall outside the classroom window. Suitable bird feeders can be made from old cocoa tins and nailed to the table. Drinking water should always be supplied and if a few drops of glycerine are added in winter it will stop the water from freezing.

Before setting up an aquarium or vivarium it is advisable to study books on the subject. Generally the best type are made with metal frames with panes of glass cemented in. The aquarium should have a large surface in relation to its depth and should have a loose cover to keep out the dust. Plants for the aquarium can be bought from a pet shop and should include Canadian pondweed (*Elodea*), *Vallisneria* species and duckweed (*Lemna*). If more than one kind of fish are introduced they should be about the same size. A useful guide to stop overstocking with fish is one inch of fish to one gallon of water. Suitable species of fish include goldfish, carp, rudd, tench and gudgeon. Sticklebacks should be kept separately from other fish because they are aggressive. To keep aquaria clean pond snails and certain plants should be kept. If the glass should become dirty it can be cleaned by scraping with a razor blade. Live and dried foodstuffs can be bought from the pet shop.

Vivaria are used to house frogs, newts, lizards and slow worms, and can be made from two biscuit tin lids and four pieces of glass, one lid forms the bottom, the other the top. The top should be ventilated. The glass is held together at the top and bottom corners by adhesive tape. Smaller vivaria can be used to house silkworms, stick insects and caterpillars.

When other animals are kept the cages or hutches should be strong and large enough for the animals to live in. The most suitable, easiest and cleanest to keep is a golden hamster because it can be left with food at the weekends. Other animals which can be kept are mice, guinea-pigs and rabbits. But all of these require feeding and attention every day and are not always suitable for school study.

ENVIRONMENTAL STUDIES
Reference Books
For the Teacher

CONS and FLETCHER, *Actuality in School*, Methuen.

EVANS and UDALE, *Illustrative Model Making for Schools*, Longmans.

JOHNSON, E. S., *Theory and Practice of the Social Studies*, Macmillan, N.Y.

MILLIKEN, *Handwork Methods in the Teaching of History*, Wheaton.

PHILLIPS and MCINNES, *Exploration in the Junior School*, U.L.P. Although this book was written about normal junior children it gives examples of projects and lists many ideas which can be adapted to a special class. Chapters on material for use in project work are helpful.

School Nature Study Union Leaflets (obtainable from A. C. Funnell, 23 Crystal Palace Road, East Dulwich, S.E.22). These are written by experts in non-technical language and are recommended for the teacher who wants information: *Nature Activities in the Junior School; Water Animal Identification Sheets; Birds in the Open and How to Distinguish Them; The School Aquarium; The Keeping of Animals and Plants in School* (includes care and maintenance of plants, aquaria, vivaria, wormery, ant boxes, mice, guinea-pigs, and golden hamsters).

For the Children

None of these appears to have been written for the slower children but all can be used.

B.B.C., Nature Study Pamphlets. To be used for picture sources for nature books and nature table.

BENNETT, *The Golden Encyclopaedia*, Publicity Products.

CROSS, *Things We Use*, Longmans. (Twenty-four books each dealing with one common article.)

FISHER, *Adventure of the Sea*, Rathbone.

— *Adventure of the World*, Rathbone.

HOGBEN, *Man Must Measure*, Rathbone.

— *Men, Missiles and Machines*, Rathbone.

JESSUP, *Puzzle of the Past*, Rathbone.

PARKER, *The Golden Treasury of Natural History*, Publicity Products.

TEACHING THE SLOW LEARNER IN THE PRIMARY SCHOOL

UNSTEAD, *Looking at History*. (Four books), A. and C. Black.

— *People in History*. (Four books), A. and C. Black.

WERNER, *The Golden Book of Geography*, Publicity Products.

WYLER and AMES, *The Golden Book of Astronomy*, Publicity Products.

Various Authors

Open Your Eyes Books: *Regional Study* (Three parts – City, County, Village); *History Book 3* (Three parts – Food, Clothes, Houses); *History Book 4* (Men's Forward March – Three parts); *Nature Study Book 1* (Come and See – Three Parts); *Nature Study Book 2* (Out of Doors – Three parts); *Nature Study Book 3* (Living Things – Three parts), Chatto and Windus.

The Book of the Town (other series include Sea, Air, Country, Football, Railways and Cinema), Evans Bros.

The Get to Know Series: *Inland Waterways; Parish Church; British Railways; Roads and Streets; Bridges; Docks and Harbours; Shops and Markets; Factories and Workshops; Houses and Flats; Post and Telegraph; Water Supply; Boundaries, Farms; Village Survey; Country Town Survey*, Methuen. The pictures in this series are clear and well drawn.

For the Pocket Books: *Bird Book; Butterfly Book; Flower Book; Insect Book; Beast Book*. Small thick books which can be carried in pocket on expeditions. Very good coloured illustrations, O.U.P.

Puffin Picture Books: *Ships; Ponies; Maps; Clothes; Motor Cars; Trains; Stamps; Birds*, and many more, Penguin. A very useful series, especially for the attractive pictures.

Observer's Books: *Fungi; Aircraft; Dogs; Ships; Horses and Ponies; Ferns; Pond Life*, Warne. Similar to the other Pocket Books.

Ordnance Survey Maps, large and small scale.

W. A. HOLLINGBERY

Chapter XI

THE KEEPING OF RECORDS

All of us know the staff-room figure who bristles when something is mentioned which can conceivably be termed a 'new-fangled idea'.

This critic is often at his best when the topic of record keeping is discussed. Sometimes the keeping of written records will be condemned as being 'a waste of time' or 'a lot of facts on paper amounting to nothing'. It is my experience that the critic often receives a considerable amount of support in his opposition towards keeping records.

We must begin, therefore, by attempting to convince our sceptical colleagues that they have a knowledge of the children they teach, which is in itself a record: and that this knowledge is of value not only to them at the present moment but will, if passed on to the future teachers of their children, enable those teachers to begin with a basis of understanding of the nature and needs of the children.

All teachers keep records and certain written records have always been kept. It often surprises the opponents of record keeping when they realize that they have always kept records of such things as the attendance of their scholars, results of class tests, notes from parents, examination results, etc.

Indeed on questioning we learn that these teachers often possess, stored in their memories, a remarkable knowledge of their children and a wealth of information about them which may include observations of character and personality, details of their interests, home background, behaviour characteristics, etc.

The tragedy is that this information, which would be of the greatest value to the children's next teacher(s), is often not written down but is either forgotten or not passed on. So as the child moves from class to class, or school to school, the teacher begins again at the beginning and by the time the child is completely known to him on he moves and so once again the process of understanding begins.

In many of the village schools of the past and present, the need for such recording, though desirable for the occasional transfers or new members of the teaching staff, is not so essential because numbers in village schools are small, and often the same family has lived in the village for generations. In addition teachers generally tend to stay longer in village schools than in urban schools. It is because of the complexity of urban life that written records are so essential.

I would like now to quote from two books in which the value of record keeping to the child's present and future teachers is mentioned.

The appendix to the UNESCO report 'Education and Mental Health' says this:

'Teachers are naturally reluctant to spend much extra time on them, unless it is clear that they are of value to themselves and their colleagues.

'They should be made to realize, therefore, that the records assist them in getting to know each pupil better, in making fuller contacts with parents, and in developing the sympathy, combined with impartiality, which is the essence of the modern approach to education.'

Of the cumulative value of record keeping, Sir Cyril Burt makes these points in his book *Mental and Scholastic Tests*:

'Last of all, let me urge, not only the need for periodic testing by the same teacher or by successive teachers, but also the preservation of the records, and their transference from one teacher to another as the child is moved from class to class. Too often the personal knowledge gleaned by his first teacher, through individual attention, through daily study a year's experience is lost when a child is promoted to a fresh class or leaves for a fresh school; and the discoveries have to be made all over again. Rather the old records should become the basis of new observations; and as the child develops, as he passes from standard to standard, from department to department and from school to school.'

Finally readers will be aware of the fact that the responsibility is laid upon local education authorities in England and Wales by the Education Act of 1944 which makes it essential for schools to keep careful and detailed records.

THE KEEPING OF RECORDS

The 1951 Statutory Instruments 1743; School Grants Regulations No. 71 for primary and secondary schools clearly states:

'Whenever a pupil ceases to attend the school and becomes a pupil at any other school or place of education or training . . . adequate medical and educational information concerning him shall be supplied to other persons conducting that other school or place.'

I have attempted to show in this introduction how the keeping of records will enable the teacher to help the children more effectively.

Before outlining in detail how these records may be most efficiently compiled, I must stress that records are of *particular* importance to teachers of backward children. Before attempting to remedy backwardness it is essential that the teacher should first study the *causes* of backwardness. It may be that the causation of backwardness is to be found in the home, in the child's physical or emotional state in the school or because the child's interests and special needs have not been catered for. In these cases, when the causes of his backwardness have been investigated and remedied he may make more rapid progress towards more normal attainments.

On the other hand the backwardness may be caused by dullness and here the teacher would be very unwise to attempt to force him to attain the standard of a child of normal intelligence.

If full records of the children in a backward class have been faithfully kept the distinction between backwardness caused primarily by dullness and the backwardness which has mainly non-intellectual causes may be made and the individual needs of the members of the class thus effectively catered for.

The teacher taking over a new class or starting in a new school will wish to know the sources from which she can obtain information about her children and these are some of them.

Perhaps the most important and most obvious source of information is the children's previous teacher(s). It sometimes happens that she is taking over from a teacher who has left the school. If good records on each child have been kept then she is greatly helped. If, however, no records have been kept she may attempt to contact the teacher and this is not always easy. It is not unknown for a class to have two or even three teachers in a year, all of whom have left without passing on records of their children and in this case the teacher is faced with a formidable task if she attempts to contact them all.

Other sources of information include the school medical record card, noted conversations with parents, various members of the ancillary services, the Head teacher of the school, various correspondence from Child Guidance Clinics and other sources, information from previous schools, the local authority's record card, record books, etc.

Having gathered together as complete a picture of her children as is possible, the teacher will ask what should she begin to record (bearing in mind that her time is limited and that the records must be of value to her and the future teachers of her children) and how this recording should be done.

Obviously there can be no set method of recording for all practising teachers but I would like to come to the aid of this teacher by telling her of a system of recording which we are carrying on in a large junior mixed school.

For the sake of clarity I propose to divide this review into two parts; records of educational progress and personal records. I will show at the end how all this information can be contained in the compact form of a record card.

All teachers in the school keep a 'week's work' record book; this contains a forecast of work to be carried out by a particular class for a week. This forecast is useful not only to the class teacher but also to the headmaster and relief teacher if the teacher concerned is absent for a few days.

At the same time, the teacher can look back and discover from comments against the summaries what work needs revision and what activities have proved to be the most popular. Hence this book proves a very valuable guide to us if we are taking the same or a similar class the following year, or to the class's next teacher.

In addition to this book which contains a summary of activities undertaken in all subjects, a 'progress book' is kept which contains details of the work carried out by individuals in the class, mainly in the basic subjects.

I find it useful to make a horizontal list of all material used in reading, writing and number. This is ticked off against the child's name as completed and comments such as 'much practice needed in

THE KEEPING OF RECORDS

money recognition' (dated), with perhaps a later comment, also dated, 'much more proficient at recognition of money – can now recognize pounds, shillings, pence – ready for more formal work', are added when necessary.

On the reading page of this progress book besides details of books read, apparatus used with dates, I record briefly any errors made in reading especially if they fall into a particular pattern, for example reversals. These observations are dated so that I can see at a later stage if progress is being made in overcoming these difficulties. A note is kept of the child's attitude to reading, speed of reading and degree of comprehension of material being read.

In the same way on the arithmetic page we record processes mastered, knowledge of time, measure, capacity and so on.

Full details of the results of standardized and other tests are recorded and difficulties discovered through diagnostic tests are noted.

We have found that the children like to keep their own records and this they do in reading, writing, spelling and number with my help. Some of the information recorded by the children is already recorded by me in a slightly different manner in my 'progress book', however, an error is sometimes made in the book and my boys and girls very quickly 'show Sir where he is wrong' after consulting their cards. At the same time I have found that it gives children a feeling of pride to actually see their progress from one book or one set of work to another.

The children have been using the Gertrude Keir's 'Adventures in reading' series which in the early books has sixteen pages.

The reading progress card in use is illustrated. My children use the work book and read to me page by page. As each page is successfully read a tick is put in the adjoining column and at the end of the reading the child date stamps his card which he then keeps in his book. At the next reading there is revision and the next pages are read and progress recorded by the child in the same manner. Adjustment in the number of pages on the card is necessary when the more difficult books of the series are being read.

The cards are produced in craft lessons and the measuring exercise is helped when the child realizes that the object of the lesson is to produce something of value to him.

Name of Child..

READING PROGRESS CARD

	Book 1	Book 2	Book 3	Book 4	Book 5	Book 6
page 2						
page 3						
page 4						
page 5						
page 6						
page 7						
page 8						
page 9						
page 10						
page 11						
page 12						
page 13						
page 14						
page 15						
page 16						

THE KEEPING OF RECORDS

It is always rather difficult for children to record progress made in written work. I have made a large number of graded question cards with attractive coloured pictures which we call 'Quiz cards'. In addition I have produced a number of question books, missing-word cards, jigsaw puzzles, 'mystery boxes', matching cards and other material.

In all there are over 200 pieces of material in daily use and we wondered how we could keep a check on what stage had been reached and what material had been completed.

After some discussion we designed a writing record card which the children cyclostyled and pasted into the cover of their writing books. They tick off work as completed and children who are completing assignments on say 'Quiz cards' can readily see what stage they have reached and find the next card.

This is the writing record card in use:

WRITING RECORD CARDS
'QUIZ' CARDS

1	2	3	4	5	6	7	8	9	10	11	12	13	14	15	16	17	18	19	20
21	22	23	24	25	26	27	28	29	30	31	32	33	34	35	36	37	38	39	40
41	42	43	44	45	46	47	48	49	50	51	52	53	54	55	56	57	58	59	60
61	62	63	64	65	66	67	68	69	70	71	72	73	74	75	76	77	78	79	80
81	82	83	84	85	86	87	88	89	90	91									

Books

1	2	3	4	5	6	7	8	9	10

Question Cards

1a	2a	3a	4a	5a	6a	7a	8a	9a	10a	11a	12a	13a	14a	15a	16a

Missing Word Cards

1	2	3	4	5	6	7	8	9	10

Question Cards

1	2	3	4	5	6	7	8	9	10

Question Books

1	2	3	4	5	6	7	8	9	10

Any other work

The children use picture dictionaries to help them with spelling but they find that they frequently need to use words like television, night, play, aunt, uncle, house, mother, father, watched, etc. They are encouraged to learn these words and record them in little spelling books easily made in craft lessons with sugar paper and kitchen paper.

In number work the children use a card, similar in shape and size to the reading progress card, on which they record all work done. They keep this card with their number workbook.

I have always found that when children derive little or no benefit from these cards they are readily 'lost' or become tattered or scribbled upon. During the long period that these cards have been in use very few such losses have occurred and the cards are kept in a very good condition.

So using this number record card the children can readily follow their progress from an arithmetic card to a more difficult arithmetic card, through the 'money recognition' stages, the measuring schemes and the time recognition apparatus.

Most teachers of backward children are now convinced of the need for understanding the child's home background and in beginning the section on the type of personal records that we keep of our children I would like to outline the records we keep that enable us to understand the environment in which the children spend the greater part of their lives.

We record all personal details in a section of our progress books allowing sufficient pages for each child to cover comments spaced over a period of one year.

In the home environment columns we include details of occupation(s) of parents, size of family, education of the child's siblings, the attitude of the child's parents to the child and to his school, details of any meetings and conversations with his parents; and the contents of parents' letters and telephone messages, especially where they give a clue to the child's difficulties, are recorded.

For instance Tommy, Fred and Mary may be giving us some concern because of their attitude to reading. They may have the ability to read reasonably well and yet in spite of our efforts show little interest in reading.

Comments by their parents such as: 'My husband and I were never good at reading, so we tell Tommy not to bother about it', or 'Oh, yes, our Fred will soon be catching up with his reading, we teach him for one hour every evening while his younger brother, who is a better reader, watches television', or (an actual example told to a teacher at a parents' meeting), 'Well, I know Mary is very backward and can read only a few words, but we have bought a complete set of *Encyclopaedia Britannica* to help her and we aim to get her to read a page every evening': give to the teacher a valuable insight into the home attitudes and such recorded facts are of great help to the children's future teachers.

Records are kept in this section of the type of lessons and activities that a child finds interesting. I have found time and time again that backward children are extremely interested in one particular aspect of school life and yet often a long period of time elapses after they have joined a new class before that interest is revealed. How often have I heard a teacher say, usually somewhere towards the end of the summer term, 'I never knew that Sammy was so interested in nature study – since we started our nature walks he has really come to life, his general work has improved as well, Oh! if only I had known this before, it's a pity he's leaving my class next month.'

A child recently came into my class who was said to have no interests and I did, in fact, find him particularly unresponsive. I decided to observe him closely over a period of time when I hoped that he would reveal an interest in one of the many classroom occupations and activities.

For some weeks my observations were unsuccessful until one day we obtained a new book dealing with prehistoric animals. The boy soon revealed, in no uncertain way, that he had an amazing knowledge of this subject. I naturally encouraged this interest and apart from making little books entitled *Animals of Long Ago*, he toured the school giving lecturettes on this topic and astounded pupils and teachers with his knowledge. He told me he had become interested in prehistoric animals after seeing a film about them.

Such was 'the dull boy with no interests'. The development of this interest was recorded and I feel sure will give an insight on his character and temperament to his future teachers.

Besides recording details of the child's home background and interests we record our observations of his social relations pattern.

In the classroom we note whether Tommy forms a member of a fairly stable group, the group's attitude towards him and his attitude to the group; whether he leads in group activities or is a follower, his acceptance or otherwise of group tasks and group decisions; his response to a difficulty or a difficult situation, for example when it is in the interest of the group that he should perform a task in which he is not interested or which is even repulsive to him.

We especially observe play habits and in free choice sessions where the children are provided with a wide range of activities from which they can choose, we note their choice of activity, their span of concentration on their particular choice and the type of group play they participate in.

THE KEEPING OF RECORDS

In other sessions we note Tommy's experiments with raw and crude material, for example, clay and plasticine. We watch for his attention and effort, the type of situation in which he is profoundly interested.

From time to time we carry out playground observations. Often little is gained from them but occasionally they reveal a pointer to the child's true personality and the cause of his difficulties of adjustment in the classroom.

Naturally the teacher who has a class of thirty-two children as I have, will not be able to observe them all, but I usually select a dozen or so children for close study in the playground. Experience is the only true guide in this process of selection but as an example I would want to observe a child who, in class, tended to isolate himself. It would be of great help to me if I could see whether in the 'free' atmosphere of the playground this tendency towards isolation was continued or not.

The teacher carrying out these observations has to make his true object unknown and with the typical curiosity of the junior child this is by no means always easy. I find it a good idea to begin by making short notes while on playground duty and then later to stroll around the playground some distance from the child being observed.

Playground observation is a technique which the humourless, unimaginative teacher intent on 'chasing and catching his bird' will find hard to acquire.

What things do I look for in these observations and what do I record? Here are a few of the things I have in mind when I come on to the playground armed with my pencil, jotter and sense of proportion.

Firstly the child's social relations pattern: Does he play with anybody? Is he isolated or does he tend to isolate himself? Whom does he play with? Whom does he group with? Does he play with children of his own age and class, or older or younger or more intelligent children? Does his chosen group generally accept him or reject him. Does he lead or follow? In what situations does he lead? Is he excessively aggressive or timid in his play? Does he 'bully' other children or is he bullied? In what situation is his interest aroused? Are his chosen groups pretty much the same or does he tend to flit from group to group? Does he 'buy friendship' or is his friendship purchased? Is his play imaginative? How much is the same play pattern repeated? Does he spend an abnormal amount of time with the adult in the playground? What action does he take when he comes into conflict with his group and what is their reaction to his action?

Other points are noted and I usually manage to decipher my hurried scribble and rescue my cup of coffee before work recommences.

It is hardly necessary to add that one short playground observation is of little use but that the true value comes in spreading out a number of such observations over a period so that they may be compared and changes in play habits noted, often giving an indication of the changes taking place within the child himself.

The fourth type of personal record we keep of our children is the physical or health record. It is, unfortunately, by no means unknown for teachers to be completely unaware of minor or even serious physical defects in their children with often grave consequences for the child.

For example a child may be partially deaf or suffer from seasonal catarrhal deafness. He may be short-sighted and will need to sit quite near the teacher and the blackboard. These are obvious examples where the teacher's knowledge of the child's defect is absolutely essential.

Other examples, perhaps not so obvious (such as a child who has a history of nocturnal enuresis, often indicating emotional disturbance; long stay in hospital; siblings with grave diseases such as pulmonary tuberculosis and so on), may be given to show the necessity for the teacher to know full details of the children's physical history and condition.

In my own experience I have known many dull and backward children who have gone to great lengths to hide the fact that they should be wearing spectacles or hearing aids.

Often when such children go into a new class it may be weeks or months before Johnny, who teachers maintain is a poor reader and 'doesn't seem to be getting on' is found, perhaps by casual conversation with his parent, to be suffering from severe myopia.

Again the shy or withdrawn child may be fearful of telling the teacher that she is unable to hear properly. Mothers may justly protest at having to write to every new teacher Joan has informing them that she had a serious leg injury in infancy and thus missed a lot of schooling in the second year of the infant stage just at the time she was beginning to read, this being one cause of her backwardness.

In fact some teachers, as we know, only receive such information at parents' meetings held towards the end of the year and possibly this situation is re-enacted every year of the child's school career!

How then can we, or dare we, blame the parents in such a situation which is by no means unknown in schools. The blame lies fairly and squarely on the shoulders of the teacher(s) or school(s) that failed to record this information.

Under the heading of physical or medical history what then do we record? Firstly we summarize the facts on the school medical card. The school medical officer is usually only too pleased to answer any queries. Our own S.M.O. is most co-operative and answers all our queries, and he recently spent part of his lunch hour talking to us about medical cards and how to obtain information from them.

We obtain information on the child in his early years from the Health Visitor, who has information, which she has recorded, on parental attitudes, home circumstances, siblings, diet and feeding, illnesses, treatment, attendance at clinics, etc.

The Health Visitor is often the school nurse and, therefore, will have an excellent knowledge of the child and his home from his earliest days. She is very often in school and will be found to be most helpful to the teacher, greatly enriching her knowledge of the child.

We record our observations of the children's muscular balance and control, their walking, skipping, hopping and balancing. I always carefully watch for any defects in vision, hearing, speech and any signs of excessive tiredness, or apathy and apart from recording any signs of abnormality ensure that the S.M.O. is speedily informed.

A note is kept of attendance at clinics with details of any treatment given, incontinence is noted and the letters 'S' or 'H.A.' are put against the name of any child who should be wearing spectacles or a hearing aid.

I have tried to show how a complete and full record of each child; what he has been taught, his absorption or otherwise of that teaching, his home background, his function as a member of a group and physical details, can be gradually built up.

The practising teacher will readily recognize the situation where some speedy, factual information on a child is called for. An enquiry is made by telephone about a particular child and a summary of all this information gathered painstakingly together is of great help.

After some discussion we decided to produce a record card for each child in the school who could be said to be receiving 'Special Educational Treatment'.

It was agreed that the card should be designed to cover the four years of the child's life in the junior school. We were to record the following information on this card: name, address, date of birth, position in family, schools attended, names of class teachers and classes, physical details, results of intelligence and standardized attainment tests, books actually read by the child, details of home circumstances, occupations of parents, the results of teachers' observations of the child's behaviour, interests, attitude to work, other children, etc. (A copy of this card is given as an appendix at the end of this chapter.)

With each set of cards was an instruction leaflet:

Tests for Special Educational Treatment Pupils

It is essential in order to understand a child's difficulties, to measure his progress and to plan a programme suited to his needs that he is regularly given standardized tests in intelligence and general attainments. Intelligence tests will be given annually and attainment tests once every term.

The results of these tests, together with physical details and other information will be recorded on the S.E.T. record card.

The following tests will be used:
Reading. Schonell's mechanical reading test.
Spelling. Schonell's test. Form A.
Arithmetic. Schonell's mechanical arithmetic test. Form A.

Any intelligence test used should be named, the result recorded and dated.

The book being read by the child at the time of the test should be briefly noted, e.g. $\frac{H.V.}{1}$ or $\frac{J \text{ and } J.}{4}$

RECORD CARD FOR S.E.T. PUPILS

Name	d. of b.	Posn. in family	Address	Schools attended

Class		Class		Class		Class	
Teacher		Teacher		Teacher		Teacher	
1961–1962		1962–1963		1963–1964		1964–1965	

Physical

Intellectual
- Int.
- R. A.
- S. A.
- A. A.
- Book

Other Information	Home circumstances,	behaviour,	attitude to work,	other children, etc.

All information should be dated and the source of information given, e.g. 12.12.57. (Mother)..............................

It is important that these record cards should be carefully locked away and any information on them should only be supplied to the headmaster, child's next teacher, etc.

At the end of each school year we are thus enabled to pass on our record books and cards to the children's next teachers and they are thereby given a complete picture of the children they are to teach *at the beginning of the school year*; we feel that by these means not only are we helping each other as teachers but we can more readily understand and efficiently teach our children than if we had no system of recording.

I would like to end with a most interesting quotation from a book which will be found on the shelves of most teachers' libraries. It comes from the 1944 *Handbook of Suggestions for Teachers*:

'The wholly satisfactory form of record has yet to be devised. If it is to be of real help to the teacher in his work, as it should be, it will not be over elaborate, nor entail excessive clerical labour; it will be more concerned with the points in which a child differs from his fellows than with those in which he belongs to the common average; it will give information, on the one hand, about the permanent factors in his make-up, his health, his physical defects, if any, and the nature of his home, his temperament, his native ability, and on the other, it will deal with the changes represented by the successive stages of achievement; it will whenever possible be based upon objective standards of assessment rather than depend on personal impressions; and it will be wide enough in scope to enable the reader to form some picture of the development of the child as a whole.'

Book List

ABRAMSON, J., *L'Enfant et L'Adolescent Instables*, Presses Universitaires de France.
ALLEN, W. C., *Cumulative Pupils' Records* (National Foundation for Educational Research in England and Wales), Newnes.
ATKINSON, M., *Junior School Community*, Longmans, Green and Co.

THE KEEPING OF RECORDS

BOWLBY, J., *Child Care and the Growth of Love*, Penguin Books.
BURT, SIR CYRIL, *Mental and Scholastic Tests*, U.L.P.
— *The Backward Child*, U.L.P.
Council for Curriculum Reform, *The Content of Education*, U.L.P.
CUTTY, H., *Learning and Teaching in the Junior School*, Methuen.
Education and Mental Health, UNESCO.
FLEMING, DR C. M., *Cumulative Records*, U.L.P.
— *Research and the Basic Curriculum*, U.L.P.
— *The Social Psychology of Education*, U.L.P.
FREEMAN, F. S., *Individual Differences*, Harrap.
GLASSET, W., *Educational Development of Children*, U.L.P.
GREENE and JORGENSEN, *The Use and Interpretation of Elementary School Tests*, Longmans.
Handbook of Suggestions for Teachers, 1946, H.M.S.O.
HAMLEY, H. R., *Educational Guidance of the School Child*, Evans.
— *The Testing of Intelligence*, Evans.
HIGHFIELD, M. E., *The Education of Backward Children*, Harrap.
HUGHES and HUGHES, *Learning and Teaching*, Longmans.
HUME, E. G., *Learning and Teaching in the Infants School*, Longmans, Green and Co.
HUNT and SMITH, *A Guide to Intelligence and Other Psychological Testing*, Evans.
Report of an Investigation of Backward Children in Birmingham, City of Birmingham Stat. Dept., 1920.
School Records of Individual Development, H.M.S.O.
ISAACS, S., *Psychological Aspects of Child Development*, Evans.
Ministry of Education Circular 151, 1947.
RASMUSSEN, V., *The Primary School Child*, Gyldendal.
SCHONELL, F. J., *Backwardness in the Basic Subjects*, Oliver and Boyd.
STRANG, R., *Every Teachers' Records*, Columbia University Press.
TRAXLER, A. E., *Techniques of Guidance*, Harper.
WALKER, A. S., *Pupils' School Records*, National Foundation for Educational Research in England and Wales, Newnes.
WARR, E. W., *The New Era in the Junior School*, Methuen.

CYRIL E. SAUNDERS

Chapter XII

EQUIPMENT AND APPARATUS

Good teachers can succeed with little or no material aids and few tools – at a price. But the teacher who can do as well by the pupils, without detriment to health, is indeed a genius – particularly if the pupils are backward.

Artists need a wide variety of tools in order to perfect a piece of work; the right tool for the specific work simplifies the task itself to some extent even though it may still remain difficult.

In recent years many and varied tools have been added to the teacher's kitbag at a bewildering speed. Each undoubtedly has a specific purpose; each will yield the best results only when the artist has perfected his skill in using it, understands the purpose for which it is designed and uses it on suitable material.

Too many of our tools have been thrown aside or fallen into disrepute because these three vital qualifications are overlooked by many teachers. Even more pupils suffer because teachers continue to use indiscriminately as many aids as possible in the optimistic assumption that the very act of using a tool is synonymous with using it correctly.

But all aids are a potential source of danger. It is quite obvious that the surgeon's scalpel is often a means of saving life but in the hands of the inexperienced could as easily be a lethal weapon. Teachers deal with less tangible material but it is equally true that while equipment and apparatus in the hands of a careful teacher often make the difference between success and failure, it will also bring disaster in its train if used indiscriminately; it is advisable to keep firmly in mind the fact that equipment and apparatus can never be a substitute for the teacher. The master hand must always select and guide the tool.

The analogy of an artist and his material is not really a happy

EQUIPMENT AND APPARATUS

one in considering education since it infers that the active part is that of the teacher while the pupil is passive material. Actually the relationship is a working partnership with equal activity on either side if it is to be satisfactory.

The backward child has found his part too difficult to carry out in the ordinary course of school work. It may be due to innate causes or to force of circumstances, but in either case he needs additional help of rather a special nature, and much of the equipment now available has been designed to supply that help.

The dull child is mentally immature and has the same need of concrete aids as the young child – though that is where the similarity ceases; to equate a dull 8-year-old with an average 6-year-old because they have the same mental age would be a serious oversimplification. But naturally almost identical equipment is to be found in use with backward junior children as with infants in the modern infant room, so that many of the suggestions which follow will be quite familiar to those who have any knowledge of infant teaching. Even so the actual use and purpose may differ significantly and it may be well worth while to make one more observation before passing to more detailed considerations.

The use of apparatus with normal children is usually confined to a specific teaching point but it plays a far more vital role in the education of slower children who must learn consciously many things which come easily to their more fortunate fellows. Social training, as Mr Bannister emphasized, is acquired slowly and painfully only as the result of patient and careful teaching which must go on all the time, every day, and take precedence over academic studies however important they may be. In designing aids for backward children care should be taken to see that as many as possible do perform the double function of furthering academic studies and assisting social education.

The following pages are written with a dual purpose in mind – to widen the concept of what constitutes apparatus and at the same time to focus attention on the vital part teaching aids actually play in the education of dull and backward children. Apparatus in connexion with the teaching of these children is now such an accepted fact that it is rapidly becoming a habit – a dangerous state of affairs for once an action becomes automatic it is no longer vital and flexible and its results are taken for granted.

The use of apparatus is not simply a question of the teacher's choice but an unchangeable necessity made so by the very nature of the dull child's learning process. The teacher may reject apparatus, or may through inexperience, prejudice or plain lack of thought, ignore the issues involved in its use, but this does not alter the situation. The degree of success and the ease with which the dull child acquires his education depends upon the teacher's realization of the function of apparatus and its potentialities for good and ill.

But fundamental principles must be translated into terms of classroom practice. A true conception of the educational value is of little use if the teacher is unable to bridge the gap between theory and practice, and for this reason the underlying principles are placed in juxtaposition to concrete suggestions in the hope that the reader will find a stimulus to thought on the one hand and action on the other.

General Equipment

This section confines its attention to materials and standard equipment needed by all backward classes, and is largely self-evident. Even so some points of interest often overlooked may justify its inclusion.

First the room itself may not be ideal for the purpose, and in many cases inconvenience will have to be endured for a time at least, but teachers should take stock of the position, make such improvements as are immediately possible and work towards the others which are desirable. A philosophical acceptance of unsuitable conditions means the perpetuation of those conditions; authorities already have more than enough demands upon their financial resources and they certainly will not look for other worthy causes. But the dull child should at least be on the list, even if in fairness he must take his turn with other children, and it is the duty of those who understand his needs to plead his cause.

Dingy paint in drab colours casts a gloom over the brightest spirit, and many dull and backward children are already depressed and miserable to some extent before they enter the classroom. In most children there is a strong reaction to colour and emotional satisfaction is derived from bright clean paint. Harmony is another matter and the question of education is involved here, but three points are worth considering. There is no justification for assuming that because a child uses the most shattering colour schemes in its own efforts, poor colour schemes in the decoration of the room do not matter. The effect may be subconscious but it is none the less there. Development of taste is a part of education and though at first a child may be quite unable to distinguish between good, mediocre and poor colour schemes he should have before him only the best as a permanent example. The teacher, too, does not remain unaffected by surroundings and is likely to contend far more successfully with the endless demands made by the children if the room is bright with attractive paint. Inspiration takes many guises and we do not often stop to analyse it, otherwise we might have been a little more careful in the past over school decorations. There are many hundreds of dull and backward children still working in the shadow of dirty, shabby depressing walls. Audible protests oft repeated are needed; redecoration is not a luxury. Meanwhile as much as possible of the area can be covered with large sheets of attractively coloured paper on which is mounted some of the children's work. Display panels of hardboard battened on the walls are also useful and not too expensive.

Ideally the room should have access to the grounds, be near the cloakroom and have a fitted sink with water supply. Few existing buildings will have these facilities but the room given to the dull and backward class is often a matter of habit and possibly conditions could be improved by a change of location. Water and cloakroom facilities do seriously affect the educational programme as well as the smooth running of the class.

Dull children need full-time supervision in the early years, with constant encouragement towards self-control, and support from their teacher in their efforts to take responsibility. They must also be helped and taught many of the social observances which bright children acquire much more easily and have often learned before reaching school age.

It is much more difficult to arrange a programme for the gradual training in self-control, which is so vital for the dull child, if cloakroom and water supply are at a distance from the classroom. The teacher's control will need to be extended over a longer period so that a reasonable level of behaviour is maintained in both cloakroom and classroom, which means that individual self-control will take longer to get established. Free and individual use of these rooms should be the ultimate goal but it will only be achieved if in the early stages the teacher exercises full-time but unobtrusive supervision over both, and obviously this is much easier where the geography of the building is convenient.

A sink and water supply in the classroom is an improvement which should be regarded as a priority. Water is needed for so many activities apart from washing that a tremendous waste of time can occur, or both activities and cleanliness may suffer, when it is in a distant cloakroom. Supervision is essential – especially as water is an attractive element and lends itself to a variety of interesting if illegitimate experiments. The pivot of special educational treatment is that it should be adapted to each individual's needs in order that that child shall realize its full potentialities however limited these may be. The teacher has therefore to utilize every opportunity for the development of self-confidence, self-control and self-reliance. These seem at first sight to have little relationship to a sink in the classroom, but if each child is to have the chance of taking increasing responsibility for himself and his needs equipment must be so arranged that he can have unrestricted access to it as the need arises. A sink situated outside the classroom curtails this freedom for obvious reasons: the individuals of a whole class cannot be constantly going in and out of their room, and any organization aimed at a compromise usually assigns more responsibility to a few members and often absolves others completely.

The system of monitors and duty rotas is quite satisfactory in dealing with ordinary children but it is much less so for the dull. They do not easily transfer a past experience to assist a present problem, and the common thread running through every aspect of their education is the need for a constant routine and daily practice over a long period. The implications here have a direct bearing on the practice of monitors. The slow child can be trained to be a very efficient monitor and he will carry his responsibility quite as well as many average children while the job lasts, but the transference of a sense of responsibility from a specific task to a general sense of responsibility for self is a difficult step for those of limited intelligence. A restricted system of monitors is necessary and has its uses but generally it is advisable to give each child from the beginning the duty of being responsible for himself and his own needs in so far as he can deal with them. There is then no question of transference – his training will be directly in line with what is required of him eventually.

Water is needed for such activities as painting, pasting, modelling, cleaning tools, etc., and washing hands at intervals, and as much of the work is individual or group work there is no lesson in which some child may not require one or the other. This provides many daily opportunities for the dull child to organize himself, think for himself, and learn to care for the equipment he uses. It also gives valuable practice in social aspects, for each child can have the free run of the classroom with all that this entails in terms of give and take, and the self-control which each must exercise for the good of all. Hence the sink and water supply in the classroom is a most important item of equipment in the room for E.S.N. children.

Furniture

Most people will agree that light easily moved furniture should be the order of the day; in addition the desk tops must be flat and washable. While it is unthinkable that education should be restricted because the furniture might suffer by some of the messier pursuits (and nearly all pursuits become messy in the hands of some children), it is also essential that proper care of equipment and tools should form a vital part of training.

Polished wood is not the ideal surface; the children can manage the necessary cleaning with due supervision but it involves unnecessary time and work. Washable paint or one of the modern plastic materials is much more satisfactory and has the additional merit of being more attractive to young eyes.

The child's desk should be his 'own' and must be a place in which he can store his private possessions. Many tables have no locker or drawer; compromise can be made by giving a drawer elsewhere in the room but this is not so effective. It entails much more running about, usually means crowding the class into one spot in the room and has not the same feeling of privacy; it is this last point which is most important.

Many of these children do not know the meaning of privacy and ownership. It is only pride of possession which in the first instance makes us take care of things; it is not till later when a higher level of social development is reached that the majority of people take more care of others' property than of their own. A child who has not been given some corner of his own to care for, and property of his own to look after, cannot be expected to develop a moral regard for 'mine' and 'thine', nor a consideration for property in general as a part of normal social living.

For this reason it is not only important to give each child his own desk, making him responsible for its care, but as far as it is practicable he should also have charge of all the books and minor tools he will need for constant use.

All equipment issued to a child must be in good condition at the start and marked with the owner's name by the teacher to ensure that no one can take another's property when his own is mislaid. All children experience a thrill when they are given something completely new and the impulse to take care of it is there, if only temporarily, so an effort should be made to see that each one does occasionally have the satisfaction of really new books or equipment. It is each child's duty to see that all his property is kept in the condition in which it was received but it needs constant vigilance on the teacher's part to ensure that this sense of responsibility is gradually acquired so that in time care of property becomes a habit.

Often children reach the secondary stage never having had an opportunity of gaining a 'property sense' This is a serious matter because the early years are the most formative, and habits acquired in the infant and junior school years are the ones which are likely to be indelibly imprinted in the child's character and conduct.

Most young children find it difficult at first to reach the required standard; there will be lost books, broken tools, dirty crumpled reading books or torn dog-eared workbooks. Lessons will be delayed while the hunt for missing articles proceeds, and the teacher will often be tempted to take over the safe-keeping of all equipment. Certainly the immediate result of collecting and giving out for each

EQUIPMENT AND APPARATUS

lesson or session would be a much better arrangement academically but it would be a great loss educationally and a confession of failure in one of the most important parts of true education.

The success of the system of individual responsibility will depend largely upon unremitting vigilance by the teacher who will have to evolve some code of regulations and penalties for lapses. The aim should be to encourage and it is wise to take measures to avoid failure rather than disciplinary action when failure has occurred. Timely reminders of what will be needed for the lesson will focus attention on equipment in advance. A warning when the signal to clear up is given will remind the children to check up on their tools and to carry out cleaning efficiently. Definite times must be set aside for duties; the dull child cannot be expected to plan his own time even in the personal details. He should know that at certain fixed times in the day hands have to be washed, pencils sharpened or shoes brushed, etc. His should be the responsibility for remembering to do these things but not of arranging his time to fit them in. The time allocated must be sufficient to allow a certain amount of freedom, and two or three duties to be fitted into one period is better training than allotting a short time to each separately.

But in spite of all precautions, encouragement and patience, there may be times when disciplinary action is necessary; too much patience over a long period and after warnings, can be mistaken for softness by the child and there must be a dividing line between patience and excessive lenience. If, after making allowance for limited intelligence, poor memory, and other relevant factors, it is plain that the child is not co-operating, more pressure must be brought to bear. Each case needs to be considered on its own merits but the deciding factor in any disciplinary measure will be that the offender suffers inconvenience as a result of his own action. Unrelated punishment does not make nearly such a strong impression as being thwarted by something one has done oneself. Lost pencils and mislaid plimsols are a fruitful source of trouble and the frequent offender often makes an effort if he is forced to sit still and do nothing when the others are engaged in an attractive activity. The vital points here are that he should be attracted by the lesson and the teacher must see that he literally has nothing to do. Boredom is far more potent than any alternative work. The action should be taken with as little fuss as possible; words mean little to the dull child and homilies are only a waste of everybody's time besides giving attention and a certain amount of limelight to the offender who may like the feeling of importance.

There are several such devices which can be used without the child feeling that he has a legitimate grievance against the teacher. Properly handled he will see that it is cause and effect and this is the first step towards future co-operation. Punishment as such is only an appeal to fear and it spoils the essential relationship between teacher and pupil often without achieving the real end towards which it is directed.

Training the E.S.N. child is a long, slow and very gradual process but juniors are fundamentally anxious to please, readily co-operate and respond whole-heartedly to encouragement. Provided the teacher recognizes their very real limitations of memory and keeps the demands within their power to fulfil, the gradual growth of control is assured and training becomes the positive and interesting activity which it should be.

Returning to the question of desks there is one last point to be made. Most rooms are furnished with dual desks or tables; a few single units are advisable. Emotional balance and power of concentration are naturally weak points with slower children and seating so that temptations are reduced to a minimum is wise. This is much easier where some seats are not in pairs; single desks can easily be moved together when groups are needed or the children are engaged in work which permits consultation but dual desks cannot be separated when temporary loss of control or lack of concentration requires a measure of isolation. With a single desk at hand many essentially constructive measures can be taken without recourse to disciplinary action which is often undesirable. Many lapses on the children's part and consequent punitive action on the teacher's would be avoided by the use of a single desk.

The modern approach rightly advocates working together and encourages children to discuss with each other the problems they are trying to solve. There are great advantages in this method, for co-operative effort demands self-control and assists in the development of many of the more worthwhile character traits, but there are also drawbacks when the class in question is dull and backward,

EQUIPMENT AND APPARATUS

and the children may already have spent some time in school in unsuitable classes. Character will be unformed and moral values uncertain at the best.

The child will probably copy or get his work done by a friend who is slightly better; he will not know how to work for himself, nor understand that the teacher is only asking for his best and not waiting to punish him for something which is beyond his control. This attitude to work and school which is prevalent among those who have had to fend for themselves in ordinary classes, must be corrected if the child is to make headway in any direction. Words are largely wasted in the face of dull intellect and painful recollections of past failures, so the teacher's problem is to prove to the child, despite himself, that success is possible to him.

But the child is his own worst enemy in this programme, and his comrades with the best motives of comradeship will aid and abet, so that it is very difficult when children are sharing a desk for the teacher to see that each child makes his own effort. Anything in the nature of displeasure or punishment simply confirms the child's previous assessment of the situation and it will do nothing to establish the confident relationship which is needed between teacher and pupil. The difficulty need not arise at all if the room is furnished with some single desks. Those who are finding difficulty in working for themselves can be placed far enough apart to make furtive collusion impossible, and open attempts are the signal for the teacher to give a helping hand in a constructive manner.

In addition to desks it is helpful to have one or two large tables for handwork, cutting out, and group work of various kinds, and for the laying out of materials, etc., which are needed for lessons in which the children will help themselves as they need them. Library shelves or bookcases are also essential; they must be easily accessible to the children so that they can be used freely at any time without a major disturbance in the room. The practice of piling books on a shelf in the cupboard, or standing them along the shelf in a double row is not a good compromise even when space is very short. It is usually not convenient and certainly not wise to have several children in the cupboard at once; sooner or later with the best of intentions – or the worst – someone will drop the books on the floor. A shelf, or better still, shelves give the child the opportunity of looking through the books comfortably; he is not in anyone's way and feels much more adult when the library looks like a library even if the books are very simple.

Two shelves in different parts of the room are very convenient. They separate the children when several want to change at once, and the books can be graded into easy and less easy. Where this organization is used an indication of the different grades of difficulty should be given the class, but it is generally better not to stipulate which one any particular child should use after he has passed the initial reading stage. There is in any case an overlapping of difficulty however carefully the books are graded and with older juniors self-respect must be preserved at all costs. Usually the child will go to the shelf most suited to his ability if left alone, and a tactful suggestion about the interest of a certain book can be made to those who continue to choose unwisely.

There should be a library shelf even where few can make any attempt at reading. Books attract all children unless experience has turned the attraction to distaste, and picture-books with captions can give a lot of pleasure – and knowledge – to the non-reader. With odd non-readers it is often helpful to let them 'share' a book with a fairly good reader in order to hear stories, or sit with a friend who is also weak so that they can discuss the pictures and possibly pick out the captions. In the case of a young class where presumably all the children will be in the initial stages of reading work in two's or three's would be a general practice.

A good collection of picture-books with simple captions will be needed, and the interest level must cover a wide range so that the more mature non-reader will not feel an affront to his dignity. Fortunately there is now a much bigger selection of books with a pictorial bias than there used to be and some of them are quite suited to the 10-year interest level.

Expense is always a limiting factor in the choice of equipment and there are two major schools of thought where books are concerned. One postulates that with cheap editions and small books a larger selection is possible, and goes on to state that dull and backward children are hard on the books they handle so that it is less wasteful for them to spoil cheap books than the more expensive variety which cannot so easily be replaced.

EQUIPMENT AND APPARATUS

This is a practical point of view and there is a good deal of truth in it; but the other side also has a strong case. Dull and backward children need the most attractive books to encourage them to make the tremendous effort reading entails. These must be well illustrated in good colours, clearly printed and very carefully laid out. The binding must stand up to clumsy and awkward handling, for the more easily a book is damaged the less incentive there is to take care of it – especially if the spoiling occurs when the child is being as careful as he can. The constant replacement of cheap books is uneconomic, for money is being spent year after year on the same books and the original provision of a wide range of cheap books actually means the limitation of new additions, apart from the fact that most cheap books do not reach the required standard in other essentials.

It is also relevant to remember that training plays a large part in any child's attitude to books, and dull children will learn to take care of attractive books rather more quickly than of cheap editions which will not stand up even to ordinary use. It is disheartening to make a great effort and then be defeated largely through shoddy materials, and generally speaking the cheap books do not repay the dull child's greatest care. Cheap paper is porous, discolours quickly, and picks up dirt and germs very easily whereas the better books are printed on good paper with a smooth finish which is far more hygienic and remains fresh in the face of time and exposure.

To conclude the furniture section a brief consideration of storage facilities is necessary. In many, probably the majority, of rooms adequate space and arrangements for storing are still not available, and small as the point may seem, it does add enormously to the task of the teacher and has a direct bearing on the training of the children.

In theory all materials required for a lesson or session are prepared by the teacher during breaks. This is a comparatively straightforward piece of organization where an ordinary class is concerned with a definite lesson, but special classes are quite a different proposition. Even the teacher with considerable foresight is likely to find someone who wants something which has not been made available. Education of the backward is such an individual matter and not the least part is seizing the psychological moment when the pupil's interest is awakened to teach some essential point which would otherwise be lost. Putting off may be for ever losing the opportunity and yet leaving the class unattended to go to a central stock room with the complication of keys and the possibility of interrupting other lessons *en route* may not be a very feasible alternative.

A second point which involves an educational principle also arises. We are concerned with practical issues of the child's life as well as with the development of the child as a person; in fact it is through the practical that we are most likely to reach our ultimate goal and we cannot afford to let slip even the smallest opportunity of pressing home those habits in which we are trying to train the child for his life in the adult world. He will not then have everything he needs given out, prepared and generally supervised so carefully that his only concern will be the actual carrying out of his task. However simple his work and environment our civilization is such that he certainly will have to do a little thinking for himself, and some unsupervised work will be expected of him. His private life too, should be his own concern if he can possibly reach that level of independence.

All the way through school life the aim must be to help the child stand on his own feet, to think for himself as far as possible, and to be self-reliant. For him the school must be a real training ground for life because he is dependent on the teacher's efforts for his future in a way that the average child is not. By the time he reaches the top of the junior school he ought to be able to fetch what he needs for a simple task and clear up properly afterwards.

In order to allow this valuable training it is essential that there is ample accommodation in or near the classroom. This does not of course mean that nothing is prepared by the teacher; considerable organization is necessary to see that material is not wasted. A dull child cannot be expected to work out the most economical way of cutting up a large sheet of paper for example, neither is it advisable to leave such operations as mixing up paste to a child if most of the class is likely to need it. But it should be possible for every member of the class to fetch and return all minor tools as and when he needs them, and injunctions to put away should only be needed at the end of a session.

This makes for a much more natural attitude to work and gives

EQUIPMENT AND APPARATUS

valuable training in self-discipline not only in connexion with the care of tools but also in the freedom to walk about and work under normal adult conditions in the classroom. But it does necessitate adequate storage facilities; a cupboard which requires the teacher to mount on a chair to reach the top two shelves does not constitute suitable accommodation! Neither does one large cupboard into which everything can be fitted provided one has time and ingenuity and shuts the door in haste immediately the last item is in. Paper stacked in a tidy pile may look all right until someone needs a colour near the bottom of the pile, and deep drawers will hold countless small boxes of apparatus and be perfect for a tidy room till the ones at the back right-hand corner are needed in a hurry! Large cupboards are a first class snare; convenience for use by the children is the touchstone, not cubic capacity. A handyman with a few tools and a little hardboard can make quite a number of improvements even in unsuitable furniture. Large sheets of paper are a problem to stack in such a way that they are easily accessible even if a shelf of sufficient proportions is available. Certainly the most satisfactory method is to have a wooden or hardboard case which stands on end with the opening at the top. It should be sub-divided into smaller sections so that the different types of paper are separated, and if a hinged flap is fitted at the top as a lid the paper will be kept clean and undamaged to the last sheet as it is a simple matter to lift out a sheet as it is needed. It also has the advantage of not taking up cupboard space and yet not being an eye-sore in the room; this leads to a third point.

No matter how short the accommodation, miscellaneous collections on tops of cupboards, in corners, under tables or even on an exposed shelf should not be tolerated; they can be disguised.

Orange boxes are now obtainable and with a few sheets of brown paper and cardboard they can be turned into reasonably serviceable lockers with doors. Large cardboard cartons are easy to come by and are very useful. They can be suitably disguised with decorative paper by the children themselves and arranged as part of the classroom furniture. Screens made from clothes-horses serve several purposes; they may shut off a pile of boxes and at the same time provide wall space for mounting some of the children's work which often cannot find a place on the limited wall space of most rooms.

Covered screens are also invaluable for dramatic work of all kinds.

A shelf on the wall can be better utilized for library books or a nature corner than for rolls of paper, etc. These can quite as well stand in a box below the shelf and be hidden from view by a curtain. In most rooms something can and should be done to avoid the 'jumble sale' look. A classroom is not intended to sacrifice use to beauty but at least it should be sanitary and have a business-like appearance. The children are taking their own standards from what they see around them; it is not much good preaching the virtues of cleanliness in a room cluttered up with dusty collections of 'useful' material, neither is it logical to expect care and tidiness on the part of the pupils when their room gives an enduring impression of careless disorder.

Order must come first from the teacher and it is quite hopeless to attempt systematic training of children if perpetual adjustments have to be made with make-shift devices for housing materials and apparatus. No matter how far short of ideal the room may be, the teacher must make a critical survey of the facilities that do exist and then take the constructive steps mentioned above to meet essential needs. Every piece of equipment should have a permanent home sufficiently accessible for the use of the children who must be taught to keep things in their proper place from the beginning. Teachers who are not naturally systematic may find difficulty at first in themselves setting the necessary standard but self-discipline is not a bad thing, and in this case the results in the children's development and achievements will be worth it.

Materials

A detailed list of paper, etc., is unnecessary and would not be of any real value, but since paper is an indispensable article and high on the list of priorities perhaps a few comments will not be out of place for they may clarify the issues involved.

Art plays a very large part in the education of backward children. Most of their learning must be acquired through visual channels and by practical means. Not only will the child need paper, colours and various tools for experiment, but the teacher equally often finds himself in need of considerable stocks for visual presentation.

Fortunately there is now a considerable variety of paper available –

EQUIPMENT AND APPARATUS

at a price. Obviously the child should not be given expensive paper at an age and stage where he would derive as much advantage from cheap paper. But the practice of limiting these children at all stages to the cheapest paper is to be deprecated. Mr Edmonds has already criticized (in Chapter VI) the over-use for juniors of wrapping paper, and advocated sugar paper when feasible, so I will merely add that the result of work on sugar paper is usually rather better than the child's ability because it is an easy medium – a direct contrast with the wrapping paper. This is an inspiration to the child; for the few who are gifted in practical work there are many more who are weak and afraid to tackle anything because they have so often been disappointed by their own efforts.

A wide range of pastel papers, frieze papers and coloured paper is now available and a little of each in the classroom makes for richness and variety in the children's work. A new kind of paper or a different colour to work on is in itself stimulating, and while the same grey paper to be used for every piece of work on all occasions may be quite adequate for the purpose it does become a little monotonous, and on the backward child tends to have a repetitive effect where the actual work is concerned.

The same remark applies to colours. Most English construction work of which backward children are capable is made more attractive to them if they are allowed to illustrate, and indeed in the very early stages pictures are an integral part of their work. With normal children this stage occurs in the infant department where crude pastel drawings with labels or simple sentences are quite satisfying to the child and serve the purpose. But the backward child may need this type of work during most of his primary stage. It is not then advisable to continue to give him a large home-made book and crayons or powder paint; he will respond much better to materials and techniques of a higher level and it is right that he should.

If he is making his own book he will want a much more finished product and his illustrations will only satisfy him if the technique is of a more mature level than that found in the infant room. In order to achieve this, poster or tablet colours are necessary, and individual boxes of primary colours are probably one of the more important pieces of equipment for the older junior. Great improvements have recently been made in the supply of paint in a convenient form and it is now possible to obtain small cakes of tempera or poster colour which fit into handy metal holders. Such boxes are ready at a moment's notice, no preparation is needed and there is very little to clear up – neither do they take up much desk room. They are useful for diagrams and illustrations in workbooks for English, R.I., practical arithmetic and any individual work the children may be doing in nature study, geography and so on.

Such boxes are rightly condemned for any large undertaking and must never be used for that purpose, but may be regarded as a piece of equipment for the type of workbooks generally in use. It is always a pity to accept current opinion on any aspect of education, and solely on that ground consign to oblivion something which has real value if used with discrimination. Nearly all aids and equipment are in themselves potentially harmless – their eventual value in either direction depends entirely on the use to which the teacher puts them.

The control of large free movements must come first with any child and the backward child needs much more practice in these than does the average child, but he also needs to progress to smaller and more exacting movements eventually. The manipulation of a smaller brush in more accurate work is an opportunity provided it is given when the child is ready for that stage. The rebellion against small cramped and finicky work in art has led to a violent swing in the opposite direction; we are in danger of losing a sense of proportion and assuming that anything requiring care and accuracy, or any piece of work with a good finish must have been obtained by the repression of the child's vital power of expression. There is a difference between freedom of execution and careless, slovenly work, but a differentiation is not always made and the implications though slight at first sight are far-reaching when traced to a logical conclusion.

The acquisition of standards is a fundamental in education and it is one of the most difficult problems in dealing with backward children. We do not want to cramp or restrict their initial efforts in an insistence on technical efficiency for which they are not ready, but eventually they have to acquire skills which will only be mastered by careful controlled effort and a determination to succeed on their part. This is an attitude to work built up gradually, which some temperaments will find easier than others, but which will be a critical

EQUIPMENT AND APPARATUS

factor when the child faces the adult world. It is not a narrow consideration limited to the world of art and the current fashion in schools. As teachers of backward children we must utilize art, as we do all branches of the curriculum, as an opportunity for furthering the development of those character traits which we know will stand the child in good stead in later life. We cannot do this to the best advantage if we do not provide equipment and materials which make increasing demands on the child who can only meet them by the acquisition of new techniques involving some measure of self-discipline.

Minor tools play a very valuable part in the development of the co-ordination and manipulative power; as many as possible should be included in the general equipment, and the curriculum so arranged that each is brought to the attention of the children in such a way that they understand its purpose and general possibilities. A class will not all be ready to use any specific tool at a given moment but they must all have the opportunity of watching those who are being taught, and no restriction should be placed on reasonable experiment. Help is always needed with technique; complete satisfaction only comes with the mastery of the tool, and while the child should be encouraged to try for himself he should not be expected to succeed by himself. Free access to tools is only good so long as the pupils are acquiring mastery, and this can only be obtained by judicious arrangements on the part of the teacher; indiscriminate experiment with one tool after another simply results in boredom, disinclination and poor work habits.

Rulers, scissors, cardboard and stencil knives, stick printing, lino cutting and modelling tools, hammers, screwdrivers, punches and stapling machines should all be part of the standard equipment of the classroom. This is by no means an exhaustive list and does not include tools for specific crafts but just those which can be utilized for various purposes arising from the ordinary work of the children.

Daily routine tasks often involve the use of a tool, and frequently they are carried out by the teacher when a child would gain so much more from doing the job. A typical example is pencil sharpening; with due consideration for age and ability the children ought to learn to do this for themselves. Naturally the organization must ensure that where pencils are needed for a class lesson sharpening is not left till the moment for use arrives, and there is not undue waste of pencil or time – but therein lies the art of teaching. The provision of an adequate number of knives is the first essential, and a set time in the daily routine for a regular check is the second.

Successful mixing of cold water paste, mounting and pinning up of work, cleaning blackboards, arranging flowers, changing perpetual calendars, etc., are all examples of little things involving the use of apparatus or hands which provide daily exercise for backward children, and train them to be reliable and methodical in their approach to living.

Modelling materials must not be overlooked in equipping a class, and the greatest possible variety should be obtained. Some materials are more suitable for general use at certain stages but they need also to be suited to the task in hand, and the greater range the child has from which to choose the more experience he obtains and his power of discrimination develops accordingly.

Plasticine, coloured clays, sand, plaster of Paris, sawdust, soft woods and the various proprietory products should be at hand. Limited materials invariably limit scope, while unsuitable materials make any task doubly difficult and less satisfying in the achievement. The practice of modelling only in grey plasticine not only limits the child's experience in many ways but is also likely to discourage his interest in a form of education which is valuable to him.

The dull junior in his early years is no different from the average junior in his readiness to reach out for new experiences. He will welcome with zest any new modelling material presented to him; he will experiment and with help and guidance from the teacher he can achieve results which satisfy him. This in turn will give him confidence to go on and though he may never reach the heights in terms of concrete results he will have made great progress in the control and co-ordination of his hands; even more important he will have a healthy attitude towards practical work at the secondary level.

The question of exercise books also repays a little serious consideration in order to give satisfaction both to the child and the teacher, for their viewpoints are not the same and both are important. A measure of permanence is required; the child derives considerable pleasure from 'looking back' provided his work satisfies

EQUIPMENT AND APPARATUS

his own standards and shows improvement. This is a very natural attitude; intelligence may tell us that it is the actual experience of doing a piece of work that contributes to our knowledge, and that once it is finished it should not matter what happens to it, but in fact we are usually very loath to destroy anything we have done at the cost of some effort except when it falls short of our own standards. No child can be expected to maintain his enthusiasm when asked to work on loose scraps of paper which may even be destroyed before his eyes when they have served the teacher's purpose. The practice of working on odd pieces of paper can have a surprising influence even on a dull child; he may not be able to explain or realize it but he still reacts to the implied suggestion. The teacher may use the scrap because the work is of the quick rough record variety, or possibly does not really fit into any of the workbooks; or it may be a disguised test where the aim is just to check the pupils' grasp of what has been done. But the fact of using an odd piece of paper implies to the child that the work is of less importance than that carried out in books and that there is less need for care in execution.

This is an attitude which the teacher of a dull class cannot afford to encourage since these children have not the power to understand and discriminate in the way that the average child can over when certain aspects are important and when they are not. The use of loose paper therefore should be strictly limited or loose leaf covers provided so that all odd work can find a recognized place in the scheme of things.

However efficient the teacher's record of progress, it still falls short in the case of the backward child of a survey of the actual work. His steps forward are so very tiny that they are imperceptible except over a period of weeks, months and sometimes years. In these cases 'looking back' is quite as stimulating and valuable to the teacher as to the child; it is so easy to feel that the very slow child has done nothing, and such a serious injustice because his effort will have been so much greater than that of the average child. He ought therefore to receive the appropriate commendation, not, as may so easily happen, either patient toleration or actual reproof.

On the other hand the faltering uncertain footsteps of the dull child often result in disaster; the demands made on him may prove too heavy on those days when he is not up to the mark in health or temper, and a permanent record of failure is most undesirable from the child's point of view even if the teacher finds it necessary to keep it for any reason. An ordinary exercise book is not sufficiently adaptable for the backward child's needs, partly for the reasons outlined above – tearing out pages to destroy a failure is a mutilation not to be encouraged – and partly because it decreases the likelihood of a satisfactory standard. In all work involving academic effort the dull child is at a serious disadvantage because he cannot successfully grapple with the purely intellectual aspect and at the same time carry out to the best of his ability the manipulative processes involved. Any one operation at a time is all that he can deal with efficiently and the best results are achieved by separating out the several demands as far as possible.

The obvious answer seems to be two books – one with the 'composition' bias and the other with the manipulative bias. The first would be used by the child as a rough workbook in which he would make his original effort without undue regard for the writing, etc. This book would take the brunt of the red ink corrections and 'off days' while the second book would provide the satisfaction of finished work carefully set out, well written and largely correct. Normally the double labour might be considered a waste of time, and it would be with normal children, but the backward child would not in fact be doing the same thing twice over since his concentration would be directed to two entirely different aspects which he could not in any case have achieved simultaneously. Illustrations would naturally be put straight into the finished book as they make so much less demand on the child's powers and would only be boring repetition if drawn twice. This two-book method also covers the problem of constructive correction of work.

Books with ten double pages are ample for backward children. Thicker ones are a waste of paper since constant handling reduces pages to an unsuitable state long before they are reached. A new book is in the figurative sense a 'clean sheet' which gives an inspiring feeling of a fresh start – something the backward child frequently needs.

In conclusion it is worth noting that most people give a good deal of time to consideration of specific number and reading apparatus

EQUIPMENT AND APPARATUS

but often neglect to give any real thought to the wider issues which have been touched upon so far. Yet a constructive and comprehensive plan based on a rational consideration of these issues and the aims and needs in the education of backward children is likely to be of much greater value to all concerned since equipment and apparatus will then be seen in its true perspective. Instead of a hotch-potch of mechanical aids pressed into service on the spur of the moment to fill a gap, it will be a vital and essential vehicle for the education of children who cannot fully succeed without it.

The Making of Apparatus

(1) The question of the desirability or otherwise of using apparatus must take into account the production of the home-made variety. The teacher may legitimately ask when it is to be made and by whom. Hundreds, both past and present, have spent hours of their leisure time and often their money in providing necessary equipment. Such a state of affairs is wrong from all points of view; if apparatus is provided at the cost of the teacher's energy, enthusiasm and outside interests it is far too dearly bought. Better no apparatus than an irritable jaded teacher who has lost contact with life, and is unfit mentally and physically to face a class full of effervescence and needing wise and careful direction. But this is not necessary; many are making their own lives a burden for the want of a little constructive re-planning.

The time factor must be given serious consideration by those responsible for the organization of schools. A great deal of harm has been, and is being, done by a short-sighted policy in this direction. Far too many people in advisory and supervisory capacities offer facile advice to harassed class teachers, point out the value of a practical approach, the need for more apparatus but never come down to the basic points of how? when? and by whom? Far too few of these same class teachers put the real issue squarely in front of those responsible and induce a little clear thinking on the problem. The result is more far-reaching than is at first obvious; the class teacher's whole attitude towards apparatus, advice and discussion of problems is coloured by the conviction that no real assistance is likely to be forthcoming.

In sober fact it is very easy to give advice if it is limited to theory and it is this that has undermined the confidence a good many class teachers of dull and backward children have in advisory bodies. It says much for the teaching profession that many do struggle on and make supreme efforts to do the impossible. But many cannot face the demands on health, time and efficiency and are forced to compromise. They may give up the teaching of dull and backward children or they may fall back on less suitable methods. Whichever course they follow, a vast potential of valuable contribution to the teaching of handicapped children is being wasted, and the working partnership between organization and practice which should be an inspiration to greater progress is bogged down by blind misconception on one side and passive resistance on the other. Each is so sure of the other's error that neither sees the possibility of constructive action.

A limited amount of 'homework' can legitimately be expected of every teacher as work has to be prepared, but every effort should be made to allow the teacher of a backward class some time during school hours. The assertion that teachers of bright children may not have the apparatus to make but need time equally much if not more to deal with the amount of marking that has to be done – an argument so often put forward – is not a valid one. A little organization, a properly balanced arrangement of lessons and an efficient method of teaching takes care of most of the marking at the primary level.

Few junior schools have sufficient staff to allow 'free' periods even were the principle recognized. A reassessment of the situation is long overdue. Statistics, valuable as they may be to organizers in remote corners, are cold comfort to the teacher of the backward class and would prove a lot less attractive to their sponsors after a period of practical experience in the classroom. Teachers are aware of all the official answers and the sympathy with which they are given usually proves more of an irritant than a sedative – teachers as well as children learn by experience!

We cannot afford in any case to wait for the golden age, which to the primary school teacher seems to recede in exactly the same ratio as we progress towards it. Children only have one school life and time is a vital element in the education of dull and backward children. What is to be done must be done at once – next year may well be too late both for the child and for the teacher's enthusiasm. The

EQUIPMENT AND APPARATUS

problem of time for making apparatus must be dealt with within the school even while the fight for recognition of the need goes on outside. There are possibilities and they should be considered on their merits, weighing up what is being gained against what is being sacrificed.

(i) Where a large classroom or hall is available lessons can be combined, e.g. massed singing, radio broadcasts, films, dancing, games, stories, all lend themselves to duplication without necessarily depriving the children to any serious extent.

(ii) Study periods. Older and more able primary children are capable of working on their own with a minimum of supervision in certain aspects of their work. It is desirable that average and bright children should acquire the habit of studying without constant supervision and one teacher can easily manage two adjacent classes with set work. The ultimate gain or loss here depends upon the training of the children and the organization of the class teacher. This adjustment is only possible for an ordinary school in which special classes are organized for the backward.

(iii) Assistance by the Head teacher and/or clerical assistant. This is likely to be controversial ground but Head teachers are much more free agents than class teachers and in view of the ever increasing burden of clerical work laid on them a break now and again for constructive work might be a good thing. Teachers are certainly in short supply in primary schools but authorities might give concrete expression to their sympathy by the provision of more generous clerical help, in which case the Head would have more time for teaching, and possibly a few hours for cutting and mounting could be spared by the clerical assistant also.

(iv) Assistance by the children themselves. As a rule children are only too eager to help and with due safeguards they can do a good deal of the work. Backward children in many cases will not have the necessary skill, but in ordinary schools, the average and bright children will be capable of all the cutting, mounting and often labelling that is needed. Their standard of performance will be high so long as they are only allowed to do a little at a time, and have been trained to accuracy and careful work.

A good deal of the work to be done is in itself educational and could well be undertaken as part of normal class work but a small group of skilled children will cover a lot of ground in their own time with very little actual supervision. Certainly there will be no shortage of pictures if an appeal is made for help in collecting; unsuitable ones can always be quietly discarded. Children's help always needs careful organization and supervision but it can save the teacher endless hours of work and leave her time to carry out the more skilled parts to complete the apparatus. With suitable training the 10-year-old dull and backward child can give a surprising amount of help provided he has a fair level of practical ability.

(v) Organization within the class. Dull and backward children, though necessarily more dependent upon their teacher, can and should be trained to good work habits. One of these is the ability to settle down to a concentrated effort on work that is within their capabilities. At special periods during the week an older class should recognize the need to work unaided, and apart from a major crisis, without reference to the teacher until after the deadline is reached. Care in setting the work is essential, and with a minority of children the initial training is not easy, but such periods can sometimes give the teacher a brief opportunity for making simple apparatus.

Here then are some concrete suggestions in reply to the problem of time; something is possible in all schools and a combination of the foregoing with a reasonable amount of homework should go some way towards a solution.

(2) But the time involved is closely linked with the durability of the material. An hour spent on something which does not survive the first half hour of use is mathematically an unsound proposition, and no amount of free periods will overcome that difficulty. Cheap materials are a false economy with most children, and unfortunately dull and backward children are usually heavy handed and clumsy in manipulation so that extra durability is essential in any apparatus to be used by them over a period. A number of factors must be borne in mind when materials are under consideration.

(i) If the equipment is something commonly needed by all backward children then the more permanent the better, provided it can be made hygienic. Plywood, millboard, hardboard or strong cardboard should be used according to which is the most suitable for the specific task.

EQUIPMENT AND APPARATUS

(ii) If the equipment is needed to meet a special situation which has arisen within a specific class the circumstances indicate a less expensive and less permanent material. Once the equipment has served its limited purpose it may quite well not be needed again as a similar situation may not arise for a matter of years. Strongly constructed semi-permanent apparatus for such occasions is a waste of material and time, and is dangerous in that temptation to fit the class to the apparatus may arise at a later date.

(iii) Hygiene is a serious problem. Much of the apparatus must be made of cardboard and cannot easily be made washable, but certain steps can be taken to minimize the danger.

- (*a*) Use a good card or paper with a glossy surface which is much less porous than the cheaper variety.
- (*b*) Wherever possible use a covering of sellotape, cellophane, or clear varnish to give greater protection; the latter can be sponged.
- (*c*) Inspect hands before allowing any child to use equipment.
- (*d*) Store in a box with a lid.
- (*e*) Destroy and replace at reasonable intervals.

(iv) Difficulty of handling means much more wear and tear on apparatus. The size and thickness of the component parts must be considered in relation to the age and ability of the children who will be using the equipment. Damage and loss occur much more frequently if this is not taken into account and the children cannot fairly be held responsible for it.

(3) Finally the acquisition of pictures, etc., may present some difficulty though recent years have seen a big improvement in this direction. But the following suggestions may be a help.

(i) The 'Pathway Picture Scheme' published by Gibsons consists of many useful pictured objects in attractive colours with labels. They are printed on high grade glossy paper and each picture is approximately three inches square.

(ii) Nursery identification pictures are obtainable from a number of publishers including Philip and Tacey. These portray a wide variety of objects in colour.

(iii) Picture alphabet books, early illustrated vocabulary books and picture dictionaries are very useful sources of supply, and are often of more value cut up for apparatus than they are as books. A study of E. J. Arnold's and Philip and Tacey's catalogues will yield several pictorial series which are worth while.

(iv) Ordinary periodical covers often carry attractive coloured pictures. For work with retarded children of ordinary intelligence *Today* cover pictures are excellent but the humour is beyond the dull as a rule. The help of friends and of the children themselves will contribute towards the collection which should be a permanent feature of the classroom.

(v) *Child Education* provides suitable infant and junior pictures with an occasional one mature enough for older children.

(vi) Calendars, especially the month by month variety, are useful as they provide topical pictures. The figures, too, in many cases are clear and large enough to be utilized.

(vii) Children's picture books of the cheaper variety have sometimes unexpectedly good pictures and are worth watching for among displays of books.

In fact there are now good sources of supply and the difficulty usually arises only because the demand has not been foreseen, and provision made before the need becomes urgent. The moral is self-evident; collect methodically as part of normal preparation for work with a backward class.

Storage

(4) Nothing is more irritating than the plaintive cry from a child, 'There's a piece missing', or 'These pieces don't belong'. Precious time is wasted while everyone tries to check up and sort out the sets. A few precautions in the making and a few more in the using can do much to prevent the occurrence.

(i) Use different coloured card to distinguish sets where this can be done. In some cases different colours are needed within the set but it is usually possible to effect a satisfactory arrangement which will indicate a 'stranger' immediately.

(ii) Whenever possible hold the loose pieces together with a thick rubber band. This is especially necessary where there are several component parts each made up of a number of items.

(iii) Loose words, labels and such small items should be stored

EQUIPMENT AND APPARATUS

in a small box or tin – a match-box is suitable – with some distinguishing mark on the outside to indicate to which set the box belongs.

(iv) Single sets comprised of a number of odd parts which cannot be dealt with by a rubber band should be kept in individual small boxes.

(v) Packs of cards, each enclosed in a rubber band, should be stored in large cardboard boxes. All the packs for one game should be kept together and the box clearly labelled on the outside.

(vi) When using the apparatus keep all boxes and containers closed until all the group is seated and ready to start. Only use one game at each desk, and after giving the signal to clear up, allow no one to move away from the desk till all the apparatus is boxed up and the table leader has checked the floor for dropped pieces.

Where isolated individuals are using the apparatus, which is usually the case with language equipment, a reminder to look round carefully when clearing up will be needed; much depends on training here. In the event of a miscalculation in the timing of a lesson it is safer to tell the children to leave the equipment as it is and pack it oneself; on no account should they be hurried or allowed to clear hastily. This not only risks the apparatus and undermines the careful training the child is receiving but leaves him in a state of mental stress and confusion which bodes ill for his next lesson.

Strong cardboard boxes with close fitting lids are an essential for safe, easy and hygienic storage. Uniform sizes for the various sets are desirable; they can usually be obtained on requisition at reasonable prices and are a worthwhile investment for the convenience and security given. Paper envelopes are not a successful alternative but strong home-made envelope containers can be made from book linen and provided they are made to fasten securely with press studs they are a possibility.

Shelves probably have a slight advantage over drawers for keeping the boxes conveniently placed for use but much depends upon the arrangement and neither need prove inconvenient. As the children will be responsible for keeping the apparatus stored in its correct place, and being backward they can hardly be expected to read the kind of labels the teacher is likely to need, it is a good plan to differentiate the various groups of boxes by a coloured label across the end of the lid. This will show up at a glance and most children will have no difficulty in putting the box into its proper pile.

Good arrangements for storing will save a great deal of time as well as safeguarding the apparatus, and once suitable facilities have been settled a rigid enforcement of regulations is necessary so that a routine of care is built up.

Conclusion

Much that has been written here will not be new to experienced teachers, and is a matter of common sense rather than any startling new approach; this is true of most aspects of education. But even experienced teachers lose sight of fundamentals as time goes on and the daily demands grow more pressing. An occasional stocktaking of one's own practices and their implications is quite salutary; surprising anomalies can creep in undetected and the fact that precept and practice have ceased to be complementary can go unnoticed.

Undoubtedly the reader will want to question and disagree on some points but in so doing he will also review his own ideas and practices and one of the aims of this chapter will have been achieved. For those with less experience this will not be a short cut but it may enable them to gain their experience less painfully; while no one denies that one should learn by experience as far as possible, the fact remains that there are some experiences which are better avoided!

I. R. MILLER

Chapter XIII

THE SLOW LEARNER IN THE INFANT SCHOOL

When is an infant to be considered backward?

First of all, one must distinguish between true dullness and retardation. Infants can be retarded for a number of reasons and it is difficult at this early stage to decide whether the child is merely retarded or truly subnormal. There must be a fairly lengthy period allowed for the child to adjust to school life and for the teacher to observe and study the child. The teacher's daily contact with the child, her understanding and encouragement will help to develop him or her as a person. I would not personally have a child tested until the final term in the infant school. If the child is discovered to be a suitable candidate for an E.S.N. school it is better to make the change at the age of transfer, 7 + years. Sometimes it is possible to retain the child in the infant school for a further year and then to review the case at the age of 8 + years. Physically the child leaves babyhood behind between $6\frac{1}{2}$ years and $7\frac{1}{2}$ years and there is a corresponding mental growth which makes the child surge forward as an independent being. Very slow children in a free environment often blossom in this growing period. Small children are not critical and the E.S.N. child will usually fit quite happily into the group.

There is a far larger group of children in the infant school who are retarded. The E.S.N. children are a very small minority in comparison with the retarded group.

Retardation can be caused by a variety of reasons. The child's physical condition on admission to school is an important factor and faults have to be corrected in the first and second years of school life. The majority of children are now much healthier, cleaner and better nourished than in pre-war days. This is partly the result of the

School Health Service, particularly of the hard work put in by the Health Visitors over a period of years and of the growth of public opinion against dirt and disease. Some progressive School Health Departments medically examine children before entry into school and this practice does help to eliminate the more obvious faults at an earlier age. Small children can lose quite a lot of school-time at various clinics for corrective treatment and while this is naturally of first-class importance, it is also a hindrance to the learning process.

Personally I feel that throat, nose and ear troubles slow children down mentally more than any other form of illness. The infectious illnesses, apart from polio, cause children to lose time in school but otherwise do not have such a serious effect upon their general well-being.

Young children are prone to coughs and colds and in the first year in school they have not developed an immunity to infection. I have found that the catarrhal conditions left after colds are often allowed to continue by young mothers, without treatment. In fact, it becomes a condition which they tend to accept as part of the general health of the child rather than a condition to treat. Children suffering from this unpleasant condition are lethargic, heavy-eyed and generally lacking in vitality and in my opinion slower to learn.

On admission to school all children are medically examined by the School Health Department. This examination can take place in the child's first term. I have found after working under different local education authorities that the extent of the inspection varies considerably. Under some Medical Departments children's eyes are tested with the 'E' or picture test at the first inspection, but other authorities do not test children's eyes unless requested to do so by the Head teacher, until children are 8 years old. From a teacher's point of view I feel it would be advisable to test children's eyes on admission to school. Indeed, it would be of great value if children's eyes were tested yearly between the ages of 5 and 10 years. All too often it is the teacher who by her daily contact with the child sees the signs which point to a deterioration of eyesight and draws the attention of the parent and doctor to it.

Defective hearing is an even more difficult condition to detect at the infant stage. There may come a day when audiometers are part of every school's normal equipment but at present, teachers have to

THE SLOW LEARNER IN THE INFANT SCHOOL

rely upon their own observations. The children with bad speech patterns want careful watching in this direction. The poor speech may be due to defective hearing, adenoidal and tonsil troubles or simply lack of correction on the part of the parents when the child was learning to talk. It is wiser I feel to let children with defective speech have a few months in school mixing with the other children before recommending them to the speech therapy clinic. Very often the child corrects itself but poor speech patterns should not be allowed to continue or the pattern will persist throughout life. It is difficult for a child to learn to read when the speech pattern is poor even though in most infant schools the visual approach is used. The phonetic method adds to the difficulty for these children.

Children suffering from psychological troubles will become apparent in the classroom. These children are either very slow to learn, because they lack confidence, or make little progress because they are extremely erratic. They may be behaviour problems and show signs of maladjustment. In some cases the infant may have made a poor adjustment to school life. The parents have not prepared the child sufficiently for the change, or the child may have been frightened by older brothers and sisters. Unfortunately the teacher is still used as a 'bogey' by unenlightened parents. For most children the commencement of school is their first experience of a mass of children and it can be terrifying and bewildering for them. I have vivid memories of my first day in a large infant class. It is a mile-stone in one's life and it is a pity that the infant teacher has not time to observe the children's reactions in more detail on this day. Sometimes these children overcome their difficulties in the classroom environment with the help of a sympathetic teacher and in co-operation with the child's parents. Other children will need the Child Guidance Clinic to find out exactly the nature of the trouble. Unfortunately in some areas when a child goes to the Child Guidance Clinic, medical etiquette forbids the discussion of the child's case with the Head teacher. This seems deplorable as teachers and doctors are working for the good of the child and should co-operate fully. I have found that one is more likely to receive a report from the county educational psychologist if a child is referred for testing and treatment. Teachers are in direct contact with the families in their area and know something of their problems. The Health Visitor is very often an invaluable ally in this direction. I feel that much more use could be made of the teacher's personal knowledge of the child by the medical profession. The teacher is in daily contact with the child and should know how the child reacts to the classroom environment and make an objective observation on the child which could be of real value to the doctor.

Social Adjustment

The period of social adjustment to school does vary from child to child. As the child learns to fetch and carry for himself, visit the toilet alone, dress and undress himself, wash his face and hands, clean his teeth, etc., so he gains confidence which he extends into the learning situations. The teacher should encourage the child to attempt these things for himself but she should also be prepared to help him, as boys do not develop the smaller muscular movements as soon as girls and they have real difficulty in coping with such things as buttons. However, some mothers and teachers tend to help boys far longer than is actually necessary.

Socially, the child who has been fortunate enough to attend a nursery school or class tends to progress at a greater rate because he has become independent at an earlier age. Usually when such a child passes into the infant school he or she is ready for new experiences and will make greater effort. Time is not used in acclimatizing the child to its new environment. I do not think it is fully realized exactly how much time has to be spent in the early stages on social education.

What is the effect upon the small child of the mother who is in fulltime work? Personally, I consider it to be be a very great one. Most working mothers are doing so for economic reasons but I do not think the material benefits gained can make up for the child's feeling of insecurity. These mothers are too tired at night to take much interest in their children. The children miss their mothers at school functions and feel neglected. During the holidays they are often left to their own devices and herein lies a very real danger. The children are not neglected materially, but emotionally and spiritually they are starved. Petty offences which would be corrected by a sensible parent in her home, go unnoticed and the children finding that their naughtiness is ignored resort to petty crime.

One 6 year old girl said to me, 'I'm fed up! Either my Daddy is at home or my Mummy is at home but they're never both there together.' That child was feeling her lack of home life acutely and was intelligent enough to put it into words.

If mothers must work for financial reasons, would it not be possible for them to do part-time work so that they are at home when the children return from school? I am sure we should see far fewer children with psychological problems if we emphasized the importance of a proper home life.

Children who are upset at home show it in their work at school. One child, fostered out all the week, returned to her parents at weekends. On Monday and Tuesday she was too tired to work and usually emotionally upset. Her progress was most erratic. She was unable to cope with the weekly upheaval and the conflicting adults.

In a changing world new factors and values are bound to react upon the nation's children. Full employment in the country has increased the standard of living for all but it has brought about a different set of problems. In many areas the school takes the place of the home and responsibilities once accepted by the parents are cast upon the teacher. To a child, nothing can take the place of its mother's care and attention. The public conscience needs to be reawakened if we are going to bring up our young to be mentally healthy.

Infant School Organization
In an infant school where the psychology of individual differences is recognized, the slow learner should fit into the classroom environment. Infant teachers in their classroom organization aim at the all-round development of the child. The environment is organized so that the child's interest is aroused and stimulated. To the layman the purpose of the classroom is not always apparent and when the children are seen playing, it is not realized that the play equipment and apparatus has been put there for a specific reason and that sound, educational theory is behind it all. The sand, clay and water, paints, crayons, constructional apparatus, large bricks and toys, house corner, nature table and pet's corner, dressing-up box, number games, pre-reading games and activities, book trolley, puppets, junk box, woodwork bench and any other kind of creative activity are all for the child's use. Naturally the materials are used in varying ways according to the age, ability and imagination of the child. The slow

child has the same opportunities to use the materials for experimental purposes and the teacher observes his or her efforts with them. Sometimes the slow child tends to play with familiar equipment and is unwilling to try any other type of material. It is then that the observant teacher must use her influence to help him or her to try new experiences. All the children in such a classroom are proceeding at their own individual rate. They are encouraged and praised for what they accomplish and spurred on to greater efforts by the teacher who is watching constantly for the right moment to introduce a new activity.

Reading maturation comes at about 6 + for the average child (I.Q. 100), but children with higher I.Q.s and good physical development, particularly eyesight, may well start before the age of 6 years. A teacher who has developed good pre-reading activities in her classroom and where a reading vocabulary has been built up with the children before a book has been presented to them will lay a very sure foundation. Shortly after the Second World War there was a theory that children would learn by themselves if there were enough pre-reading activities and reading material in the room for the child's use. Personally I think that the majority of children need definite teaching when it comes to learning to read. The teacher may use informal methods, but the children need to be taught individually, regularly and carefully. There needs to be plenty of reading material in the room other than that used in the reading scheme, which the children can use freely. In their zest, infant teachers tend to urge children on from book to book and there is a danger here in not allowing sufficient time for consolidation. Every infant teacher is delighted when one of her pupils suddenly reads without apparent effort. Such children have good eyesight, above average I.Q.s, a greater power of association, obviously much better memories and probably come from homes where they are read to and encouraged in their efforts. Such 'natural' readers are rare, just as there are few, if any, word-blind children.

The Choice of a Reading Scheme

A great deal of research work has been done both in this country and abroad on this subject, but the choice of a reading scheme still largely depends upon the method of teaching employed in the school.

THE SLOW LEARNER IN THE INFANT SCHOOL

A large number of schools use the 'look and say' method combined with the 'sentence' method in the early stages. Phonetics may be introduced when the child has a considerable vocabulary, is becoming more conscious of sounds, and is able to help himself. However, our language is not a phonetic one and if the method is overemphasized, poor spelling in the junior school will be the result. From my own experience I would say that the vast majority of children in the infant school learn to read by the direct approach provided that the teacher has given many pre-reading experiences, has provided a stimulating environment and has not forced reading upon them at too early an age. At the end of the last war, I had a class of backward girls age 7 + years in London. They had had practically no infant schooling owing to evacuation and re-evacuation but they were rich in experience. I had to start from scratch with them, and at the end of the year most of them had reached the stage they would have been at if they had attended an infant school. It was a salutary experience for me and I realized how much we had expected from infant children in pre-war years and how difficult we had made it for the children and for ourselves.

The fact that there is a definite maturation point for reading is still unrecognized by far too many teachers.

The reading scheme adopted by the school should be carefully selected and there are now suitable books available on the market. It should have a graded word-list for each main book and supplementary material for consolidation. Some schemes developed for infants tend to teach too many new words at a time and there is too great a gap between readers. If such a scheme is in use it is at this stage that the teacher must make sure that the children really consolidate their reading or they will be discouraged by failure. It is important that the scheme should be bright and colourful. Infants and indeed all children love colour and to present an attractive book to the children immediately arouses their interest. The scheme should also be rhythmical and repetitive. Rhythmical reading for the child in the early stages and particularly for the E.S.N. child is a great help. Certain American schemes emphasize this point. Naturally the content of the scheme should be within the child's grasp and comprehension. Reading for comprehension is after all the whole point of learning to read. Words are meaningless on their own. It

TEACHING THE SLOW LEARNER IN THE PRIMARY SCHOOL

always seems a pity to me that many schools test children's reading ability on lists which consist of isolated words. To the average child the whole business is stupid. A reading test which attempts to estimate the child's power of understanding gives a far truer picture of the child's ability. The importance of regular daily teaching of reading I have previously emphasized and this particularly applies to the retarded infant. Children who are retarded require more individual attention. I have found that it is best for a teacher to take these children in small groups of six or eight pupils. The child must not be allowed to feel that he or she has failed and the teacher must use a little diplomacy when the arrangement is first made. The children are taken from their classes for about one hour daily for extra tuition. (In some schools this tuition is given by the Head, in others by a supernumerary if available.) Sometimes it is wiser to give the children a fresh start on a new series of books if the children for one reason or another have made little progress on the class-reading scheme. The individual tuition includes pre-reading games and allied activities such as drawing, writing, etc. Whoever teaches these children must be prepared to adapt herself to the needs of the individual child and to devise apparatus to help the child in the learning process. It all takes time, unlimited patience and a lot of thought on the part of the teacher. Above all she must win the child's confidence, provide the incentives and ensure that each child succeeds. Retarded children thrive on this extra attention and the teacher has a far greater opportunity of detecting individual defects. If at the end of 6 month's regular teaching some children are still showing no signs of learning to read the teacher will suspect that they are the educationally sub-normal children and will recommend them for assessment. Little can be done for these children in the infant school as to try to force them would be unwise. Maturation point will be reached in the junior school and therefore if the child remains in a primary department the junior school must be prepared to teach it to read. Not all local education authorities have sufficient places in their Special Schools for E.S.N. children and many of these children remain in the ordinary schools. Provision can be made for them in remedial classes, recognized as such and staffed by specially chosen teachers. I have always strongly advocated infant-trained teachers for first and second year forms in the junior school. The severe break between schools can then be somewhat eliminated.

There is a strong body of opinion which feels that the transfer of children at 7 years to the junior school is at the wrong time in the child's mental and emotional development. It is entirely an artificial division. Infant teachers feel that just as children are gaining some skill in the basic subjects they are subjected to a break in continuity and very often a change in teaching methods. Average children make rapid progress between 7 and 8 years. The first form junior teachers see this rapid growth of mental ability. Since the war many children have had a bare two years in the infant school owing to the large increase of numbers. Two years is not long enough to lay the foundations of the basic subjects. Some children born in the latter months of the year may get a three year period in the infant school and these children have a greater chance.

The problem of retardation throughout the country would be partially solved I am sure if we had smaller classes in primary schools, ideally between twenty to twenty-five pupils. How often this is repeated and yet little progress in this direction has been made over the last fifty years! Primary schools are still expected to have an average of forty on roll by the Ministry and yet classes for the senior age groups are allowed to have thirty children per class. The physical and mental strain upon the teachers in primary schools has not been emphasized nearly enough. Small children demand constant attention from the adult, particularly in an environment where children are being encouraged to develop their own interests. The individual approach to children has not been with us for many years and a number of infant schools developed their creative activity methods at a time when the child population was enormous. These methods in spite of all the criticism which was levelled at them have persisted. The recent Ministry survey on children's reading has shown that the percentage of illiterates in the country has considerably decreased, and with smaller classes I am confident this percentage would decrease still further. It is the slower children who will always suffer most in a large class. One must face the plain fact that a teacher delights to see his or her pupils progress. The quicker children are bound to be kept busy or chaos will result. The less able children in a large class will fall by the wayside unless special educational treatment can be given to them.

TEACHING THE SLOW LEARNER IN THE PRIMARY SCHOOL

The E.S.N. child in the infant school should be able to fit into the classroom environment provided the teacher is sympathetic towards him. His efforts, however poor, must be praised and his self-confidence increased. He should receive as much individual help as possible with the basic subjects, but be allowed to take his part in the classroom activities. His limitations are then only known to his teacher.

Finally, it is a poor educational policy which spends vast sums of money on a child at the end of its school life and only pays lip-service to the most important step of all – the beginning.

Book List

BOYCE, E. R., *The First Year in School*, Nisbet, 1953.
GARDNER, D. E. M., *The Education of Young Children*, Methuen, 1956.
— *Education Under Eight*, British Council, 1949.
— *Long Term Results of Infant School Methods*, Methuen, 1950.
— *Testing Results in the Infant School*, 2nd edn., Methuen, 1953.
Scottish Council for Research in Education, *Studies in Reading*, U.L.P., 1950.

MARY E. MIDDLETON

Chapter XIV

BACKWARD CHILDREN IN VILLAGE SCHOOLS

The village school presents its own particular problems of organization and curriculum. In considering the wider aims of providing a suitable education for its children, it may adopt the same ideals as the larger schools in the town area, but in carrying out these ideals, its methods of approach may be totally different. For example, it may well be that it is the aim of the school to help to equip its pupils for the life they may lead, or to help them to use their leisure time both profitably and well. Because the country child may live a life very different from his town counterpart, much of the work of the school must be approached from a different angle.

The country child no longer lives a life of solitary isolation. Wages are better than they were, so that there are likely to be some opportunities for journeys away from the village. Wireless and television are in many homes. Modern developments in methods of farming are demanding a different type of skill from the farm worker. All these have definite implications on the future of the country child, and modern educational developments must consider these implications in planning his school work. Much can be done in the schools to break down the barrier of misunderstanding and prejudice which still exists between the town and the country. In buildings and in general amenities, the village school is often far behind the schools in the towns, but if the curriculum is well planned, the rural school has a wealth of natural materials, readily available at its own doors, so that it has advantages as well as deficiencies. Although the work may have a rural bias it is not intended in any way to be vocational training. Some children can walk through the countryside observing very little. This applies more to the less gifted

TEACHING THE SLOW LEARNER IN THE PRIMARY SCHOOL

children, and by using the countryside as a basis of learning we are teaching the child to live more abundantly in his own environment. For a long time parents have tended to look upon the years spent at school as a period which must be endured before the child can go out to work to add to the meagre family earnings. Fortunately, many parents are realizing that the schools have something of real value to offer their children. They are taking more interest in the work of the school. Their interest and help can be of the greatest value, and where the relationship is good between parents and school, then the school will become a true and lively centre of the community it serves. In my own experience as Headmistress in the same village for a long period, I have seen a very definite change in the attitude of parents towards the school in general, and towards their own children's education. This may seem to paint too rosy a picture of village school work. Anyone who is well acquainted with teaching in a village will realize that there are very many difficulties to be overcome, but the trend is in the right direction, and in planning the curriculum, all these points have to be considered.

In the rural schools, the classes are usually smaller in numbers than classes in town schools, but there is almost invariably a wide range of ages and abilities in each class. For example, in a two-teacher unreorganized school, there will probably be children ranging in ages from about 8 to 15 years in one class, and in a school which has been reorganized the range will probably be from 8 to 11 years. This of course, presents its own particular problems. Class teaching in any formal manner is virtually impossible. The whole class has to be reviewed more as a family unit, with each member claiming his rights and privileges. It is good social training for the senior members of the school to realize that the younger members of the community have also to be taken into consideration. Here it may be emphasized that the slower and less gifted children, and even those who are educationally sub-normal, are usually accepted quite freely into the family unit. These children have been accepted by the outside village community. They and their families have probably been known in the village for many years, and they are accepted quite naturally. No one will expect from them very high standards of academic achievement, and they can generally take their place in the communal life of the village. There are exceptions to this, but it has been my experience that the slower children can adapt themselves more easily to school life in the country, than their counterparts can in the town schools, and serious behaviour problems are less common.

In rural areas, provision of Special Schools presents a very difficult problem. Because the population is spread over such a wide area, the schools provided must be residential ones, and these can cater for only a small percentage of the children who are in need of special education. Most of the children have to be catered for in the ordinary school. There may be, in each small school one or two children who will eventually be transferred to a secondary grammar school, but there are usually quite a number of children with rather less than average intelligence, especially in the more isolated districts.

The teacher has to work out a plan so that she is meeting the individual needs of each child. It is important to see that the right type of work is provided for Mary who is a potential grammar school pupil, and although her needs may be very different from John who is 10 years old, and unable to read fluently, both must be catered for in the same class and both must be given the individual attention they need. Another very common problem in the more isolated schools, is the 'floating population'. These are the children of parents who change their jobs frequently and it is not uncommon to admit a child of about 8 years who has already attended three or four other schools. This child may present very real difficulties, not only with his limited attainments, but also he may have difficulty in adjusting himself to still another different school routine.

Such are the problems presented by the children. Staffing in the rural schools also presents its difficulties. A staff of two or three teachers have to be responsible for all subjects in the curriculum, and in planning the work of the school, it is essential that each teacher can develop her own special interests at all levels. She thus maintains contact with the children and there is once again the feeling of unity within the school, rather than in isolated classes. The infant teacher is not merely a teacher of the infants' class but she is also available for help in subjects such as art, needlework, or music.

I have given considerable time to the general background of the village school, because I feel that this is of the very greatest importance to the slow learner, or the educationally sub-normal child.

TEACHING THE SLOW LEARNER IN THE PRIMARY SCHOOL

The infant teacher is usually well trained to deal with reading difficulties, and if there is free interchange of children from the various classes, there is no feeling of 'being sent down a class', if the slower child spends part of his morning with the infant teacher. Other children may go to the infant teacher for help in other subjects, at other times. This can work admirably, but there are two very important points to bear in mind:

(1) The infant teacher must provide the child with material that is not at infant level in content. Although the child's reading ability may be very limited, it is essential that he is not presented with an infant reader, on which he may already have failed. Here again close co-operation between the teachers is necessary. If the child has shown some particular interest, this may be utilized in arousing an interest in reading. For example: A boy with a keen interest in farm work came to school with the news that his father was driving a new make of tractor, which had recently been purchased by the local farmer. This boy who was 9 years, had been attending my school for about six months. His reading age was $5\frac{7}{12}$ years, and he had shown little desire to read. He made a drawing of the tractor, putting in quite a surprising amount of detail. Fortunately at the same time I came across a farming magazine with a review, and detailed pictures of the new tractor, and the infant teacher was able to supply pamphlets, from the firm. With the help of these pictures the boy made an illustrated 'tractor booklet', which he could 'read', to all who would listen. The boy had memorized the reading in the book and the pictures were so vital to him that immediately he knew the association between the picture and the writing. I must emphasize, that all this did not happen quickly. The boy had been given time to adjust himself to our methods, and we were fortunate in finding something which was of interest to him. This was only an approach to reading, but the boy soon began to show more interest in reading, than he had done at first. The tractor book became to him a reference book, and he remembered every word in it, and he would refer to it when he wanted to spell a word that was written there, turning almost at once to the right page. This boy worked quite happily with the infant teacher, and his reading was improving slowly, but steadily.

(2) The second point to watch, when cross-classifying children for

reading, is also extremely important. Careful recording must be made of the child's progress, and reactions. A boy who was apparently working very happily with the infant teacher seemed to reach the point where he was making no further effort or progress. Although his reading age was still low, he was transferred again to his own class, and progress restarted. It is most essential to watch out for these individual reactions, and make the change when necessary. The same teaching method with each individual must be continued as far as possible in the senior school, for there should be no break in continuity once the method which is achieving results for the individual has been found out.

The country child who seems to have very little aptitude for academic work often possesses an interest and a wealth of knowledge about the work of the countryside. He often works on a farm himself, or he hears his father discussing the farm work. If this interest can be enlisted and applied to the art of learning to read, the child will approach the subject with much more zest. This approach also serves another very useful purpose, for school is no longer an isolated unit, but it becomes so much more closely related to the life of the child. Here the slow learner can often feel a real sense of achievement, for he can often give information which is quite technical in content. I have known of many occasions when I have had to verify the accuracy of some detailed knowledge given to me by children with very little reading ability. A farmer friend can be most useful.

Unfortunately there are very few early reading books which cater for the country child. We have compiled readers of our own with some success, but we have found it almost impossible to ensure a sufficiently well graded vocabulary, but our books and the books the children have made themselves have provided very valuable supplementary reading material.

Individual and class dictionaries for various ages, are very useful. A dictionary of 'Farm words' – 'Words about the Home', etc., make for easy reference. Pictures of farm machines and implements are stuck into a book with their names underneath, or an older child may compile his own dictionary, using pictures or drawings when appropriate. Farming magazines are also useful for reference. When the range of ability is so great, the child has to learn methods

TEACHING THE SLOW LEARNER IN THE PRIMARY SCHOOL

by which he can help himself when the teacher is occupied. If this method is carefully fostered and developed the child gains confidence, self-reliance and initiative.

The approach to number work is organized on similar lines to the reading, with free interchange between the classes. For the dull and backward child, the number work must be very practical. Many opportunities occur in the ordinary school routine when the children can be given opportunities for counting. The number of children present in the class and issuing the milk bottles are real situations when counting is necessary. Laying the tables for the midday meal can be an extremely useful number lesson, when the knives, forks, spoons, etc., have to be counted out. An older girl can be taught to supervise, and to help the younger ones when necessary, and it is often quite surprising at times to find how much a young child can learn from an older one.

Handling of money is a very difficult problem when teaching the dull children, especially in the country. They do not often go far from their own village. If they go to the village shop, it is usually to give an order which will be delivered later in the day and payment is made on delivery. If the child is given money for shopping, she will hand the whole of the money to the shopkeeper, and the change is returned to the child wrapped in paper, or in a purse. The shopkeeper will certainly know that the child is 'not so bright', and in her endeavour to be helpful, she takes away from the child the valuable experience of using money in a real situation. Customs may vary in different areas, but after discussion with other country teachers, I am convinced that most of these children have very little opportunity to handle money in real situations.

It is essential then, that opportunities must be devised in school. Shopping with a small 'group shop', or individual shops, and simple shopping cards are all useful. This work I have found to be one of the real difficulties when dealing with a big age-range. The real E.S.N. child needs so much individual help, and there is so little time to spare. I used 'shopping cards', which can be checked quickly. For example, three children in a group of four would be given five cardboard shillings, and five prepared cards. The fourth child would be shopkeeper. The first card might read – 'Buy chocolate for 7d.' (all things in the shop would be priced less than 1s.). After buying the child would then leave on her desk the card, the chocolate and the change. This would be repeated until all five cards were used, and the teacher could check. The shopkeeper would then be changed. Written records of the transaction can be kept if desired.

Cards can be graded in difficulty, and can include the buying of two or three articles, and giving change.

The slower child can have additional practice with her own individual shop. This will give her confidence, so that she is able to join in with the group without fear of complete failure. Wet play-times and dinner-times are invaluable. The older girls love to act as teacher, and if the material is easily available, they will play shops quite happily together. If a true friendly relationship exists between the older and the younger children, the 'play-work' together also provides valuable social training for both ages.

A great deal of the usual school arithmetic must be omitted from the curriculum of the slower child. Before he leaves school, he should be familiar with the weights and measures he is likely to meet in everyday life. This he must acquire in a practical way. It is not unusual to find a child who can work out fairly complicated sums, involving yards, feet and inches, without having any conception of the real length implied by the term 'yard'. The same applies to other measures. A boy who was working sums from a textbook, involving pints, quarts and gallons, had no conception of the capacity of jugs in use in the school kitchen.

During the period in which I taught in the village, I was approached on different occasions by parents of children in school, who have been unable to measure the amount of material needed for curtains, the length of linoleum needed in a small room, and even to measure the lengths of stair carpet required for a perfectly straight stair-case. Some of the this work may be beyond the comprehension of the slowest children, but many of them do become quite proficient in using the ordinary weights and measures, but this can only be achieved through constant and continuous practice.

Each school will develop its own approach according to its own activities. I have found that gardening can be extremely useful for this practical approach to number work. Seeds can be planted three inches apart, and one foot between rows. For this purpose sticks can be cut to the correct length for measuring. If the plot to be sown is only small, newspaper can be placed on the floor in the classroom, the same size as the plot, and the child can be supervised when he is cutting the measuring sticks, and marking the holes for the seeds. This method will apply only when using large seeds such as peas and beans. When it is time to go out in the garden, there will be many eager children, all demanding attention at once, but the slower child will be able to do a useful job of work, with much less attention, if he has practised well in the classroom.

Later on, garden produce can be weighed to find out how many pounds of potatoes from one seed potato, or the weight of carrots from one packet of seeds. All these are real situations, and in the day to day routine of school work, many opportunities will occur. Every advantage must be taken of these situations, but the greatest care must be taken to see that the practical work is well planned and not a series of isolated incidents. The brighter child will soon learn the technique and practical application of the weights and measures but the slower child must have opportunities to repeat many times.

At the senior stage, the boys often spend one session at a woodwork centre, whilst the girls may go to a domestic science centre. These slower children will be at a very great disadvantage, if they have not learnt to weigh or to measure, and much of the value of their practical work may be lost.

I have tried to emphasize the importance of using real situations whenever possible, so that the purpose of the work is easily apparent, and it is all too easy to overlook these opportunities in the busy routine of school work, but once the value has been realized, the slower children will derive much benefit.

Preparatory work needs to be done before the use of the actual weights and measures. This needs to be carefully graded, and allowance made for plenty of repetition when considering the slower children. For example, in weighing it is essential to understand the meaning of the terms, heavy – light, and the principle of balance is not always understood. Home-made scales with an easy and exaggerated balance are the best to use in the preparatory stages. Before the weights are introduced, there should be plenty of experimentation with simple exercises, e.g. How many shells weigh the same as three small bricks? etc.

Simple cards with drawings can be used so that the reading

difficulties are reduced to a minimum. A little ingenuity is required in order that the children can be kept happily and purposefully occupied, when the teacher is working with other groups. With careful training from the early stages this can be achieved quite satisfactorily.

In the country school, the craft work should play an important part in the education of the child and many of the mentally handicapped children can achieve satisfaction in this work, which can be so closely connected with reading and number activities.

We gathered our own materials for many of the traditional crafts, such as weaving, simple basket-making, and for chalk carving. I found that some of the local farmers were most co-operative. We were given unlimited quantities of baler twine, which we made into ropes and mats of various types. By plaiting the twine we made simple coil mats. Rope-making, plaiting, and simple join splices (for joining the twine together) are all processes which are simple enough for all the children to learn and often two or three children could work together. The general principle was that each child should have an individual piece of craft work, and there were also two or three class articles in the process of being made. These might include the making of wool rugs, coir mats, rope, or any other craft which requires simple repetitive processes. This again avoided the waste of time by individual children waiting for help in the more difficult processes of their individual craft. It also enabled bigger articles to be made without the children becoming bored by completing a lengthy piece of simple repetitive work. The slower children could fit easily into this system and they felt a real sense of achievement in the work they accomplished.

With the individual craft work which varied considerably, each child made his own 'How I made it', booklet. The form of the booklet was not always the same, but often there was some written work about the material used, followed by detailed notes of the method of construction.

This work in itself I found extremely valuable, as it provided the children with a real incentive for writing. Having realized the care needed to write out each stage in the method, it was good training for the reading of instructions, such as cookery recipes, or knitting patterns. Much of the work in craft was done by experimenting with various material, and a child making a basket might begin by writing in his booklet, 'I brought some sycamore twigs for my basket, but I could not use them because they would not bend.' The booklet might then continue to state that she had chosen hazel, ash or willow which are straight and pliable. The booklets are entirely individual and so they can be kept well within each child's capabilities and understanding. Perhaps an example will emphasize this point. Rope-making needs three children to work together as a group. All can do the simple practical work, but the booklets will be varied. On one occasion the practical group included one very bright boy, and another with very limited ability. After describing the making of the rope, the first boy used reference books to find out about sisal and hemp ropes and how they were made and used. The slower boy drew pictures with simple sentences to show how the local farmers used the ropes we had made for them in school. Incidentally the slower boy was extremely interested in the other boy's book, and probably learnt something from it.

Measuring and very simple scale drawing can be worked into these booklets. For example the children can measure the lengths of the twigs used in basket-making and draw these in their booklets, to half or quarter scale. I have seen some extremely useful work done by children of all ages, and of very varied capabilities.

It is difficult to classify the work of the school under various subject titles, and even more difficult to work to a planned time-table to meet the individual needs of the children. So many different methods of approach are needed, and many different types of work and activity will be in progress at the same time. It is very helpful to group together for assembly, for News Time, or for some informal dramatization work, in which all may take part, but there are few occasions when a class lesson can be taken. In my own class, reading, number, craft work, needlework, individual topic booklets may all be going on at the same time with everybody busily occupied. This may sound like chaos, and it is not a system which can be introduced quickly. It will only work satisfactorily if the children have been accustomed to working independently.

Careful recording on the teacher's part is of the utmost importance. With the comparatively small numbers it is not difficult to work out a simple recording system so that individual difficulties

can be noted, and the next period planned so that help can be given where it is most needed. Besides the simple individual records of children's work, at the end of the day my own record might include the following items:
(1) Find magazines, with pictures of ploughing for T—.
(2) During the day give D— (an E.S.N. girl) opportunities to tell the time at half hours.
(3) Put out books about weaving for S—.

A few minutes at the end of the afternoon will ensure a smooth beginning for the next session.

I find it difficult to explain explicitly the methods I adopted for the dull and backward children, because they seem to merge so naturally into the general class routine.

Project work, or topics of interest can form a very useful part of the rural school curriculum, and once again, the slower children can take their part with the more gifted ones. I have used with some success such wide topics as 'A Village Survey' or 'A Farm Study'. These topics have a very varied scope. They can include map-making and the drawing of plans by the more able children, whilst the slower children can help in the making of models, with their accompanying booklets.

In choosing a topic, it is usually better to choose something of local interest. All the children can find out information from their homes, and the local workers. The work needs to be very carefully planned, so that each child is working to capacity, but once the system is really established, and the children know what is expected of them, there are unlimited possibilities. The choosing of a local topic is not such a narrow choice as may at first seem apparent. In a farm survey, on which we worked for a whole year, two or three children worked together on the topic 'What the Farmer Buys, and Sells'. This included quite a detailed study of imported feeding stuffs, and their country of origin. Another boy studied the history of the plough and he made some very creditable models and paintings. The slower children may need a great deal of help in writing down the information they gather. I can recall some very useful pieces of work, done by slow children. One boy whose father was a gamekeeper, made a booklet about pests on the farm, and wild birds and animals which help the farmer. Another girl helped with the poultry on the farm, and with some encouragement she was able to keep a poultry record. Once interest and enthusiasm are aroused, the work progresses rapidly, and there is the added stimulus of feeling that the work will be included in the class effort.

These children do often become very proud of their work. They know it must be good to be accepted by the class. Children can be ruthless critics. On one occasion, I remember the efforts of a 10-year-old boy, who was eventually transferred to a residential school for educationally sub-normal boys. He was making a picture booklet about his father's work on the farm. He drew a picture of his father carting kale, and with some help, he made up a sentence about his picture. I wrote this out for him to copy. After a few minutes he came to to me with the sentence written out quite neatly, and obviously with effort. I was quite prepared to accept his work, and to praise his effort but he remarked, 'I can do it better than that.' He was given an opportunity to try again. Four times he came to me with the same remark. Finally the work he produced was better than any I had seen him do before. He had become his own critic. A high standard of work was being done in the rest of the class, and his effort was to be part of the whole work. He was not satisfied by anything less than the best he could produce.

I am sure that this project work is extremely valuable where there is a wide age-range, and a wide ability range. It can cover all subjects in the curriculum, and it does provide good social training. The children learn to work together, and to help one another, and the efforts of all are acceptable. I have often spent two or three full afternoons each week on this type of work, but if it is a new approach for the children, it is better to introduce it gradually, and allow it to develop slowly. The most essential factor is, that the teacher must have a clear plan of the work to be attempted. She must be ready to feed in new ideas and information when it is needed, but the plan of work must be flexible enough to allow the individual children to develop along their own lines.

It will be necessary when working on these topics to pay visits to the local farms, etc., and if arrangements can be made, longer journeys to such places as the egg-packing station, or the grain stores. It is on these visits that the children can often find the answers to queries that have cropped up in the work. These journeys with careful preparation beforehand, can provide opportunities for the widening of a limited outlook.

In the country school the teacher has a unique opportunity of getting to know the children as individuals. To be able to accept them all with their differences in personality, and in ability, is a challenge that has to be met, if all are to work together happily and harmoniously. There is no change of class, at the end of the year, with a completely new start. The changes are slow and gradual, and the same children are in the same class for several years, but the work is extremely satisfying. To see the children leave the school, find suitable employment, and take their part in the life of the village is indeed a satisfying experience. The slower child will probably remain in the village, doing a very useful job of work, whilst the more gifted child may seek his employment further afield, but all will continue to meet together in the Youth Club, or village social activities.

K. I. MARSHALL

Chapter XV

REMEDIAL TEACHING

Some remedial teaching is part of the work of most teachers. Many children, at some point in their school career, need help over work they have not understood or missed through absence. It frequently happens, however, that even with good teaching and timely attempts at assistance, some children fall so far behind their fellows, that they are no longer able to take their place satisfactorily in their group.

If this has happened, or seems likely to happen, consideration must be given as to what measures can best help to maintain progress. Sound judgement can only be given on the basis of the school report and of objective tests. These should consist of a medical examination to eliminate such possible causes as poor sight or hearing, an individual intelligence test, given by a qualified examiner, usually an educational psychologist, who may also give tests such as the Rorschach if maladjustment is a possible factor, and attainments tests in basic school subjects. As a result of these tests, it may be discovered that a child is:

(a) Physically handicapped.

(b) Mentally handicapped with an I.Q. so low that he needs special educational treatment in an E.S.N. school. (In general I.Q. 70 or below.)

(c) Not as handicapped as in (b) above but dull and backward, so that he needs permanent placing in a slow-moving group. According to district arrangements, this may be a special school or central special class, but is much more likely to be the lowest group for his age in his own school. (In general I.Q. 70–85.)

(d) Mentally capable of work at least average for his age, but socially immature, so that he needs some time in a special adjustment class or group.

(e) Mentally capable of work at least average for his age, but maladjusted and in need of psychiatric help.

(f) Working below his mental capacity, although apparently normal for his age emotionally, and of normal or above-normal intelligence.

Children of all these groups may well be found in any infant school. Fortunately, most infant school teachers are keen observers, and by the time the children reach 7 + and are about to enter junior school, most deviant children will have been noted. It is of course especially important that children in groups (a) and (e) should be noted and referred for treatment at the earliest possible moment. Failure here, may cause years of avoidable backwardness. Linda came into the district Opportunity Class at 11 +. She had an I.Q. of 89 (Terman) and an arithmetic age of $8\frac{1}{2}$, but was a non-reader. She spoke badly, and had such mispronunciations as 'sidders' for 'scissors'. Her mother was illiterate. Her school record card followed her transfer, and it was noted that on leaving her infant school her reading age had been 5.7, not unsatisfactory for her I.Q. With her mispronunciations as clue, an audiometric test was asked for, and she was found to be partially deaf.

Maladjusted children too, frequently present backwardness in school as part of their problem, and, although some form of remedial teaching may be given them as an aid, it should not be given as a substitute for the clinical treatment they need. It is unkind, as well as inaccurate, to term a child maladjusted unless he has been so ascertained by a qualified psychiatrist, but, should any teacher find such a child in his charge, it is essential that teaching should be in full co-operation with the guidance clinic.

Returning to the categories above, it can be seen that, since remedial work implies a restoration of a child who has failed to make the most of his resources, it is not suitable for a child whose resources are very limited. There is a danger that children who ought, for sound reasons, to be accommodated in an E.S.N. school might be offered remedial teaching instead. True, a short period of individual help can assist such a child in gaining confidence and may help him to fit in more quickly with his peers, yet it appears unjustifiable on three good grounds. First, remedial teaching with such a child may mean delay in his going to the E.S.N. school for the attitude may well be taken 'John is at least getting *some* help, whereas here is Jim in a class of forty-five, brighter than John by 10 points of I.Q. to be sure, but getting no help at all. Let Jim have the E.S.N. place and John can make do with remedial teaching for the time'. Secondly the giving of remedial teaching may raise false hopes in John's parents. 'Perhaps he is not really E.S.N. after all – Mr B. the remedial teacher had a pupil who passed the 11 + last year – maybe John will be all right and this special school business is just the doctor's silly idea?' Thirdly, a child of low intelligence needs to be constantly in a school environment adapted to his special needs, and withdrawal for a fixed and limited period of remedial teaching, does not meet this requirement.

In a lesser degree, remedial teaching is also unsuitable for the slow, dull child, at least if he is young, though a case may be made out for the dull child of secondary age, or a dull child who has had long illness and perhaps never made a start on basic work.

The child who is young, and emotionally or socially immature, is another subject unsuitable for remedial teaching. He is best catered for in an adjustment class. If the junior school he attends is run on infant lines, with plenty of active work, and opportunity for acquiring experience and vocabulary, such a child will come to basic work in his own good time (probably by the time he is 8) with no headache to himself or anybody else.

The child pre-eminently suited for remedial teaching is the one in category (*f*) whose powers are near average, or above, and who, for some reason, is working below capacity.

To summarize – actual examples from cases taken on for remedial teaching, or refused, are shown below.

SUITABLE CHILDREN

(Tests are on Terman Merrill for I.Q. Schonell word reading test and arithmetic tests for attainment.)

Name	I.Q.	Mental Age	Reading Age	Arithmetic Age	Notes
James 9+	113	11+	nil	8.8	Deprived home. Mother has deserted.
Beryl 10+	100	10+	5.7	9.3	Has attended nine schools and had ten months in hospital after being savaged by a dog.
Tom 12+	85	10+	5.4	9.0	Poor intellectual standards at home. Poor speech.
Lesley 13+	108	13.9	12.9	8.2	Several changes of school. Mother died when Lesley was 8. Now has a stepmother whom she likes.

UNSUITABLE CHILDREN

Name	I.Q.	Mental Age	Reading Age	Arithmetic Age	Notes
Agnes 11+	62	6.8	5.1	nil	E.S.N. – should be in Special School.
Jane 9+	80	7+	6.1	6.7	Should be catered for in slow moving group in own school.
Richard 10+	100	10+	9.2	9.5	Not very backward. Has older brother at grammar school, and parents are pressing because of 11+.
Rose 7+	80	5+	nil	nil	Physically handicapped. Parents very upset. Is too immature for formal work, and also needs provision in P.H. school, as her condition is progressive and incurable.

TEACHING THE SLOW LEARNER IN THE PRIMARY SCHOOL

Before deciding on remedial teaching, one more difficult problem may arise. What is the best procedure with a child who, while average or bright, is retarded over the *whole* field of school work? Clearly, he cannot be given individual help, or even help in a small group, for all his basic work, unless the school is exceptionally fortunate. If he goes out to a clinic or remedial centre for a large part of his time, he is going to miss much social contact in his own school, and his loyalties may be divided. Compromises which may be found workable in such a case are:

(1) If the area is fortunate enough to possess one, transfer him to a special school for such children, e.g. Leicester's school 'for children of unfulfilled promise', a form of help which, at present, is very seldom provided.

(2) To include him in a slow-moving group, with as much individual help as the teacher can give, but with the emphasis on his return to his own stream as soon as he has a chance of keeping up – the dangers of an average or bright child being retained too long in a slow moving stream are self-evident.

(3) To tackle one subject, usually, since it is so important a tool, reading, by remedial teaching, and to turn to number work after the reading has become satisfactory. In practice, the acquiring of reading skill often does so much for a child's confidence, that all-round improvement in other subjects often comes of itself.

Therefore, remedial teaching may be defined as the rehabilitation of a child who, as the result of properly administered intelligence and attainment tests, is found to be capable of school work appropriate to his age, or nearly so, but is working below his capacity in part of the school curriculum. It is, in essence, a temporary measure, and should not be provided for any child who, for any reason, needs permanent special provision.

Having decided that a child needs remedial teaching, decision must be made as to what form it should best take.

This will depend on two main factors, firstly, how retarded the child is, secondly, the resources available.

It seems common sense, that if a child is not very retarded, say about a year below his mental age, the first measures should be taken in his own class by his own teacher. Such first aid is of, course, given by any teacher of experience as a usual procedure, but in the case of a young teacher, the head, or more experienced member of the staff, may be able to give helpful advice. The advantages of a child not being removed for this help are obvious. It can be given unobtrusively, and the backwardness will not be emphasized.

If a child is, however, say one and a half or two years retarded, more comprehensive measures may be taken, and he may be given help in a special group or individually. No hard or fast rules can be laid down; each child must be considered as an individual and judged on common-sense lines.

(1) Remedial teaching should be given individually or in a small group. (Maximum effective number probably about five.)

(2) It should be regular and frequent, and the group should be as homogenous as possible for age, interest and maturity, and should be in charge of one teacher.

The kind of group that is taken by any member of staff who happens to be disengaged, and which is discontinued whenever there is a domestic crisis in the school, is of doubtful usefulness, to say the least.

(3) The time chosen should be such that it is not equated with punishment, preferably the same time that the rest of the class does similar work, certainly not in recreation time, or in such lessons as art, craft or games.

(4) The teacher should be interested and technically skilled. This is definitely not the task for the weakest member, or for a member of the staff who is untrained for, or dislikes working with, the less advanced children. Junior schools usually have on the staff one or more teachers with infant training, who may well be capable of and willing for this work. (In secondary modern schools this can be a really difficult problem.)

(5) The teacher should have available stocks of suitable teaching material.

(6) He should be given the complete confidence of the head, and should have access to *all* available information on the children in his charge. This, which appears so obvious, is by no means always found in practice. Rightly, psychologist's reports and similar documents are highly confidential, but, if a teacher is mature enough to be entrusted with special work, he is mature enough to be trusted entirely. Lack of confidence of this kind can be very discouraging.

(7) The parents should be contacted, and their co-operation sought. They should meet the group teacher as well as the head, and it is of advantage if they can be seen with and without the child. Observation of the child and his parents, can often throw a light on difficulties that can be seen in no other way.

(8) The rest of the staff should be consulted, and should, if possible, visit the remedial teacher during working time, so that they can see what is being done, and so that remedial and class work can supplement each other.

Such remedial teaching as has been described, has been an integral part of many schools since long before the Second World War.

Since that time, however, and especially since about 1950, there has been growing up a more specialized conception of remedial teaching. Places as far apart as Exeter, Manchester and Kingston upon Hull, among others, have set up remedial teaching services, and two universities, Leeds and Birmingham, have opened remedial education centres. The remedial teaching is not the charge of a teacher serving the children in his own school, but is done by a specialist teacher (working either in a centre, or on a peripatetic basis) who is engaged full-time in remedial work.

How has this arisen?

In some cases, it can be attributed to the 1944 Act, under which local authorities were encouraged to provide a psychological service for their schools. This meant that in many areas, objective testing began to be done on a much greater scale than hitherto, and backwardness that was 'acquired' and which appeared in pupils in ordinary schools, was spotlighted. Often, psychologists found that children referred by heads as problems, showed wide gaps between ability and attainment. In the Borough of Ealing in 1950–1 some fifty children were found, who presented no problem needing psychiatric help, but who were seriously retarded in school work. The appointment of a teacher who could deal with this retardation, filled a need, and released the psychologist from some routine work.

Publication of the paper 'Backwardness in Reading' and a considerable amount of publicity and outcry about 'illiteracy' also tended to focus attention on the problem of the non-reader, and remedial teaching was one way of answering the demand that something should be done.

REMEDIAL TEACHING

Going somewhat deeper than this, it does appear, too, that with the advent of the welfare state, and the assumption by the community of many forms of care formerly undertaken by voluntary effort, there has, as it were, been an 'overspill of concern' for many groups formerly overlooked – the deprived, the spastic, the deaf, the problem family, and many more, have been the focus of public attention and concern as never before. Coupled with this, has been a growing emphasis on the common needs and rights of all children, and their common humanity. So we tend, today, to say 'children who are backward' not 'backward children', 'children who are physically handicapped', rather than 'physically handicapped children'.

Interest in the common needs, rights and attributes of all children, has been the starting ground here, and although individual differences have been studied as never before, they too have seemed to emphasize the 'childishness of children' whereby all children are seen as a whole, differing from each other in degree, not in kind.

Thus, coupled with a demand for help, the demand for segregation has been played down. All treatment of children tends to swing towards the norm. Children who are physically handicapped, tend more and more to attend ordinary schools, orphaned children are fostered or brought up in homes which resemble a family unit, the blind and the deaf take up careers which would once have been completely closed to them.

Remedial teaching is perhaps another straw in this wind that blows towards the norm, since it seeks to help a child without removing him permanently from his school environment. In this lies its possibilities and its dangers. These concern the child, the teachers of his own school and the remedial teachers. Some are comparatively minor, some are major. They will presently be summarized, but, before this summary, it is necessary to detail the more usual arrangements for teaching by a specialist remedial teacher.

A child recommended for such teaching, may receive it either at a clinic, or at a remedial teaching centre in a school or other convenient place, or may be visited by a peripatetic teacher in his own school.

All these have advantages and disadvantages, and the desiderata outlined in discussion of remedial teaching in a child's own school still of course hold good.

Summary of Problems and Considerations

(1) Remedial teaching may be offered as a substitute for other forms of special help, and so deprive a child of his real need.

It seems that as, in time, more provision is made for the handicapped and the dull, and classes are reduced in size, remedial teaching will be less in demand, though in large districts, there will always be enough children handicapped by absence or similar cause, to make such provision worth while. As the 'bulge' disappears from the schools, the need for remedial teaching seems likely to diminish, since class teachers will have more time to give first-aid to the individual in difficulties.

(2) Where remedial teaching is arranged in a child's own school by his own teachers, lessons can easily be fixed, frequently when his class is doing similar work, and can be for a duration suited to him. Reintegration, when he improves, is easy. At an outside centre he may have to take the only available time vacant, and, if he has far to travel, may attend only once a week, and the usual hour session may be too long, even with varied skilful teaching. Reintegration may be difficult.

(3) Divided loyalties between school and centre may be set up in the child. He may, if he enjoys the centre better than school, actually hold up his own progress, as he knows he will miss his trips to the centre as soon as he improves. Margaret, a 13-year-old, went for remedial teaching to a centre in her previous junior school. She was welcomed, and often said she wished she could come back. She had to be tactfully transferred to another centre, before she could progress very much.

(4) Where the teaching is given by his own teachers, he may have little consciousness of his backwardness. A special visit to an outside centre will emphasize it. However, such a visit may prove a break that will give him a respite from the atmosphere where he has failed, or may, in the case of some children, bring them face to face with their failure, which may prove salutary.

'I *can* read', said Gerald aged 9 + I.Q. 102. 'I don't know why I've got to come to you, you only teach the ones that can't read.' 'All right, we'll see how you can do this test,' said the teacher. 'Yes – Now see this line, you did that, and you also did two words on the next. That section is for 5-year-olds. You see you *can* read but just

REMEDIAL TEACHING

about like a child between 5 and 6. Now most 9-year-olds can read to here.' For some children this would be utter cruelty – but for Gerald who had been a 'headache' to both teachers and fellow pupils, the shock of calling his bluff was what he needed. Needless to say, he was immediately told that he was just as bright as all the other boys of his class, and that he could soon learn to read as well as they, with a little help and effort. In his case, his reading improved as his truculence decreased, over a period of several months.

(5) Where the remedial system is integral in a school *all* children are likely to be considered. Where the child goes outside, a head may hesitate to send a child who is not robust, or not reliable, and, indeed, with a child on the borderline of delinquency, the journey might give opportunity for mischief.

Recommendations may depend also on the social climate of a school, and cases tend to come from the same schools, unless based, say, on a general survey of an age group.

(6) There is unlikely to be parental opposition to remedial teaching in school, but there may be much to visits to an outside centre. This is particularly true where the centre is a child guidance clinic, since some parents still think of these as places for what they call 'mental' children. On the other hand, if this can be overcome, such visits may be the means of solving difficulties far deeper than backwardness in the classroom, and may be the means of rehabilitating the whole family.

(7) Where the child attends an outside centre, the remedial teacher sees and gets to know the parents. Because the child has been withdrawn from his school, the parent may feel that this is in itself, criticism of the school. This may reinforce his own feeling that the school has not done what it might for his child. Most reasonable parents will see, when it is pointed out, that the school must be interested if it has singled out his child for special help, but the remedial teacher must be on guard not even to seem to criticize the school. This is not merely a matter of professional etiquette, but plain common sense. The parent has, perhaps, no faith, or a very wavering faith in education. If the remedial teacher is going to try to create or rebuild that faith, it is a poor start to condemn the thing he is trying to establish.

(8) While the child is being helped by a colleague, it is easy for

his class teacher to discuss his problems and progress. He may feel more diffident with a stranger – he may be discouraged that the child has been removed to be helped by an 'expert' and feel consciously or unconsciously slighted. Perhaps this is especially so, in the case of the elderly teacher, who has given years of devoted service, and seen many 'fashions' come and go in the classroom. A teacher may feel too, that since the child is getting special help, he is no longer his own responsibility.

If the teacher is peripatetic and visits his pupils in their own schools – many of these points will still be relevant.

In addition, he will need to be able to maintain easy relationships with both staff and head. Even in a school with a good social climate and a happy staff-room, this will, at times, present difficulties. For example, a teacher may ask the remedial teacher's opinion, in all good faith, or ask for help over a difficulty. This help may well be given, almost without a thought, but some other member may well feel that he has a bigger problem that has not been offered any help, or the head may feel that the teacher has asked the remedial teacher something that should have come to him. The remedial teacher has no status, and his position can be difficult in a good school, and in a school with a poor atmosphere, it can be impossible. However tactful, however experienced he is, however self-effacing he tries to be, he will inevitably 'run across somebody's bows' sooner or later, probably sooner.

Having considered the pros and cons, which, in a comparatively new departure in teaching, are important, what of the teaching itself? The remedial teacher, working as a specialist, will probably get the outstanding cases of backwardness, and because of its importance, will most often be asked to deal with reading.

The advantages and disadvantages of the various methods of teaching have been perhaps, over-discussed.

Most experienced teachers of reading to younger children, have their own favourite schemes and methods, and teach best if allowed to follow these. So the remedial teacher will get children who have been 'brought up' on visual, phonetic and perhaps kinaesthetic techniques. He may also get the odd case who has not learnt at school, but whose parents have attempted to teach perhaps by the 'ABC' methods of an older generation. Whatever the child's past teaching, the remedial teacher must take him as he finds him, and build on whatever he has, little though it may well be. A child will sense if a teacher 'looks down' on what he has learnt, and if such a feeling were to be produced, it would not be a hopeful outlook for the remedial teaching pupil.

Given that the remedial teacher is technically competent, and has an adequate supply of material his task will be:

(1) First, and above all, to convince the child that there is point and pleasure in learning to read.

(2) To build up the child's vocabulary and understanding of words, and to enlarge his speaking vocabulary.

(3) To fill any gaps in the child's background of experience, in as far as may be done.

(4) To equip the child with the necessary techniques for studying new material, and to fit him for independence as soon as he is ready.

With the younger child, it will usually be best to begin as nearly as possible with work he already knows, and the teacher can read stories to him, and talk about them. This, though it may not raise his reading age, will build the link between previous and present teaching, and prevent a cleavage. Gradually he may be introduced to features of other techniques which have relevance for him. If, as well may be, the child cannot read at all, then the remedial teacher will get to know the child's personal interests and use these as a starting point.

With an older child, who has, perhaps, failed over the years, it may be better to give a new 'slant' to teaching. The kinaesthetic method is not greatly used in schools, since it is difficult to adapt it to the teaching of class or group. Individually, however, it can be of great assistance, since, although it allows a child to use any particle of skill he may have acquired by the more usual methods, it is itself novel, and the writer has proved time and time again, its use as a 'tonic' to the older child who has hitherto failed.

The method, adapted from Fernald's, is as follows:

(i) The child writes his own story on *a subject chosen by himself*.

(ii) The teacher gives him each word he needs but cannot spell, written in large letters on a slip or card or paper.

Letters should be about three-quarters to one inch high, and if the child can do cursive or joined script, should be in this style, although if the child can only manage unjoined writing, this will serve.

(iii) The child traces over the letters 'feeling' them with the index finger of his writing hand *not* with a pen or pencil.

(iv) When he thinks he can reproduce it without looking, he tries the word on a separate sheet. He then checks it and, if correct, enters it in his story. If incorrect he tries again.

(v) The teacher may have a typescript made of the child's completed story, if it is felt that this will help bridge any gap to reading the printed word.

(vi) The child keeps the cards with the words written, and puts them in an alphabetically indexed file or suitable box, in case he needs them again, or makes for himself an indexed notebook, into which he enters the words.

(vii) As he gains facility, the teacher introduces further material, either constructed by himself from the child's vocabulary, or chosen from the reading books at his disposal. The writer has found Miss Keir's *Adventures in Reading* and the *Pathfinder* series by Bradley good in this connexion, especially for older boys.

Advantages of this method are as follows:

(1) The method is novel enough to arouse interest, and can use whatever the child has, and new techniques may be gradually brought in, e.g. a child able to do so, may sound the letters as he traces them, and the child who cannot do so may be gradually helped to do this.

(2) The child chooses his own subjects and vocabulary, therefore, both are meaningful for him. He may, of course, be encouraged to illustrate his story as he goes, which will add to his interest.

(3) The tracing encourages good left to right habits, and strengthens visual acuity in those children of confused laterality, who form a sizeable proportion of backward readers.

(4) Expression, reading, spelling and handwriting are built up together and given relevance to the child.

(5) He learns a practical use for alphabetical order, in his index or notebook of the words he has learnt, and this can lead later to dictionary work.

Whatever method the teacher uses, reading and written expression should develop in parallel.

Some reading books have suitable workbooks, which may be

REMEDIAL TEACHING

employed as an aid, but care should be taken that the child also does original work of his own. Some workbooks, while providing good introductions to the books they accompany, are mainly made up of work which requires underlining or drawing as answers to questions. These, while they may be stimulating and useful, are not a 'full diet' and should be used with this fact in mind, and supplement provided.

Ours, in spite of records, films and television, is a verbal civilization, and it is of vital importance that a child should be brought to a personal encounter with the written and printed word as soon as he is ready. Ingeniously devised systems of teaching reading, by 'reading machines', elaborate matching and the like, are out of place save as 'extras'. They may have their uses in strengthening a child in some weak spot in his technique, but they are no more relevant to reading than the constant use of a climbing frame, and nothing else, would be to a child's physical health. The child must equate his reading with reading books. His reading must mean a *book* to him, whether it be his own handmade story-book, a teacher's individual book made for him, or a simple printed text.

Jim – aged 9 + I.Q. 88 – could read a few words in the style sometimes described as 'barking at print'. He had been brought up on strictly phonic lines, and his teacher had spent many hours making cards for matching and learning word families – a prodigious task, for she had a B class of forty-nine. Jim's spelling age was a little above his reading, being 5.9 and 5.3 (Schonell) respectively. He was asked to say a sentence, anything that came into his mind, and said, 'Bill and I are going to play football at dinner-time'. This was said several times and then written. Although Jim knew perfectly, by this time, the contents of the sentence, he read it in his old jerky style. He was then asked what he had been saying, and could not reply. Suddenly, the remedial teacher realized that Jim had never made connection, either between the printed and spoken word, or between the words he had laboriously learnt from cards, and anything that was meaningful. The work he had been doing, was to him, something one did in school, for some reason best known to his teacher, but meant neither speech nor printed sense to him. For Jim, it would have been better if his teacher had spared herself heavy work card-making, and instead of giving mechanical matching exercises, had spent more class-time reading stories, encouraging acting, original work and the reading of very easy books. This is an extreme instance, but illustrates the point fully.

What should one expect of remedial teaching? This will be much what one would expect of any successful work in school.

(1) First an increased confidence, an increase in powers of concentration and readiness to work, which should spread to all the child's work and may first be shown in more mature behaviour.

Tim, age 9 + I.Q. 106, R.A. 5.5., a remedial reading pupil, had made very little progress in four months remedial teaching. The headmistress and the visiting remedial teacher, were, therefore, somewhat puzzled by his mother's appreciation of his 'great improvement' until they realized that he had unaccountably stopped his nightly bed-wetting (of which the school had been unaware). Mother had been able to take the family for a holiday, which she had previously been too embarrassed to do. Subsequently the reading itself showed a similar rapid recovery.

(ii) Progress in actual reading of approximately two–three months per month as shown by standardized tests. Gain will, of course, not usually be uniform. A very usual pattern is rapid gain from 0 to about $7\frac{1}{2}$ years of reading age, followed by a slower progress.

This 'second stage' can be recognized very clearly in some children by a new tendency to confuse known words – e.g. said/and, of/for, out/our, etc. It is at this time, that a carefully applied course of phonics can really help a child, particularly, the writer has found, a course on diphthongs and long vowels.

The child should finish remedial teaching at the moment when he is ready, and each case must be taken on its merits. As some children of equal ability will vary from each other in starting reading, so some remedial teaching pupils will vary in their readiness to work without extra help. By and large, the average junior who has reached a reading age of about $8\frac{1}{2}$–9 on a standardized test, should be able to continue improving 'under his own steam', and an average senior likewise, with a reading age of approximately $10\frac{1}{2}$; or a useful criterion is, perhaps, that a reading age, not more than a year lower than the child's mental age, may be a safe finishing point.

The aim should be to give the child his independence, and, as soon as he is ready, to return him to his own group with such information to his own class teacher as will ensure maintenance of progress. Provision should always be made for a re-test, either by the school or by the remedial teacher, after a reasonable time (say six months) and the way be left open for further help if necessary.

Where a child is transferring from junior to secondary school, it will probably be wiser to let him discontinue remedial teaching if he is possibly able to cope without it, so that he can give all his attention to his new environment. Full details of his record, and present standard, should, of course, be forwarded to his new school before he enters, so that he may be appropriately placed, and enquiry should be made when he has had time to settle, say at the end of his first term, to see if the school considers he can manage without help. Frequently a 'new beginning' will stimulate a child, and if the school is aware of his needs, he may be found to have made accelerated progress. If not, arrangements should be made for him to have additional help, either in school, or at the centre, as a matter of urgency.

Conclusion

Remedial teaching is an individual remedy applied to the individual, and so will vary from child to child. Reading has been discussed here, but the same principles of giving meaning and reason for learning, and then furnishing needful techniques, apply to remedial teaching in all the basic subjects. It is not an educational assembly line, where the children start as non-readers and end equipped with 'reading age', nor is it coaching or cramming. Its aim is to ease or redistribute pressure, to reshape what is out of proportion, to supply what is missing. There is something 'amateurish' in such teaching, in the real meaning of that word, and it calls for a teacher who, as well as being technically competent, is emotionally adult and something of an individualist. This last has its dangers – for, seen from the outside, the work has attractions for the person, who does not, for reasons of personality, fit in well in the average staff-room. Also, seen from the outside, the work may seem easy, free as it is from large numbers. True, the remedial teacher is free of much routine work, but is involved in the tactful dealing with perhaps thirty different, and it may well be, thirty difficult personalities, from perhaps as many schools. The work involves being a keen observer for the full teaching time. One cannot sit back and relax for a few moments, as one can, for instance, sometimes in the classroom, when all the children are happily busy. Some slight hesitation, some half-given hint expressed in word or tiny action, may answer a question on a child's difficulties that have been puzzling the teacher, or may give the clue to the next phase of teaching that will be necessary. To relax observation is to miss this, and perhaps waste months of effort thereby.

The opportunity of close individual study, is one of the greatest privileges of the remedial teacher, but it can only be enjoyed by constant vigilance.

He must also be ready to take help from any source where it may be found.

Thomas, a loutish 13-year-old began to read when he was encouraged to tackle a gardening job at his church with the active co-operation of the minister. Alan, a sensitive, restless boy, made anxious by the desertion of his schoolfriend's mother, and the discovery of a similar situation among his own relatives, settled down, when his mother, friendless and unsettled in a new council estate, was visited by the local deaconess, and introduced to some of the neighbours. A long way round to improvement in school work perhaps, but the remedial teacher, who has time to talk to his pupils, and to get to know their worries, must also find time to alleviate them, inside school and outside it, if that be possible.

Like all teaching, remedial teaching is, when all is said and done, a means of adapting a child to his environment. It can be a stimulus and a help to children who have fallen behind, as long as suitable pupils are chosen, and suitable teachers undertake it.

It cannot be systematized, for it is essentially a service for individuals, therefore, it is likely to be of most use in large centres, where sufficient children, backward because of causes such as illness, are to be found. It cannot, and should not, be offered, or used as a substitute, either for good teaching in a child's own school, or for special schooling for those children who need it. If it is so used, it will defeat its own purpose, and cease to be remedial.

Book List
Advisory Council on Education in Scotland, *Pupils with mental or educational disabilities*, H.M.S.O., Edinburgh, 1951.

REMEDIAL TEACHING

CLEUGH, M. F., *The Slow Learner* (Chapter 10), Methuen, London, 1957.
GATES, I.A., *The Improvement of Reading*, Macmillan, New York, 1950.
HARRIS, A. J., *How to Increase Reading Ability*, Longmans, New York, 1947.
IRVINE, E. D., LEWIS, EVE and HOWARD, J. L., *Adjustment Teaching for Educationally Subnormal Children in Exeter*, City of Exeter, Special Services Sub-Committee, 1956.
MINISTRY OF EDUCATION, *Education of the Handicapped Pupil, 1944-55*.
— *Language*, 1954.
— *Reading Ability*, 1953.
— *Standards of Reading*, 1957.
SCHONELL, F. J., *Backwardness in the Basic Subjects*, Oliver and Boyd, London.

The following articles on remedial teaching in various localities published in *Education*:

THOMAS, DR ELFED, *The L.E.A. contribution to Remedial Education*, Vol. III, No. 2869, 17 January 1958.
Exeter, Vol. 106, No. 2747, 16 September 1955.
Kingston-upon-Hull, Vol. 110, No. 2855, 11 October 1957.
Swansea, Vol. 110, No. 2860, 15 November 1957.
Manchester, Vol. III, No. 2870, 24 January 1958.

JOAN M. GORDON

Index

achievement 6
activities 136 204
  see also Chap. II, III, IV & V
age, mental, 17 47 48 118
aids 17 212
  auditory 60
  mechanical 57
  visual 60 182
amorality 2
apparatus, *see* equipment and—
appearance 5
ARITHMETIC Chap. V, 92-114 130 256-258 260
  book list 114
  games 103-105
Arnold, E. J., 238
ART Chap. VI, 115-133: 12 22 36 51 52 76 148
  book list 133-134
  correlation 184 228
ascertainment 17
Assembly 11-14 29 32
aural stimuli 64
authors 48 52 53
automatism 119
awards 28-30 32

backward family 21
behaviour 17 148 216 243
belonging 2 41
Bible 10-12 14 158
book assessment 66-67
bookmark 74
broadcast programmes 57-58 59
Buhler, Karl 118
Burt, Sir Cyril 196

Child Art 119
Child Education 238
child guidance 23 243
Christ 11 12
Christian
  community 10 15
  faith 11 12
  festivals 13 15 174
church 1 15
Cizek, Franz 119-120

class
  opportunity 265
  readers 18
  size of 18 173 249
  unstreamed 18 152
classroom,
  activities 204 245-246
  arrangement 61 99 145 180 214-216
  atmosphere 2 56 60-61 152 153 172
  chores 3 6 100 170 180 224 230
  discussion 40 52
  games 53 55
  shop 100
clerical assistant 235
clinic 23
collections 2
colour book 125
communication 41 45 55 62 130
community 1-5 9-10 56
comprehension 51 76 86
conduct 1 9-10
confidence 3 10 41
continuity 3
co-operation 9 23 26 167 184 185
co-ordination 17 110
  muscular 33 131 229 230
correlation 130
craft 7 33 36 130 161 199 202 259 260
  see also Chap. IX, Handicraft
crossword 76
curriculum 55 56 97 115 130 251

dancing 34 35 142 145 146 147 148 149 156
delinquency 1
dentist 23
development,
  emotional 136-137
  moral and spiritual 36
  personal 151
  physical 136
  of taste 215
Dewey, John 107
diaries 88
dictionary 69 202 255
discipline 43 98 138 139 172 175 219-220

DRAMA Chap. VIII, 152-163: 34 52 59
  book list 163
  miming 34 188
  plays 11-13 188
  puppets 12 52 133 171 183 188
  dramatic work 155 156 183
  dramatization 136 142

education,
  Atavistic Theory of 118
  definition of 21-22
Education Act, 1944 36 196-197 270
Ellisdons 160
emotional release 157
Eng, Hilda 118
environment 22 25 167-168 203 244 245 250 252 280
ENVIRONMENTAL STUDIES, Chap. X, 179-192
  book list 193-194
EQUIPMENT AND APPARATUS Chap. XII, 212-240
example of teacher 2-5 9 61 129 171
exercise books 230-232
eye movement 63-64 78-79
eyes 206 242

family, problem 37
Fernald 275
film 12 57
  strips 12 51 57
flannel graphs 12 51 150
flash cards 75-76 77 106
Fridayitis 24

games 96
  arithmetic 103-105
  Classroom 53-55
  football 27
  lesson 26
  skills 27
  team 30-32
gardening 257 258
gardens 174 183 186
geography 43 44 46 184 188
God 12 13 14
gramophone 137 146
  records 149 150 156 160
groups,
  arithmetic 110-112
  model 4
  play 4 53
  reading 68-69 73
  remedial 17 18 268-269

habit 168 171
Hadow Report 94
HANDICRAFT Chap. IX, 164-175: 52 191
  book list 176-178
  correlation 184
Head teacher 23 167 235 248 269 274
health 241 242
  inspector 186
  records 206-207
  rules 25
  see also Chap. II, 21-38
hearing 23 105 206-207 242 243
Hemming, J. 55
history 43 44 46 136 184 188
homes 23 24 39-40 155 167 168 179 203 244-245
house system 28-33
hygiene 24-26 237
hymns 13 14

illustrations 2 11 13 57 72 182
images,
  abstract 50
  visual 51 60
imagination 97 129
individual
  differences 94 108 263
  needs 139 223 253 260
  treatment 3 70 279
  work 18 179 182 248
illiteracy 37
INFANT SCHOOL Chap. XIII, 241-250: 26 34 63 66 99 156 265
  book list 250
Isaacs, Susan 45-46

justice, 9

Keir, Gertrude, 'Adventures in reading' 199
Kinaesthetic
  method 274 275-276
  sense 108 131

leadership 4 33
library 65 66 175 221-222
Ling Physical Culture Association 149

Mackley, Geo. E. 120
maladjustment 265
manners 5 6 14
map-making 261
maps 185
maturation 15 47 63 67 68 174

INDEX

mental
  age 17 47
  images 118
modelling 230
models 2 12 13 51 171 174 175 182 185 188 191 261
monitors 8 10 16 173 216-217
morale 161
MUSIC Chap. VII, 135-151: 13 155
  songs 58
  and movement, 26 27 34-35
musical instruments 155

nature study 46 181 189 190 192
news 87-88 89
Newton, Robert 159
non-reader 50 103 222
notice board 182-183
number 199 202 256
  sense 130
  see also arithmetic

Ostwald, Colour Range 122
  Colour Wheel 124 125

parents 1 5 16 17 21 23 24 26 37 90 167 179 203 207 243-245 252 270 273
percussion bands 142-143 146
Philip and Tacey 238
phonetic elements 75
PHYSICAL EDUCATION AND HEALTH Chap. II, 21-37
  book list 37-38
  apparatus 33
  drama 155
  music 143
physical inability 117 121
pictures 50 53 55 64 71 99 100 182 193 236 237 238
  collections of 54
picture association 130
play 26 59 99 141 205
  ground 166 183
  ground observation 205-206
  groups 4
  time 59
poems 51 154 162-163
poetry 35 144 158
poise 3 35
Pope W. Macqueen 160
prayers 13 14 15
projects 56 69 73 130 171 179 184 261-262
psychologist 23
publishers 47 48

punishment 9

radio 57 58 139 146
rapport 131
READING, Chap. IV, 63-91 18 41 43 46 51 53 59 60 61 130: 131 198-199 246-248 254 255 274-278
  book list 91
  broadcast 58
  choral 11
  material 222 223
  pleasure 6 7
  progress card 199-200
RECORDS, THE KEEPING OF Chap. XI, 195-210
  book list 210-211
  arithmetic 108 113
  card 209-210
  handicraft 168
  individual 17 179 190 260 261
  reading 67 69 70 74 75
Reid, L. Arnaud 21
relationship, teacher and child 3 4
REMEDIAL TEACHING Chap. XV, 264-280
  book list 280-281
  classes 248
repetition 53 66 127 128 132 154 169
rhythm 35 155
  see also Chap. VII, music
Rorschach Test 264
Rouma 118
routine 5-8
ruler 101
rules 9 121 125-126

school
  community 14
  functions 6 32 152
  health visitor 207 242 243
  keeper 167
  meals 6 24
  medical officer 22 23 207
  medical service 23 242
  special 26 161
  village 196, *see also* Chap. XIV
  visitors 175
scribble 119 131 143
self 6-7 15
  consciousness 52
  control 215
  discipline 225 226
  expression 52 120
service 8 10 14-15
services 9
  ancillary 23

285

sight 22
skills,
  basic 4 7 36 179, *see also* Chaps. III, IV, V
  physical 145
  tests of physical 28-29
Slade, Peter 159
SOCIAL, MORAL AND RELIGIOUS TRAINING, Chap. I, 1-19
  book list, 19-20
social relations, 205
  training 99 148 180 191 213 218 252 262
speaking, choral 35
special educational treatment 17 18 117
SPEECH, ORAL VOCABULARY AND, Chap. III, 39-62: 14 76 152 153
  book list 62
  defects 243
  therapist 23 61
spelling 61 202
staff 16 18 33 268-270 274-275
stories 47 58 59 125 150 162-163
story
  acting 153 183
  film strips 51
  illustration 52
  telling 43-45 48-51 53 60 154 155
syllables 75
Syllabus, Agreed 10
symbols 78-9 130

tachistoscope 76
tail-ender 16
tape-recorders 57 58-59 159
teacher, example of 2-5 126 129
telephone 59
templates 128
tests 21 199 208 264
  physical skill 28-29
  vocabulary assimilation 77
  word recognition 67 70
textures 128 131
time demands 10 72
timetable 55 56 173 185 235 260
togetherness 5

UNESCO, Report (Records) 196

VILLAGE SCHOOLS, BACKWARD CHILDREN IN Chap. XIV, 251-263
visitors 6 175
visits 9 40 187-188 262
visual
  aids 60 182
  experience 108
  patterns 75
  stimuli 64
vocabulary 67 70 72 77 78 101 275-276
  controlled 65 66 70 71
  enrichment 86-90
  graded 255
  lists 67 68
  oral 99
  see also Chap. III
vocational training 251
voice 159

water supply 216-217
weather 183 189
Whittier, J. G. 14
word
  attack 74 75 78-79
  form clue 75
  games 80-89
  lists 67 72 247-248
  perception 80-81
  recognition 70 71 72 74 76 81-84
words 50 52 55
  recognition 63 78
work,
  expression 12 52
  graded 3 17
  group 18 111 182 185
  individual 18 182 220-221
  occupation 76 77 190
  written 52 68 69 71 72 75 87-90 111-112 187 259 276
work book 8 64 77 111 202 228 277
work habits 236
work sheets 78 106
worship 10 13 14
writing 41 45 130 131 143 161 201